COMING OF AGE

The Advanced Writing Curriculum

D0001203

Edited by

Linda K. Shamoon • Rebecca Moore Howard
Sandra Jamieson • Robert A. Schwegler

CrossCurrents

New Perspectives in Rhetoric and Composition

CHARLES I. SCHUSTER, SERIES EDITOR

Boynton/Cook Publishers
HEINEMANN
Portsmouth, NH

Boynton/Cook Publishers, Inc.
A subsidiary of Reed Elsevier Inc.
361 Hanover Street
Portsmouth, NH 03801–3912
www.boyntoncook.com

Offices and agents throughout the world

© 2000 by Boynton/Cook Publishers, Inc.

Library of Congress Cataloging-in-Publication Data
Coming of age : the advanced writing curriculum / edited by Linda K. Shamoon . . . [et al.].
    p.   cm. — (CrossCurrents)
   Includes bibliographical references (p. 151).
   ISBN 0-86709-567-9 (acid-free paper)
   1. English language—Rhetoric—Study and teaching.   I. Shamoon, Linda K.
  II. CrossCurrents (Portsmouth, N.H.)
  PE1404 .C6174 2000
  808'.042'0711—dc21   00-026205

Editor: Lisa Luedeke
Production: Elizabeth Valway
Technology project manager: Dan Breslin and Eyeon Interactive
Cover design: Darci Mehall/Aureo Design
Manufacturing: Louise Richardson

Printed in the United States of America on acid-free paper
04   03   02   01   00   DA   1   2   3   4   5

To our colleagues at the Conference on Future Directions for Programs in Rhetoric and Composition Studies (Rhode Island, 1998) whose words, ideas, and challenges helped create this book; to Charles Schuster, whose excitement and advice kept us going; and especially to Robert J. Connors, whose research, scholarship, and humanity will continue to guide us.

Contents

Preface

Coming of Age: The Advanced Writing Curriculum is a print-linked publication. Print-linked publishing combines the print mode of publishing with at least one other, such as a CD-ROM or the Internet, in presenting the full contents of a single work. Central to print-linked publishing is the concept that both modes taken together constitute the full publication. The CD-ROM or Internet material is not ancillary to the printed material. In print-linked publishing, the contents of both modes are of equal importance, and they are thoroughly synthesized with each other. Integration of content is a core principle of print-linked publishing.

We present *Coming of Age* as a print-linked publication in two media: print and CD-ROM. The disk that is shrink-wrapped with this book is not subordinate to the book; it is part of the book. The Preface, Parts I, II, the Afterword, the Works Cited list, and a list of Contributors of *Coming of Age* appear in print. Parts III and IV, the Works Cited list, a list of contributors, and a course description for each type of course discussed in this collection appear on the CD-ROM.

A print-linked publication differs from the numerous print publications already on the market that have ancillary CD-ROMs or websites. The material in the electronic component of such texts is an add-on that enriches the printed contents of the freestanding publication, and the print publications themselves have typically been textbooks or journals. In contrast, using the principles of integration as well as interactivity, print-linked publishing is more experimental and future-oriented than these other combinations of printed material and electronic attachments. Its integrative principle is experimental: the contents of the print and electronic portions of the book cannot be separated from each other; neither the print nor the electronic portion makes sense alone.

It is future-oriented in two ways. First, it invites a high level of reader interaction with text and authors. Most of the essays in *Coming of Age* are presented in electronic form. Readers may move linearly or non-linearly between the print and electronic portions of the text, and they may immediately download, use, adapt, and transform—or, in Jerome McGann's words, "deform" (1998)—those portions of the text that are presented in the electronic medium. When essays on the CD-ROM refer to websites and other Internet resources, the corresponding URLs appear as hot-links, allowing readers to move fluidly between the essays in this collection and the additional resources their authors recommend. And in the list of contributors on the CD-ROM, hot-links to each author's e-mail account encourage readers to correspond with and ask questions of the authors.

Second, print-linked publishing is future-oriented in that it solves a vexing economic problem for scholarly publication. As readers of the *Chronicle of Higher Education* know, scholarly publishing faces an economic crisis: only very short books can be marketed at modest prices. As the page length of the book increases, so does the selling price, and the increase in that price can be dramatic (Heller 1999). But by using all publishing modes available, print linking allows for the full presentation of scholarly arguments and materials at an affordable price.

Because *Coming of Age* is intended to instigate direct, immediate, curricular, and pedagogical action, print linking is especially well-suited to this book. The theoretical framework for the argument of *Coming of Age* is presented in the solid, stable medium of print. And the generative course descriptions and program recommendations are presented in the volatile, interactive electronic medium. Taking advantage of additional available space on the CD-ROM, we are also able to follow already-established practice, appending ancillary materials such as a full list of course descriptions for the courses discussed in *Coming of Age*.

Coming of Age has four sections: Part I proposes the move from "advanced *composition*" to "advanced *writing*," and along with Part II, it argues for what the advanced undergraduate writing curriculum should accomplish; Part III provides essays that explain and demonstrate how to accomplish these goals and challenges readers to develop their own pedagogical and programmatic options; while Part IV discusses ways to implement such a curriculum and provides concrete suggestions from a variety of campuses that have done so. The Preface, Parts I and II, and the Introduction and Afterword of this work are printed in the volume you hold in your hand. Parts III and IV are on the CD-ROM. The Table of Contents lists all essays in all parts of the publication, and in the print portion of *Coming of Age* you will find excerpts from and course descriptions for each of the selections that appear on the CD-ROM. Then as you read the CD-ROM essays and compose your own curriculum and course proposals, you will be able to cut and paste from the CD-ROM essays and the ancillary materials included on that disk into your prose.

The editors of *Coming of Age* developed this book and the notion of print linking around the concepts of integration and interactivity. We believe that it is appropriate to present a rethinking of the discipline of writing in a format that amounts to a rethinking of the structures of publication.

Introduction

History, Politics, Pedagogy, and Advanced Writing
Rebecca Moore Howard

Writing in 1997, Suzie Jacobs worries about the ways in which composition theory devalues composition pedagogy. Theorists, she says, buy into English department hierarchies in which pedagogy—and by extension, composition studies—ranks last.

Jacobs' concern is hardly new, nor has it been laid to rest since 1997. As composition studies has gained disciplinary status, it has developed an increasingly troubled relationship to its own pedagogy, the pedagogy from which the discipline grew. Compositionists who are "only" practitioners have a decidedly reduced status. Moreover, those compositionists who count as publishing scholars are differentiated according to whether they are publishing "mere" reports of pedagogy or whether they are "real intellectuals."

Coming of Age: The Advanced Writing Curriculum complicates this bifurcation. When we editors solicited essays for this collection, we asked composition theorists to describe ideal advanced writing courses, and we asked them to reflect on what those courses contributed to their students, to the university's advanced writing curriculum, and to composition studies. Thus many of the essays in this collection implicitly enter the long-standing debate about the relationship of pedagogy to theory: they demonstrate that pedagogical practices—in this case, course design—are driven by theory that can be articulated and can then propel further theory, pedagogy, and curriculum design. The boundaries between pedagogy and theory blur when practice and pedagogy articulate the field. Just as the work of writing program administrators counts as intellectual work (see Council of Writing Program Administrators 1998), so does the articulated work of teachers.

Coming of Age also enters into historical debates in the discipline. The history of writing studies in the United States is the history of first-year composition at American colleges. Some people date the beginning of the discipline with the Morrill Act of 1862, which created land-grant American colleges. The Morrill Act was part of a move to encourage larger numbers of students to attend college; no longer was higher education the exclusive provenance of a small, hereditary elite. But the expansion meant that college students could no longer be counted on to be in possession of a predictable sort of literacy; hence Harvard president Charles Eliot and others believed that such literacy—or at least its surface niceties—should be transmitted to the new initiates. Thus was first-year composition born at Harvard, soon to become the norm at most American colleges.

First-year composition (FYC) has since identified and defined the discipline of writing studies. Scholars of composition—as well as the larger public—have debated the whys and hows of composition instruction, but even in the cyclical calls for the abolition of FYC, first-year pedagogy has remained at the center of writing studies as a discipline. Some people date the beginning of the discipline with the 1960s rise of published scholarship, but even then, that scholarship focused on FYC.

Advanced undergraduate writing courses have, in this environment, been an afterthought. They played no role in the nineteenth-century beginnings of composition studies, and they play only a minor role today. Many colleges have no advanced courses, and among those that do, many limit those courses to technical writing, tutor training, the literary nonfiction essay, and/or an amorphous beast called "advanced composition."

We editors began our work on *Coming of Age: The Advanced Writing Curriculum* (a book that has gone through many subtitles) with the modest objective of offering a more imaginative set of possibilities for advanced composition. In our early work on the volume, we had some preliminary ideas about how our book might contribute to the always-emergent history of composition studies. In our early conception of the book, we accepted the term *advanced composition* as transparent and usable. As we read the published scholarship on advanced composition, however, we began to realize that it was obsessed more with rendering a universal definition of the term than with designing vibrant courses. Thus we began, among ourselves, to challenge its validity. Instead of generating our own universalized definition of advanced composition, we decided to discard the term altogether. We have come to regard advanced composition as baggage left over from a period in which advanced undergraduate writing instruction was either very specialized (e.g., technical writing), an extension of the literature curriculum (the nonfiction essay), or an extension of FYC (more of the same, but harder). *Advanced Composition* disappeared as a possible subtitle for our book and as a focus of its argument.

Hence we began to think in terms of the "advanced undergraduate writing curriculum." As our contributors began to submit first drafts of their essays, we saw that they, like us, were struggling to imagine what a fully developed undergraduate writing curriculum might look like. Many were teaching their advanced courses under the undifferentiated, unitary rubric of "expository writing" or "advanced composition." But as contributors' first drafts accumulated, we began to see a sort of collective wisdom emerging, one that enriched our preliminary argument and our sense of its contribution to the development of composition studies. Some of the essays describe advanced undergraduate instruction as preparation not for graduate studies in English nor for teaching school but for a career as a writer. Others, speaking from the civic discourse tradition, describe the advanced undergraduate writing curriculum as a preparation for public life.

Reading these first drafts, we began to ask not how *advanced composition* should be defined, but what an advanced undergraduate writing curriculum should accomplish. We offer *Coming of Age* as an answer to that question: the advanced undergraduate writing curriculum should prepare students for careers as writers, with the term *writer* broadly defined, and it should also prepare students for highly rhetorical participation in public life. Essential to such preparation is providing students with a theoretical and historical understanding of writing, writers, and writing studies. We therefore recommend that writing faculty who are contemplating the revision or institution of an advanced writing curriculum strive to establish courses that provide writing students with a historical and theoretical awareness of writing as a discipline; that prepare students for careers as writers; and that prepare them for using writing as a means of participating in the public sphere. Essays in this collection by Robert A. Schwegler ("Curriculum Development in Composition"), Thomas P. Miller ("Rhetoric Within and Without Composition: Reimagining the Civic"), and Linda K. Shamoon ("The Academic Effacement of a Career: 'Writer'") offer persuasive arguments for these three curricular objectives.

The balance among the three parts of this curriculum will vary from one college to another. At some institutions, faculty might focus the advanced undergraduate writing curriculum on the civic; others might opt for a professional focus; and some departments might find it most appropriate—or politic—to concentrate on discipline-oriented courses in theory and history. Still other programs will offer a representative selection from all three fields. We recommend that the question of balance be decided according to local constraints but that every program strive to have some representation from each category, so as to provide undergraduate students of advanced writing with a reflexive sense of themselves as writers; with a historical understanding of the profession of writing; with a sense of the writer's responsibilities to audience, self, and community; and with tools for entering the profession of writing.

We recommend, moreover, that every advanced writing program consider establishing core requirements from each of the three fields. Toward that end, Part II of this volume offers our suggestions for possible core courses. We offer three potential core courses from each of the three fields (disciplinary, public, and professional). Because we believe that the advanced curriculum must serve a local constituency and be determined by local needs, we do not propose a single course for each field. Instead, the three possibilities that we offer for each field demonstrate how the selection of core courses derives from and in turn determines the direction of the advanced writing program.

Our point is that no single set of core courses could possibly be appropriate for all advanced writing curricula. Nor can the level of difficulty for advanced courses be the same at all institutions; readers of this volume will quickly realize that some of the courses described herein may be too basic or too difficult for the advanced students at their institutions. It is our expectation that anyone adapting these courses to their own advanced curricula will necessarily be making the appropriate local adjustments to level.

But we do assert that certain guiding principles—that is, instruction in the disciplinary, public, and professional dimensions—may be widely applicable.

As faculty consider what might constitute an appropriate core course in the public focus, for example, the three possibilities we offer—Yameng Liu's course in contrastive/comparative rhetoric, John C. Bean's course in argument, and Richard Leo Enos' course in the history of rhetoric—provide a provocative range of possibilities. Any one of these three courses would provide advanced writing students with essential core skills, knowledge, and perspectives in preparation for writing in the public sphere, as well as for additional study of civic literacies.

Part III of *Coming of Age* then showcases a variety of courses that might serve as electives in the advanced curriculum. Again, these courses are organized according to the three-part structure (disciplinary, public, and professional) that we recommend for the advanced curriculum.

The courses described in Parts II and III of this book amount to a dazzling array of possibilities. Readers will no doubt react as we editors did: with excitement. Reading our contributors' course descriptions, we often found ourselves eager to teach the courses described. But even as we proffer these course descriptions to readers of *Coming of Age,* even as we invite others to share our excitement, we must also offer a word of caution. We believe that the primary organizing principle of the advanced writing curriculum should not be faculty interests. Instead, the desired learning outcomes of the curriculum should be its primary organizing principle. Rather than choosing a selection of courses from a smorgasbord of possibilities, we suggest that faculty develop a structure for the advanced curriculum, and then within that structure, choose courses that match faculty and student interests.

The curricular feat of establishing a curriculum that incorporates discipline-based theory and history, that situates writers in public discourse, and that prepares students for careers as writers can only be accomplished by redirecting the field that has heretofore been called "advanced composition" but that we believe should be renamed "advanced writing." The change in terminology asserts that the advanced curriculum is *not* simply "more of the same, but harder," a fallacy that the term *advanced composition* too easily reinforces.

In Part I of *Coming of Age,* Lynn Z. Bloom ("Advancing Composition") offers a history of advanced composition courses that eloquently demonstrates the need for redirecting the field. We editors of *Coming of Age* believe that redirecting the field means asking fresh questions about the *purposes* of advanced writing instruction. Long-established courses in advanced composition have tended to be offered as discrete courses that respond to student demand but that do not present writing as a field, a discipline, or a coherent professional category. Where more than one such course is offered, the courses are typically not designed to be in dialogue with one another. This leaves the writer with no clear identity as Writer, the advanced composition course with no clear institutional or intellectual purpose beyond the course itself, and composition studies in general with only a shaky claim to disciplinary status. When the knowledge base of a discipline—its history, theory, research, and practice—is used only to inform skill-oriented pedagogy and is never shared with undergraduates as a field, the riches of that discipline are being only partially used. Regardless of how they want to engage with the world as writers—professionally, socially, or politically—students of advanced writing need to understand the nature of writing and to join the conversations of the discipline, just as they would in any other discipline. The advanced writing curriculum that we describe can facilitate that understanding and invite those conversations. Students wishing to pursue a career in writing or to increase their civic participation through writing need a purposeful curriculum that prepares them to meet their goals as thoroughly as does any other curriculum in the university.

In addition, advanced writing instruction must be more than an occasional, miscellaneous digression from the main task of the required FYC curriculum. It must have a rationale other than that of offering exhausted FYC teachers a respite from their labors. It must have a goal other than that of increasing students' cultural capital by increasing their command of high literacy. The advanced writing curriculum must explain in concrete terms how it contributes to its students' lives by giving them a sense of disciplinary membership, by preparing them for public life, and by preparing them for careers in writing.

In his essay "Curriculum Development in Composition," Robert A. Schwegler establishes why the advanced curriculum should provide its students with a sense of disciplinary membership: a successful advanced writing curriculum must present writing not just as a skill but as a subject matter. Courses oriented to the public dimension and to the profession of writing must be supported by courses in the history and theory of composition; otherwise, the long-established default perception of writing as a skill will inevitably assert itself. In Parts II and III of this volume, the subsections "Preparing Students for Participation in the Discipline of Writing Studies" suggest courses that might accomplish this task of presenting writing as a subject matter—core courses in Part II, elective courses in Part III. Andrea Abernethy Lunsford ("Histories of Writing and Contemporary Authorship") describes a course that conveys a sense of how the author functions in and is constructed by society as well as a sense of the ways writing itself has developed and the roles it has played in society. Sandra Jamieson ("Theories of Composing") describes a course that would teach undergraduates some of the leading theories of composing that have commonly been taught only to graduate students. Her course would not only provide disciplinary knowledge to advanced undergraduates, but it would also invite them to formulate their own ideas about the relationship among writing, thinking, and learning. Gail Stygall's course, Discourse Studies, provides advanced writing students with "specific tools with which to analyze aspects of larger rhetorical approaches," in addition to offering perspectives on contemporary problems in rhetoric and composition. The course that Mary R. Lamb describes ("The Rhetoric of Gender as Advanced Writing") takes students beyond essentialist gender politics and into a dialogue about the complex ways in which gender and writing intersect. Arthur E. Walzer and David

Beard's "Rhetorical Theory: Major Figures in the Aristotelian Tradition" connects writing to the history and theories of rhetoric, a connection too often neglected in advanced writing curricula. Deepika Bahri's "What We Teach When We Teach the Postcolonial" uses postcolonial theory to illuminate writers' work and also demonstrates that literature can, indeed, be taught so that it increases writers' understanding of their social roles and construction. Her essay serves another important purpose, as it provides an answer to an issue that Min-Zhan Lu (1999) raised in the pages of the *Journal of Advanced Composition*: Lu asks that the relationship between composition studies and postcolonial studies be two-way, and Bahri shows that the study of education practices provides the field in which that relationship can develop. Dennis Baron's "Literacy and Technology" makes writers aware that technology is not just a neutral tool but one that affects their very conceptualization of their work. Chris M. Anson ("Below the Surface: A True-to-Life Course in Editorial Practice") can take students beyond the notion that attention to correctness is an annoying last stage of the writing process and toward an understanding of error as a community construction. In "Computers and Communication," Johndan Johnson-Eilola describes how to heighten students' understanding of computer applications and theories of electronic discourse.

In addition to including students in the disciplinary construction of writing studies, we recommend that the advanced curriculum orient them toward public forms of writing. In Part I of *Coming of Age*, Thomas P. Miller ("Rhetoric Within and Without Composition: Reimagining the Civic") explains how the rhetorical tradition articulates and enhances writers' involvement in public discourse. Essays in the Parts II and III subsections "Preparing Students for Participation in Public Writing" then demonstrate ways in which students might be guided toward using writing as a means of participating in the public sphere. Yameng Liu ("Contrastive Rhetoric/Comparative Rhetoric") explains that in a global economy, training in contrastive rhetoric is advantageous and even essential to the writer. John C. Bean's "Seeking the Good" teaches students not just how to win arguments or write persuasively but how to see the philosophical and moral implications of their efforts to argue and persuade. The course described in Richard Leo Enos' "The History of Rhetoric" would "introduce . . . writing students to the ways that meaning is made and shared with others" and provide them with "the opportunity to study the ways in which rhetoric can be used as a resource for solving—and for judging solutions to—problems." Such a course offers advanced writing students invaluable techniques for understanding and participating in the rhetorical situations in which they will find themselves. Bruce Herzberg ("Civic Literacy and Service Learning") provides a rationale for teaching civic or public discourse in advanced writing curricula. Beverly Wall ("Political Rhetoric and the Media") crosses a boundary that has been artificially maintained in writing curricula: she describes an advanced writing course in which students use rhetorical analysis to engage in—not just analyze—American politics. Instead of using analysis to distance themselves from the political scene, Wall's students use it as a means of becoming involved and implicated in American politics. In "Writing About Race and Ethnicity," Valerie Balester asserts that as pressing national concerns, race and ethnicity are issues that students must engage if they are to become successful writers in the public sphere. Patricia Bizzell then argues for teaching advanced writing in the contact zone as a means of enfranchising all the students in the course. In "Writing as a Means of Social Change," she describes a course in which students "talk about what different audiences are likely to accept as logical or what kinds of deviations from standard usage they are most likely to censure or welcome." Such discussions are the first item on the agenda of the business communications course described by Kitty O. Locker ("Writing for and About Business and Nonprofit Organizations"); they are an essential component of learning to write in the corporate sphere, as well as in the realm of nonprofit organizations. Describing a capstone course, H. Brooke Hessler's "Constructive Communication: Community-Engagement Writing" explains how we can teach students that writing—and writing instruction—can be central to constructive and active citizenship.

The third component that we advocate for the advanced writing curriculum is a set of courses that prepare students for careers in writing. Linda K. Shamoon, having interviewed professional writers, adds surprising texture to received notions of careers in writing. Her Part I essay reveals that professional writers tend to think of themselves not as just one kind of writer (creative, technical, and so on) but as multifaceted professionals; they long for a sense of community with other professionals; and they wish that their college educations had prepared them for their careers. Illustrating how Shamoon's findings might become pedagogic action, contributors to the Parts II and III subsections called "Preparing Students for Participation in the Profession of Writing" describe a wide array of possibilities: genre theory (Kathleen Blake Yancey, "More Than a Matter of Form: Genre and Writing"); contextualized style instruction (Rebecca Moore Howard, "Style, Race, Culture, Context"); visual as well as print literacy (John Trimbur, "Theory of Visual Design"); technical communication taught not just with an eye to marketplace skills but also from a position of historical awareness (Mary Lay, "Technical Communication"); cultural studies taught in such a way that students preparing to enter the profession of writing understand that all writing, however instrumentalist in its purposes, is situated in cultural practice (Diana George, "Cultural Studies: The Rhetoric of Everyday Texts"); creative writing, which, as Shamoon's professional writers assert, is a form of professional writing (Mary Ann Cain and George Kalamaras, "Taking the Rhetorical Turn in Advanced Creative Writing"); writing about the arts as an exercise in moving from one discourse community to another (Joseph Trimmer, "Writing About X: The Arts"); writing in the specialized legal genres (Richard Fulkerson, "Teaching Writing Like a Lawyer"); and writing in the publishing profession (Libby Miles, "Working in the Publishing Industries").

The courses described in *Coming of Age* are not an exhaustive collection. Many other courses could have been included in this volume or are yet to be imagined. What about a course in film literacy, for example? Here we provide examples and invite readers to imagine or reinvent their own curricula and courses. Each institution must fill in its advanced writing courses, but in a principled rather than opportunistic way. As Robert A. Schwegler argues in his Part I essay, advanced writing curricula should be developed not according to happenstance but according to the purposes that the curriculum is to serve for its students and for the discipline of writing studies.

Nor do we expect our three-part curricular taxonomy to be the last word on the topic. Rather, it represents our present thinking as well as the direction suggested by the courses that our contributors describe. We hope this taxonomy will prove useful to readers of *Coming of Age,* but we also hope it will generate further conversation.

In Part IV, the final section of *Coming of Age,* we turn to program design. In this section, five essays speak to the experience of developing programs of advanced writing instruction: John Ramage's "From Profession to Discipline: The Politics of Establishing a Writing Concentration"; Theresa Conefrey's "Needs, Numbers, and the Creation of a Writing Studies Major"; Ruth Overman Fischer and Christopher J. Thaiss' "Advanced Writing at GMU: Responding to Community Needs, Encouraging Faculty Interests"; Kathleen McCormick and Donald C. Jones' "Developing a Professional and Technical Writing Major That Integrates Composition Theory, Literacy Theory, and Cultural Studies"; and David Schwalm's "Getting Approval." These essays describe several advanced writing programs and describe them in sufficient detail so that readers can adopt or adapt them in their own program development. As in Part III, these essays are published on the CD-ROM, enabling ready cutting, pasting, and sharing.

But the story of program development extends far beyond issues of good pedagogical and curricular design. As many writing faculty have learned to their sorrow, developing writing curricula—and especially advanced writing curricula—is an activity deeply embedded in institutional and intellectual politics. The stories are legion: An independent writing department is created at a large state university, but only after its curriculum undergoes ten reviews. The director of a writing program at another large state university returns from vacation to discover that he has been replaced in the directorship by a literature specialist. A writing specialist is hired to develop a writing program at a small liberal arts college. The program she designs is multilevel (advanced as well as introductory) and interdisciplinary, with writing specialists as well as faculty hired from a variety of disciplines. But within a few years the writing specialists' positions, including that of the program designer, are gone, replaced by interdisciplinary faculty, leaving a "writing department" with no tenured members and no faculty trained in composition or rhetoric.

The institutional and even departmental quandaries that writing faculty, programs, and curricula face daily are well-known and much lamented, and the struggles often surface when writing specialists propose a program of advanced instruction. At one large state university, a year and a half of rhetoric and writing specialists' work resulted in a "reformed" English major that includes merely a writing "strand" without courses in creative writing, memoir, or autobiography. Such exclusions indicate the kind of compromise—and tongue biting—often required of writing specialists.

Chillingly, the struggles emerge, too, when advanced writing curricula become successful. In yet another large state university's experience, the established advanced writing curriculum came under fire when literature faculty saw it as siphoning students and majors from the literature curriculum.

Programs of advanced writing instruction are difficult to implement and difficult to protect. Whether such a program takes the shape of a major within English studies, a second major available to all students, a certificate program, an independent department, or some other arrangement, the path to implementation may be painful, and it most certainly will be long. The essays in Part IV of this work endeavor to help faculty imagine and prepare for the future of such programs.

Even in the face of much-discussed, debilitating experiences, the proposals for unified writing programs, majors, minors, and other advanced configurations continue to emerge across the country. We predict that these programs will become reality, endure, and grow in number, precisely because so many writing faculty recognize the argument made in this book: there are compelling intellectual, occupational, and disciplinary reasons to establish writing as an advanced program of study. If we faculty who hold such a vision are to succeed, however, not only must we be aware of the opposition we may encounter in our efforts at implementation, but we would also do well to respond constructively rather than defensively to that opposition. Program developers working in a political vacuum or playing the victim role—the downtrodden, unappreciated compositionist fighting on the side of Right—may otherwise find themselves with an exemplary program design that is never, or only briefly, implemented.

Once it is developed and enacted, the advanced undergraduate curriculum serves many constituencies. *Coming of Age* focuses on the ways in which advanced writing instruction serves advanced writing students. But this instruction also benefits the students and teachers of FYC; no longer do one or two required courses have to provide all the needed writing instruction for an entire university. Instead, the first-year course can modestly start students on the path to becoming fully developed writers. In these circumstances, moreover, the writing program can, at its option, focus the required sequence on academic literacy practices, in the confidence that the advanced curriculum will prepare students for post-baccalaureate writing.

Coming of Age has been written in a period characterized by lively conversations about advanced writing instruction—conversations at conferences, on listservs, in faculty meetings. In these conversations we read a widespread interest in developing instruction that derives more from disciplinary than lay senses of need. We believe that establishing an advanced undergraduate writing curriculum serves undergraduate students who will take these courses and who will major or minor in writing. But we also believe it serves the discipline of writing studies. First, it asserts presence, not absence, for writing pedagogy. In an advanced curriculum, instruction in writing responds not to the absence of students' skills but to the presence of expertise that can be acquired through instruction. Second, the advanced writing curriculum fills in the "middle" of writing instruction. American universities have a flourishing first-year composition along with flourishing graduate programs that train people to teach FYC well. In his Part I essay, "Feathering Our Nest? A Critical View from Within Our Discipline," Richard Bullock explains some of the self-serving motives for offering graduate degrees in writing studies—motives that pose a danger as well to advanced undergraduate writing curricula. A current debate is whether graduate degrees in composition and rhetoric should prepare students for other careers, which would break the circular relationship of those graduate degrees and FYC. Purposefully designed advanced undergraduate writing instruction further contributes to the rupture of that circular relationship; it opens up writing studies by asserting curricular outcomes such as civic engagement and professional writing. Finally, the existence of an advanced undergraduate writing curriculum asserts beyond question the disciplinary status of composition by challenging the premise that writing instruction is a normative enterprise that should be required of many or all college students. The normative model makes any talk of a discipline of composition studies a futile gesture in which thwarted, unsuccessful literary scholars attempt to reconcile themselves to their fate. Until the discipline of composition has a highly articulated, coherent field of instruction outside the required curriculum, and outside the graduate programs that train people to teach in that required curriculum, it will have only a tenuous claim to disciplinary status. An advanced undergraduate writing curriculum provides the missing piece in the argument for the disciplinary status of writing studies.

Thus emerges a growing historical awareness among us editors of *Coming of Age:* richly imagined, fully developed advanced undergraduate writing curricula help to move the discipline of writing studies out of the confines of the first-year sequence that has defined the first century of the discipline. Now writing studies becomes something other and more than a first-year sequence and a graduate curriculum that trains teachers for that sequence. Now writing studies comes of age, taking its place as an intellectual discipline with instruction that is driven by disciplinary rather than lay exigence and methods and asserting its place as a discipline in which pedagogy and theory are mutually constructed in a rich, complex relationship.

COMING OF AGE

Part One

Redirecting the Field
from Advanced Composition
to Advanced Writing

Advancing Composition

Lynn Z. Bloom

I'm calling this chapter "Advancing Composition" instead of "Advanced Composition" for a number of very good reasons. Wherever "advanced" composition is, we're not there yet. The participle *advancing* implies a process—things in motion—that seems to be the perpetual state of this area of composition that is, we hope, moving forward. This book, and the colloquy therein, is advancing what we know and identifying areas that we will need to know about to understand this ever-evolving subject. *Advancing* also connotes movement—promotion, if you will—of the subject from the periphery to the foreground of curricular consciousness. If the title conveys multiple meanings in a subtly witty way, then it too embodies the spirit of its subject. If it fails to do so, at least I've taken the risk—and that's part of the ambience of this elusive subject as well.

Definitions: What We Talk About
When We Talk About Advanced Composition

If the advanced undergraduate writing curriculum has truly come of age in or around the new millennium, as the title of this book promises, the view of the Conference on College Composition and Communication (CCCC) 1963 "Workshop on the Undergraduate Advanced Composition Course" represents the amorphous, adolescent state of its predecessor, Advanced Composition—as a course and a concept—during the past fifty years:

> We don't agree as to what Advanced Composition should be, or is. We all do different things, which are all good, but none of it seems to make any difference. Most students can't write when they enter college, and write worse when they leave. . . . We do not agree about the objectives of the course, the content, the order of topics, the number or length of essays, the emphasis. . . . We do not agree about the sorts of topics to assign, or whether to assign topics. We do not agree about in-class versus outside writing, examinations, and certainly not about criteria for grading. We find no practices which are generally effective, no agreement as to who should teach the course [. . . or on] optimum size or effective texts.

> Individuals, of course, had certain things they liked to do, and planned to keep on doing, despite majority opinion. . . . We all plan to go on teaching Advanced Composition (whatever *that* is) and talking about it. (Committee Reports on Advanced Composition 1963, 190)

Desperately seeking closure on this open-ended subject, I have read as much as a body can tolerate on advanced composition. The materials include a fifty-year sample of college catalog course descriptions; all of CCCC's Advanced Composition Workshop reports and position papers, from 1954 until they stopped in 1970; the results of various studies and surveys (Kitzhaber 1963; Hogan 1980; Dicks 1982; Adams and Adams 1991; Adams 1993); a heap of textbooks (a fifty-year span of major freshman—Why freshman? Read on—and advanced readers and rhetorics designed for writing with, and without, teachers; books on writing in specialized fields and across the disciplines; style and publication manuals); student papers; the Writing Program Administration (WPA) Annual Bibliographies, from their inception in 1984 to the present; syllabi, mostly current, sent by colleagues nationwide on the WPA listserv; and definitions proffered by colleagues on the same listserv. These materials provide a remarkably broad and varied supplement to my own experience of teaching and writing for and about advanced composition since 1970. Yet in 1999 they continue to corroborate the 1963 CCCC report, which concludes, with charming conviviality, "We adjourned to the Statler–Hilton bar" (190).

Thus although advanced composition, as a concept and as an academic subject, cries out for a definition, it is impossible to provide a global one. Indeed, in trying to map the territory, I had originally thought of an analogy with a map of western Europe, using Greece as the starting point. But I soon got stuck on deciding whether style should belong in Paris or Rome and debated extending the map to North America to accommodate New Journalism and creative nonfiction, but where? The West and East coasts? Iowa City and Chapel Hill? From there on the analogy became compromised by an incompatible mix of national and ethnic stereotypes, cultural hegemonies, and border crossings fraught with contact—if not combat—zones, and I packed it in. An analogy far more appropriate is a buffet table provisioned by chefs of various levels of expertise, loaded with opportunities to combine an array of choices of substance, and style in varying amounts—or even to choose but a single dish.

Although new dishes appear on the table from time to time, classic and current cuisines remain constants on the menu, giving little sense of either dramatic change or conspicuous progression during this fifty-year period. The changes that do occur in advanced composition appear to be instigated primarily as reactive responses to external phenomena—for instance, state accreditation requirements for high school English teachers, demands by business and industry for specialized writing courses, university mandates for a sophisticated computer-based course in every department—rather than the result of any theories or developmental concepts of either the field or the students taking the course (but see the discussion of Haswell at the end of this chapter).

Consequently, I have chosen to organize this discussion topically, which sorts out and emphasizes the major strands, rather than chronologically, which mixes them all up, as they are in real life. Thus after definitions, I'll proceed to types of courses, course aims, textbooks, and teachers' qualifications, and close with a developmental approach, which also draws some conclusions about where we've been, since much of the rest of this book talks about where we're going.

Attempts at global definitions of advanced composition founder because ultimately advanced composition is a concept—and a course—with a variety of local options. If there were a professionally agreed-on set of things student writers across America should know and be able to do by the time they complete freshman composition (as, say, a knowledge of algebra precedes calculus), then it would be possible to establish a common understanding of where advanced composition should start. However, all freshman courses don't stop at the same place. This is as true today as it was in 1967 when an illustrious CCCC invitational workshop, including Jacqueline Berke, Francis Christensen, Glenn Leggett, Richard Lloyd-Jones, Robert Slack, and Darwin Turner, tackled the issue. They began "Guidelines and Directions for College Courses in Advanced Composition" with a "relative and operational definition [that] admits that the freshman course at one college may be more advanced than the advanced course at another one." Thus their definition is advisedly local: "An Advanced Composition course should be . . . open only to students who have at least passed the freshman course at the same college or who have demonstrated equivalent ability." Recognizing that "even an 'A' student from a weak college might not be ready for the advanced course at a strong one," the authors assert that "the advanced course should represent substantial progress beyond the goal of the local freshman course." Then comes the bugaboo in this and nearly every pragmatic discussion of advanced composition: the demand on such courses to (re)train students who have passed freshman English but whose writing still doesn't satisfy institutional standards for graduation. Although the Committee clearly prefers to remand such students to "clinics, workshops," remedial courses, or freshman English (again!), bowing to necessity, they leave an insidious loophole: "Advanced courses may on occasion include some ['remedial'] material . . . if [it] is brief and incidental in response to an individual's need" (Committee Reports 1966–67, 266). But exactly! Advanced composition with a soupçon of Remediation.

Types of Advanced Composition Courses: From Here to Infinity

What exactly the advanced composition course should include, besides a grammar review, is an issue that perplexes every discussion of the subject during the past half century—every survey, every statement of theory and curriculum, and every CCCC committee report. Again, the 1966–67 CCCC report summarizes the range of opinion on the variety and focus of advanced composition. The course, especially when conceived of as "Advanced Exposition," may be construed to cover "the range of the freshman course but in greater depth," with emphasis on "alternative strategies in solving writing problems" and analysis of the "reasons for choosing among verbal forms and theories of rhetoric." Or the course may be more specialized. Using somewhat overlapping concepts, the report discriminates among *forms* of advanced composition ("e.g., report writing, verse writing"), *situation and content* ("e.g., technical writing, business writing"), *types of students electing the courses* ("e.g., prospective teachers"), *modes* ("e.g., discursive writing, persuasive writing"), and *special problems* ("e.g., theories of style or history of English prose style") (Committee Reports 1966–67, 266).

Given such a broad spectrum—cynics might say absence of principle or of content—it is not surprising that Hogan's 1980 survey of 311 American colleges and universities nationwide revealed "50 different types of courses" regarded as advanced composition: Intermediate Composition, Advanced Composition/Exposition; Genre and Techniques of Writing; Stylistics; Research; Argument; Criticism; Theory and Practice of Teaching Composition; Creative Writing; Journalism; Technical and Professional Writing; and Business Writing (1980, 21). Hogan's 374 respondents taught (in descending order of frequency): analyses (202), personal essays (195), reports (145), research papers (145), articles (132), reviews (129), expository essays (71), argument (47), descriptive essays (43), narrative essays (37), correspondence (33), criticism (27), persuasive essays (22), evaluative essays (15), summaries (14), exploratory essays (13), journals/diaries (12), autobiographies (10), definitions (7), personal narratives (4), classification essays (4), interviews (4), style (3), investigative reports (1) (21–23). This plethora of overlapping labels reflects the general confusion about the course: a lack of clear and discriminating descriptive language that tells what the writing actually does and doesn't do and a failure to acknowledge the mixed modes and techniques of much nonfiction, exacerbated by the concept of pure, pristine modes of discourse that determines some of these labels.

A 1990 survey by Shumaker, Dennis, and Green of advanced composition courses in 300 "representative" American institutions yielded 124 responses reflecting the same diversity, or confusion,[1] of opinions about "what we mean when we label a course . . . 'advanced composition,'" and an even broader variety of courses than Hogan's and Dicks' sixty-college survey (1982) had discovered: "Anything that can serve as the matter of a writing course appeared somewhere among the responses." Among the common types of courses indentified by Shumaker, Dennis, and Green were writing for publication, re-

1. Of course, what survey takers and interpreters consider "confusing" might also be construed as evidence of institutional sensitivity to the widely varying needs, desires, and abilities of students beyond the freshman year.

search writing, personal or autobiographical writing, writing on a particular issue du jour, literary criticism, traditional grammar, family histories, the "basic
paragraph," and "study of the sentence; correctness in the use of parts of
speech, punctuation, capitalization, syntax, and idiom"—as well as many versions for "narrowly defined audiences: Scientific Writing, Technical Writing,
Business Writing, Writing for the Professions, Writing in the Disciplines." Although survey respondents generally agreed that advanced students needed to
encounter "rhetorical theory, ancient and modern," taught by faculty "trained
in contemporary and classical theory," there was no consensus on whether "advanced" meant "fuller engagement with processes"—although "process" itself
was scorned by some faculty, who claimed, "The 'process' people . . . are sub-
jective, romantic, anti-intellectual, and arrogant, as a rule." Or might "advanced" mean "more experienced in the composing role, or able to participate
more fully in a writing community or even able to engage in a writing community that continues past the class," a series of alternatives I find tantalizingly
opaque in their very vagueness. "Some stressed attention to style and grace as
the hallmark of an advanced course," while "others regarded the turn to argumentation as the demarcation between freshman writing and advanced discourse," although in other colleges the turn away from argumentation might indicate the same division. The authors conclude that their survey "uncovered
little genuine conviction about what [advanced general writing courses] should
do." They nevertheless detected a call "for more professional dialogue" (136–
44), which *Coming of Age* may provide.

   Despite the Eastern bias of my sample, the spread Hogan, Dicks, and Shumaker, Dennis, and Green found in their nationwide surveys of a particular
year is replicated in the fifty-year span of catalogs from fifteen institutions that
I consulted: two two-year colleges; six private four-year colleges, including
Amherst (for 100 years) and Dartmouth; five public four-year colleges, primarily though not exclusively teachers colleges; and two public research universities.[2] This spread is also reflected in the CCCC committee reports over the
years, in Penfield's analysis (1991), and in the textbooks commonly used.

   I examined the course descriptions decade by decade in order to determine
when particular types of courses entered the curriculum and disappeared from
it, as well as to see how the courses were described. To cut to the chase, as in-
dicated by the varied titles above, a common title does not designate a common
course (and why should it, given that change is the prime constant in a living

---

2. I used catalogs from the following institutions: *two-year colleges*—Capitol Community College, Manchester Community College; *private four-year colleges*—Amherst for 100 years, Dartmouth, Hampshire College (est. 1970), Mt. Holyoke, Smith, University of Hartford; *public four-
year colleges,* primarily though not exclusively teachers colleges—Keene Teachers College (later
Keene State College), Millikin University, New Haven State Teachers College (later Southern Connecticut State University), Quinnipiac College, Willimantic State Teachers College (later Eastern
Connecticut State University); *public research universities*—University of Connecticut–Storrs,
University of Massachusetts–Amherst.

curriculum?), either at a given school over a fifty-year period or among schools during any given decade. Beginning in the 1950s, many colleges introduced "advanced writing," particularly to accommodate state certification requirements for prospective teachers of high school English. Thus Advanced Writing students at Keene Teachers College in 1951 were to "become fully acquainted with the problems of composition in the high schools" while perfecting their own writing and understanding "the practices of good writers" (1951, 44). Advanced Composition students at New Haven State Teachers College, having been warned that "this is not a course in creative writing," studied "grammar and usage" and wrote in familiar types of prose models: "argumentation, definition, formal essay, familiar essay, narration, description, critical analysis" (Committee Reports 1956–57, 46). But otherwise the advanced courses with specific labels such as "expository writing," "business writing," and "technical writing" emerged randomly throughout this fifty-year period at all types of schools except the Ivies. At Amherst and Dartmouth, on the other hand, "advanced composition" was largely restricted to various sorts of belletristic (i.e., creative) writing or literary criticism, when the type of writing was specified at all.

The composition programs at Amherst and Dartmouth are of particular interest in the twentieth century because faculty with national reputation in rhetoric and the teaching of writing were associated with them. John Genung, an English professor at Amherst from 1882–1917 whose highly influential *Practical Elements of Rhetoric with Illustrative Examples* went through printing after printing between 1886 and 1910, was among the "big four" (Kitzhaber's term, 1990)—the last of the rhetoricians with classical training whose books considered rhetoric "an essentially conscious application of carefully learned abstract principles" rather than treating it as a subject to be learned by rote use of rules of grammar and mechanics (Connors 1997, 82). Indeed, Genung himself placed considerable reliance on the students themselves, explaining in his Preface, "Some elements of rhetoric, though very real and valuable, are not practical, because the ability to employ them cannot be imparted by teaching. They have to exist in the writer himself." Although "literature is . . . infinitely more than a mechanism . . . it is as mechanism that it must be taught—the rest must be left to the student himself" (Genung 1886, xi–xii, quoted in Connors 1997, 83). Of comparable influence was Walker Gibson (at Amherst from 1946 to 1957 and 1967 to 1987), whose *Tough, Sweet, and Stuffy* (1966) and *Persona* (1969) emerged as jazzy sailboats skimming over a grey sea of undistinguished rule-bound grammar books.

Amherst students under Genung took the prototypical sequence of lower-division composition courses of the first half of the twentieth century, a two-year sequence of courses that progressed from words, to sentences, to paragraphs, to style ("figures—diction, prose and poetic; rhythm"), to invention, to "the composition as a whole," and to literary types (1990–1901, 57). Despite Genung's theoretical confidence in the students' self-reliance as the best way to learn to write, the course sequence involved applications of theory in the form of "written exercises," "practical drill," and "discipline in the principles of style" (Committee Reports 1900–1901, 57). A half century later, advanced composition at Amherst appeared to begin where freshman composition left off, although the advanced courses diverged in a number of directions. Walker Gibson's students at Amherst in the '50s took "a course in disciplined writing, both prose and verse," and worked "independently" on their writing, "without specific assignments" (Committee Reports 1950–51, 63)—a description that persisted into the '60s. By the 1970s, "prose and verse" had been eliminated from Amherst's description of Advanced Composition, but in the '80s Advanced Composition under Brad Leithauser was a seminar in "reading and writing poetry" (1984–1985, 133). By this time Amherst had also initiated a course titled Composition, designed to prepare juniors and seniors to "write an autobiographical essay assessing their own intellectual and social experiences" according to the course catalog (1984–1985, 133). By 1998– 1999 all of these courses persisted, although Advanced Composition had been retitled Poetry, and parallel courses had been added, named Fiction Writing and Non-Fiction Writing—with topics varying annually. In 1999, for instance, in what appears to be a variation of the 1980s course, students wrote their memoirs as well as cultural criticism—"analyses of society and its institutions" (1998–1999, 135).

Dartmouth attained considerable reputation in composition circles in the 1960s and 1970s because it was the site of an elaborate two-year study of freshman composition funded by the Carnegie Corporation in 1960 and 1961. The "Dartmouth Study of Student Writing," written by Albert Kitzhaber of the University of Oregon and published in 1963 as *Themes, Theories, and Therapy,* explored two questions: "Can English composition at Dartmouth be taught more effectively in the required freshman English courses than it is now?" and "Can anything be done to ensure that students will continue to write at least as well after they have left freshman English as they do while they are taking it?" (ix–x). Given the care with which the study was conducted and the thoughtfulness of the Kitzhaber report, we might expect the post-study catalog descriptions of writing courses beyond the freshman year to reflect the principles Kitzhaber articulated.

But such is not the case. Had they been in a college with world enough and time, the Dartmouth faculty would have required a two-year writing sequence for lower-division students, comparable to the grammar/nonfiction prose/belles lettres sequence required by Amherst a half century earlier. However, apparently bowing to necessity, they compressed the entire sequence into the freshman year (see Kitzhaber 1963, 143), and recommended a writing-intensive requirement across the disciplines for upper-division students, so that "each student in at least one course every year is expected to write often and well" (Kitzhaber 1963, 154–55). Yet from 1951 through the 1980s, writing course descriptions in the Dartmouth catalog are minimalist at best and reveal no overt accommodation to the principles articulated in the Kitzhaber report.[3] The 1963–1964 catalog describes the "Intermediate Course in Writing," (taught by Noel Perrin), as "intensive practice in writing, both fiction and nonfiction" and the "Advanced Course in Writing," (taught by Richard Eberhart), as "informal guidance for men who wish to develop ability in creative writing" (1963–1964, 135). By the late 1970s the intermediate course had been titled "Essay Writing," "intensive writing" for students "not satisfied with the papers they have been writing in courses" (1978–1979, 232). By 1984 this description had been revised to identify the subject as "analytic and expository writing" (1984–1985, 247). Throughout the years, Dartmouth's "Advanced Courses in Writing" remained devoted to the writing of fiction, poetry, and "other genres," including "the informal essay" (1978–1979, 232–33).

As Katherine Adams concludes in her historical overview of advanced composition in the twentieth century, in each decade American colleges offered two somewhat antithetical models of this "composite course." One version offered "advanced remediation" for students who needed more freshman composition; the other version was "a challenging arena for young professionals." Because, says Adams, "our notion of advanced education implies a narrowing, an immersion into one specific field, this general type of advanced writing instruction never found a secure niche. For upper-division writing instruction to flourish, it would have to be designed by specialists who could gear it to one student population and to one type of writing." The very virtue of this course, this "capacious hold-all" as Virginia Woolf might have said, is "its lack of precise definition," explains Adams, and consequently its ability to be "shaped and reshaped by individual students and classes and teachers." But in its virtue resides the inability of this loosely defined entity to become "the primary paradigm for advanced college writing instruction" (1993, 59–60). How could colleges require a pig in a poke?

Course Aims and Content:
Where Are You Going, Where Have You Been?

Given the variability of advanced composition courses around the country, it's not surprising that the CCCC guidelines are extremely vague—and possibly contradictory, although because they're vague it's hard to tell. The course should have a "humane emphasis," the 1967 committee said: "Crafts must be mastered, but the goal is understanding how the uses of language define human beings." Because "the primary content of any advanced course is writing itself," the "insights of modern studies of language, rhetoric, and psychology should be made explicit." Nevertheless, while in many courses "no text will be necessary" other than student writing generated in the class, teachers who wish

---

3. The Kitzhaber report contains the germs of the Writing Across the Curriculum movement that began in the early 1970s and has gradually gained nationwide acceptance.

can find prose models in historical, contemporary, and literary collections or in the fields of the students' specialized professional orientation. The danger of such collections, warned the guidelines, is that these texts may "entice" the class to shift its focus away from "the process of writing," and toward ways of reading (presumably explications de texte) dictated by "the apparatus of well-meaning" but overly directive editors (267).

The beauty of vague goals is that they can be translated into whatever aims a particular instructor wants. Or they can be ignored altogether, which is more likely the case. In fact, within three years the CCCC advanced composition workshop had repudiated the 1967 claim to a truly advanced course. The 1970 workshop report asserted that advanced composition is "merely a continuation and extension of freshman English, differing in that it had a more highly motivated student, in that it presented a more structured treatment of style, and in that it offered a variety of writing experiences." A true child of its time, the 1970s advanced composition course was to teach "expressive" and "intellectualized" writing, both intended to provide students "with an opportunity of self-discovery and developing [their] own personal voice" (289–90). Irrespective of diverse good intentions, the only acknowledgment of either the 1967 guidelines or the 1970 (or any other) CCCC report that I have found appears in histories or in surveys of teachers of the course, not in syllabi or catalog descriptions. Whether the goals of advanced composition differ significantly from the top five "real goals" of freshman composition, as identified in Witte's 1981 survey of writing directors, is uncertain. Teachers expect freshmen to learn to (1) write mechanically correct prose; (2) write coherent prose; (3) explore the topic adequately; (4) write in various modes; and (5) write syntactically fluent prose and (5—tie) understand one's composing process (Witte 1981, cited in Penfield 1991, 23). A contemporary update would surely include critical thinking and multicultural awareness as major goals of contemporary freshman composition, as well as the course's pervasive, though often tacit, reinforcement of the middle-class virtues of self-reliance, decorum, moderation, economy, efficiency, and order (see Bloom 1996).

Hogan's 1980 survey asked advanced composition instructors to rank order the following course aims: "[1] Develop mature writing style (325); [2] Develop awareness of audience (297); [3] Teach expository forms (234); [4] Teach modes [of discourse] (180); [5] Improve skills in punctuation, grammar, mechanics (122)." Without amplification, it is hard to know exactly what the respondents meant or how closely the terms in this survey corresponded to the language of Witte's study. Consequently, it's hard to tell from either survey how closely freshman and advanced composition resemble each other, just as it is from catalog course descriptions. Hogan's respondents supplied a number of other objectives. Twenty-five listed "Rhetoric," but what do they mean by that term—to teach rhetorical principles, rhetorical strategies, a history of rhetoric, more grammar, or something else entirely? Although only sixteen people listed "Revision and editing," I surmise that since the survey took place when the process movement was paramount, revision was required in many more courses than this number indicates but that teachers simply didn't bother to list it. The same is probably true of such matters as "Invention (11)" and "Writing as Process (5)." Nevertheless, since "Organization (10)," "Analytical skills (6)," "Sentence combining (6)," and "Logic (4)" are listed as separate items, it's hard to know what "Develop awareness of thought and language relationships in writing" meant to those eleven respondents who identified this as a course aim (1980, 26).

Hogan concludes that "emphases in the courses appear to be largely traditional and . . . repetitive of those things we do in freshman composition." The foundation of the course was "traditional" rhetoric; the "research paper assignment" was paramount, although Hogan himself couldn't tell whether students were "learning skills in invention, analysis, and synthesis" beyond those they had acquired in freshman composition. The advanced composition courses were small, averaging seventeen students, and a great deal of writing was assigned—eleven papers per semester on average, nine per quarter— surprisingly, "the primary mode of instruction is the lecture" (41.7 percent), and another 34.2 percent combined lectures with individualized instruction. Fewer than 10 percent of the courses were conducted as workshops, discussions, or seminars (Hogan 1980, 28)—a percentage that, according to Shumaker, Dennis, and Green (1990), had risen to 30 a decade later, with 60 percent of the 1990 courses also incorporating peer groups. Shumaker, Dennis, and Green's survey revealed that the amount of writing varied wildly: one to five papers in 33 percent of the classes; six to eight papers in 37 percent; more than eight in another 30 percent of the classes. In addition, more than half of the respondents expected two or more revisions of each paper, and the same percentage also required a journal or portfolio. Although this potential forest of revisions (spare the trees!) embeds its own argument for small classes, in fact only 53 percent of the institutions limited the class size to twenty; 28 percent authorized classes of twenty-one to twenty-five students; and 19 percent exceeded that number (1990, 138–39). Given the labor-intensive nature of the course, all these numbers—of students and of papers—are excessive. Verifying Hogan's and Dicks' earlier findings—Dicks says, "unfortunately, the wealth of models suggests again that advanced composition may well prove impossible to define once and for all" (1990, 186)—Shumaker, Dennis, and Green conclude that "a student, an advisor, or an administrator examining a program could legitimately ask what common experience will be shared by students in different sections of such courses" (1990, 141). And the fifty-year span of my survey moved no closer to a consensual or operational definition of the course by 1999 than it had been in 1950.

Textbooks: Once More to the Essay

The diversity of course definitions is manifested in the diversity of textbooks used in advanced composition during the past half century. Although some courses take as their texts the students' papers exclusively, most require a college dictionary and a style manual, and many adopt other combinations of books. Indeed, the books lend themselves, once again, to a variety of course models—many repetitive of freshman English. Dicks' review of the meager professional literature on the subject in 1982, aptly subtitled "One Genus, Many Species," reveals a range of the characteristic types of textbooks that I myself have located in studying more recent course descriptions, syllabi, and listings in The WPA Annual Bibliography of Writing Textbooks (every Spring issue since 1981). Because publishers won't release their sales figures, breadth of adoption must be inferred from endurance and from multiple editions of books. So I turn now to the volumes piled on my study floor. These may be sorted into style manuals, rhetorics, and readers, most of which are used in freshman composition as well. There are smaller numbers of treatises on rhetoric, such as Plato's *Gorgias* and *Phaedrus;* works of nonfiction prose by individual authors, such as Robert Pirsig's *Zen and the Art of Motorcycle Maintenance* and Lewis Thomas' *The Lives of a Cell* (Dicks 1982, 183, 185); and collections of essays by single authors such as George Orwell, Virginia Woolf, and Stephen Jay Gould. Shumaker, Dennis, and Green note that of the 65 percent of their respondents who use textbooks, two-thirds are dissatisfied with their choices (1990, 139); however, the reasons for this displeasure are not specified. Since Advanced Composition is generally an autonomous course, as well as a highly individualized one, it is curious that the instructors—largely an experienced faculty—did not make more felicitous choices.

Style Manuals

Clarity, brevity, sincerity—Lanham's C–B–S formulation (see Introduction to *Analyzing Prose* 1983, 2–12)—and concern with sentence-level discourse dominate the concept of style as it has been taught in advanced composition, and for that matter, freshman English, for the last fifty years. Strunk and White's *Elements of Style,* if not the clearest and most sincere stylebook on the market since 1959, is certainly the briefest, even when bulked up from its initial forty-three pages to its current eighty-five. Too well-known to require analysis here, it is widely cited in syllabi and course descriptions and remains a strong contender today, despite the sexism of its illustrations. My 1979 edition fell open to the following advice for **noun used as a verb** ("not all are bad but many are suspect"):

> Be prepared for kisses when you gift/give your girl [with] this merry scent.
> The meeting was chaired by Mr. Oglethorp./Mr. Oglethorp was chairman of
> the meeting.
> She debuted/made her debut last fall. (54)

Two other popular sentence-level books are Richard Lanham's *Revising Prose* (1979; 4th ed. 1999) and Joseph M. Williams' *Style: Ten Lessons in Clarity and Grace* (1981b; 6th ed. 1999). Both are clear and sensible; Williams offers lucid, linguistically based explanations designed to produce—in those with an ear and an eye for elegant prose—the clarity and grace proffered in the title. For space reasons, a single example must suffice:

> *Here's the point:* With every *sequence* of sentences that we write, we have to find the best trade-off between the principles that make individual sentences clear and the principles that give a passage of sentences a sense of cohesive flow. *But in that compromise, we always give priority to those features of style that help readers create a sense of cohesion.* Readers may understand individual sentences just fine, but if they cannot see how they "hang together," those individually clear sentences will add up to no coherently cumulative meaning. (1999, 104)

Although between half and two-thirds of the advice in conventional freshman handbooks and rhetorics is devoted to words, sentences, and paragraphs—often in hundreds of pages—the advanced style manuals cover the same territory with greater clarity, brevity, and elegance—and pragmatic logic of the sort exhibited in the above quotation from Williams.

Rhetorics

Some rhetorics intended by their authors for freshman composition have been used primarily in upper-division or even graduate courses, notably Young, Becker, and Pike's *Rhetoric: Discovery and Change* (1970) and Edward P. J. Corbett's *Classical Rhetoric for the Modern Student* (1965). Sophisticated in concept and execution, they look and feel "advanced," whereas Richard Coe's *Form and Substance* (1980; revised as *Process, Form and Substance: A Rhetoric for Advanced Writers* in 1990) and Maxine Hairston's *Successful Writing* (1981; 2d ed. 1986; 3d ed. 1992), both identified as "advanced rhetorics," cover territory familiar to freshman composition in familiar ways. For instance, Coe's first edition moves from the writing process to paragraphs, words, sentences, modes of discourse, and term papers and concludes with writing critical papers, business letters, and proposals.[4]

Terminology is often the tip-off. Freshman rhetorics focus on the parts, as Coe does, referring to the final products of the students' writing by such textbook-y terms as *drafts, exercises, pieces, papers, themes,* or *assignments.* Advanced rhetorics, on the other hand, concentrate their advice on style and on the writing of whole works, *essays* (they use this term, which freshman books dare not name), and label them as recognizable nonfiction genres (the logic of sparing freshmen this conceptual language escapes me). Thus the few advanced books on the market, my own *Fact and Artifact: Writing Nonfiction*

---

4. Coe does devote five pages to professional activities, presenting papers and publication, his most conspicuous departure from the substance of freshman composition (1990, 417–22).

(1986; 2d ed. 1994), Lee Jacobus' *Substance, Style, and Strategy* (1998), and William Zinsser's far more widely used *On Writing Well* (5th ed., 1995) explain how to write biographical and autobiographical essays; direct and implied arguments; familiar essays and critiques of literature, society, the arts, and sports; essays on science and technology; and humor. They assume an audience beyond the teacher and the classroom, together with a professional's willingness to write and rewrite until the result looks inevitable—and easy. Zinsser derives his "favorite definition of a careful writer" from Joe DiMaggio: "I marveled at how effortless he looked because what he did could only be achieved by great effort. A reporter once asked him how he managed to play so well so consistently, and he said: 'I always thought that there was at least one person in the stands who had never seen me play and I didn't want to let him down'" (282).[5]

Readers

Advanced composition readers are of several types, largely distinguished from freshman texts by the absence or minimalism of the apparatuses including study questions, suggestions for writing, and elaborate discussions of writing and reading processes. The oldest, published in 1965, is a collection of several essays apiece by a small number of belletristic essayists, pioneered by William Smart's *Eight Modern Essayists*—Max Beerbohm, E. M. Forster, Virginia Woolf, James Thurber, Edmund Wilson, E. B. White, George Orwell, and James Baldwin. Another common type is the collection of belletristic or New Journalistic essays by diverse hands. For a while Tom Wolfe's *New Journalism,* nonfiction written with "techniques usually associated with novels and short stories" (1973, 15), was popular, exposing prospective feature writers to the work of such authors as Gay Talese, Truman Capote, Hunter S. Thompson, George Plimpton, Joan Didion (Didion and Barbara Goldsmith were the only women), and Tom Wolfe himself—"But exactly!" (21). More contemporary reading texts include collections of nonfiction by a variety of distinguished thinkers and stylists, a mix of women and multicultural authors that challenges white male authors' two-decade domination of these texts. Robert Atwan's college edition of *Best American Essays* (1998), with contemporary essays by Judith Ortiz Cofer, Henry Louis Gates Jr., Garrett Hongo, Jamaica Kincaid, Chang-Rae Lee, Judy Ruiz, Amy Tan, and Lé Thi Diem Thúy, among others, is marketed as a textbook, in contrast to Atwan's trade-oriented *Best American Essays* (annually since 1986). Alternative textbook possibilities

---

5. Unique among freshman textbooks, John Trimbur's *Call to Write* has the real-world orientation of advanced texts, envisioning actual audiences and occasions for addressing them in a variety of genres formal and informal: "letters, memoirs, public documents, profiles, reports, commentary, proposals, and reviews" (1999, 5). Unlike other freshman books, Trimbur's concluding section on editing spends a mere thirty-five pages on sentences, language, and problems for second-language writers (681–715). Whether this will strike potential users as a book for advanced writers instead of freshmen remains to be seen; it is marketed as a freshman text.

include spreads of personal and familiar essays, classical to contemporary and largely written by white men, in collections edited by Joseph Epstein (*The Norton Book of Personal Essays* 1997), John Gross (*The Oxford Book of Essays* 1991), and Phillip Lopate (*The Art of the Personal Essay* 1994 and *The Anchor Essay Annual* 1997). *Creative Nonfiction* (three issues a year since 1993) offers classroom subscriptions and auxiliary materials. Nevertheless, the syllabi I have on hand (I don't have creative nonfiction syllabi for M.F.A. programs) do not show that any of these alternatives to textbooks are actually used in advanced composition courses.

Who Teaches Advanced Composition?

Who teaches advanced composition? The 1969 CCCC report identifies advanced composition teachers, "with few exceptions," as literary or linguistic scholars who "by circumstances or inclination" learned how to teach the course by teaching it, either in an English department (Committee Reports, 254) or in courses across the curriculum (Committee Reports 1971, 291). The status remains quo thirty years later. The fact that conventional academic faculty—not usually the TAs and part-timers who teach freshman composition—with an academic orientation are the usual teachers of advanced composition, in whatever form, is borne out by the CCCC reports; the Hogan (1980), Dicks (1982), and Shumaker, Dennis, and Green (1990) surveys; the few research volumes on the subject (Adams and Adams 1991; Adams 1993; Haswell 1991); and all but three of the articles in two decades of the *Journal of Advanced Composition.*[6] All consist of academic prose written by authors, mostly English professors, with academic affiliations. Even three of the four authors of *JAC* articles who in other contexts write creative nonfiction or other expressivist prose (Wendy Bishop, Peter Elbow, and myself) write academic articles in an academic mode—even my own article that exhorts, "Why Don't We Write What We Teach? And Publish It?" (*JAC* 1990, 87–100). This academic bias is partly a reflection of the editorial policy of Gary Olson, *JAC* editor from 1987 to 1994, who promoted theory in concept and in language; his successors changed the journal name to *Journal of Composition Theory,* although it still retains the *JAC* monogram. This academic bias also reflects the location of advanced composition among the regular undergraduate course offerings of English departments, for the course is usually not seen as a form of creative writing unless the individual teacher so defines it.[7]

---

6. The three exceptions are Harriet Malinowitz's "David [Bartholomae] and Me" (*JAC* 16.2, 1996, 209–24), Dawn K. Dreyer's "In the Margins: An Exploration of Boundaries in a Student / Teacher Response Dialogue" (*JAC* 16.2, 1996, 225–40), and Jane Tompkins' "Postcards from the Edge" (*JAC* 13.2, 1993, 449–58).

7. However, as "creative nonfiction," the graduate version of this course is often integrated into M.F.A. programs in creative writing, where it is taught by creative writers and some more conventional academics who also write creative nonfiction.

A Developmental Approach: A Tale of Two Courses

Richard Haswell's *Gaining Ground in College Writing: Tales of Development and Interpretation* (1991) is the only work I know—except the book you're reading—that attempts to break away from the prevailing linear curricular model of advanced composition reflected in virtually all of the materials surveyed above—definitions, course descriptions, syllabi, textbooks. Haswell's theoretical work systematically addresses differences between freshman and advanced composition by proposing a developmental framework designed to accommodate the student's growth rather than to replicate a linear rhetorical model. In an elaborate "cognitive, affective, psychological and social" construct, derived from a combination of Kohlberg, Perry, Gilligan, and Whitehead, among others, Haswell offers a developmental writing curriculum that takes issue with the instrumental "linear syntax of learning to write" that conventionally postulates a linear curricular sequence for undergraduate writing, and thus a "'best' order to beginning and advanced courses"; a "best syllabus, or order to the parts of each course"; and a fine-tuning to individual student need. He also takes issue with syllabi that answer the question, "what should any one student do first?" second, and so on (288).

At the outset of the conventional linear freshman course, says Haswell, "students are made to write, the writing shows what they cannot do, and that inability tells the teacher where to begin." The first course "'covers' all the major component skills and knowledge," and the advanced course follows by "refining" the same machinery, "invention, argument, audience awareness, support, and so on. Discourse, that vehicle of thought, is brought around for its annual . . . tune-up" (289–91). Yet, as Haswell points out, the "best" syllabus sequence can be almost anything, "so complex a tool is rhetoric," allowing one to start (or end) with words, sentences, paragraphs, or whole essays; or with one (or another) mode of discourse; or with one (or another) element in Burke's pentad. Such instrumental orderings "authorize sequences without much educational sustenance" (292).

Haswell offers the alternative of a developmental frame that is focused first on the student and only secondarily on the material. Thus "optimal instructional sequence" no longer refers to complete coverage of the material, but to "the way to get students to develop their writing the furthest." In its transformative orientation, this developmental approach assumes that "both matter and student have been and will keep on changing." If anything is instrumental, says Haswell, "it is all the evolving aspects of the human—material, emotional, intellectual, social, linguistic" that sensitive mentors elicit from their students to "produce the lifework of the student, a creation that never stops developing" (294). Haswell provides a long list of pre- and postcollege changes that a developmental curriculum should foster (301–7). For instance, in opposition to the precollege "assumption that principles have *universal application*" is the postcollege "assumption of *contextual application,* appropriate in different ways under different circumstances" (301).

Haswell concludes *Gaining Ground* by applying these principles to an ideal "curriculum sensitive to lifework sequences," an integration of "student, mentor, lifework, and field" (diagram, 295) intended to reinforce the developmental changes he postulates. Thus his curriculum would do all of the following: It would teach "skills" that will become part of the student's "uncoerced life history," and it would avoid direct instruction "where students seem to progress on their own." Sequencing would focus on "key points," rather than attempting "full coverage" of an issue, to accommodate the students' differential development of individual characteristics. It would teach "tactics and strategies" together when they "cluster and interact generatively." Skills would be taught in congruence with changes "in student impulses and needs." The "more inclusive" skills would be taught first. Thus the advanced writing syllabus "treats flow first, syntax second, and diction third," assuming that the more "inclusive principles of flow (e.g., the dynamics of given new information) will automatically prompt beneficial changes in syntax and that some of the principles of syntax (e.g., parallelism) will intuitively foster improved choice of words." Sequencing in this curriculum will begin and end "proleptically," allowing students to begin by taking on "tasks a little ahead of their competence" and to end with the recognition that "what they have learned will be augmented, contradicted, and transformed in the next course" (324–29).

It is not clear from *Gaining Ground* or any subsequent publications in the field that Haswell's scheme has actually been applied to a sequence of freshman and advanced composition courses for which it is designed. His illustrations refer to research on one course or the other, as in sentence combining, but not to actual curricula in actual schools. His hopeful evidence is largely piecemeal, for the curriculum research he cites deals with such matters as composing processes, sentence length and structure, and vocabulary choice—matters usually associated with freshman composition rather than the advanced course—and not with the writing of intellectually or morally sophisticated whole essays. Indeed, Haswell's scheme, if implemented, could provide a coherent configuration for a freshman composition course or course sequence. But he remains vague about what advanced composition courses might be and do.

Which brings us to the innovations presented by the rest of *Coming of Age*. These materials, proffered by a panoply of master chefs—writing scholars and teachers—should either verify, test, or challenge both Haswell's (psycho)logical paradigm and the rhetorical paradigms, however precise or vague, of his more conventional twentieth-century predecessors. Bon appetit!

Feathering Our Nest?

A Critical View from Within Our Discipline

Richard Bullock

[O]ur own desires, practices, and situations are inevitably mixed . . .
they contain tensions, and possibly even contradictions, that we may
not wish to acknowledge.

—Lisa Ede, 1996

The Apple Doesn't Fall Far from the Tree?

Like many of my generation, I "discovered" composition studies when I was in
graduate school. I thought I wanted to become a scholar of eighteenth-century
British literature, but after a couple of punishing semesters, I found some professors who had developed an interest in writing and its teaching. I began tutoring in the writing center, and I found myself more at home there than when
cozying up to Pope and Swift. Luckily, my school had just developed a program
that combined pedagogical study with literary study, so my hybrid degree made
me marketable as a composition specialist, but one who could also teach lit
classes and (it was hoped) understand my colleagues' allusions.

In those days, having a pedigree as a writing specialist with a Ph.D. made
getting a job relatively easy; my six Modern Language Association (MLA) interviews looked very good to my friends with lit degrees, who had one or two
and who knew people from other schools who had one, or none, for the second
year in a row. Indeed, some people in the lit program began taking courses in
the pedagogy program in hopes that some of the cachet—and potentially, a
tenure-track job—would rub off on them.

Yet, when my fellow writing specialists and I got over the euphoria of having jobs and started living them, we often found ourselves marginalized: usually the only writing specialist in the otherwise totally literature-oriented department, burdened heavily with administrative duties and committee work,
barred from teaching most graduate courses and advanced undergraduate
courses (what would we teach, except for the TA training seminars and first-
year composition?), facing uncertain futures because tenure depended on A
Book, and it couldn't be a textbook or an edited collection. At my first job, my

well-meaning chair arranged for me to edit a volume of *The Dictionary of Literary Biography* on a subject I knew nothing about, so that I'd have credentials my English department colleagues could understand.

Were we resentful of our treatment? You bet we were. Were we complicit? You bet we were. We had jobs, after all, and they weren't one-year term contracts with no benefits and no moving allowance. We had teaching assistants recruited by our literature colleagues who were motivated by momentum or inertia, desire for the status of a thriving graduate program, the lure of teaching well-enrolled graduate seminars, and the institutional money that accompanies graduate students—as well as the need for TAs to teach first-year writing courses. The lit profs taught the undergraduates, the *English* majors. We writing folk, the writing program administrators (WPA), kept the first-year program running smoothly, sometimes sacrificing our own careers along the way. Charles Schuster paints a vivid portrait of the self-sacrificing WPA as an analogue of Orwell's Boxer the horse:

> Like Boxer, they believe in "working harder." Like Boxer, they are committed to improving the condition of the farm and know that it is they—and no one else—who can accomplish this goal. . . . Moreover, English department faculty find it easy to let them assume this role of Boxer: Who else would choose to do all the work of teaching writing and administering freshman composition? (That is, after all, part of their "stupidity.") Who else is better equipped to administer composition programs, serve on college and university committees, direct the writing center? Isn't that their training? After all, that's why a composition specialist was hired in the first place—to haul the stone and get up an hour earlier every morning even if it means career death at the age of seven. (1991, 87)

Schuster's scenario says much about the mindset of composition specialists, but it also says much about the English departments that hired, used, and then discarded many of them. Remember who ran the place in *Animal Farm:* the pigs. Unlike their literature colleagues, composition specialists were ill-used, disrespected, and expendable—certainly not fit for tenuring or promotion.

Those of us who survived have found ourselves in an interesting new world these past few years. Composition studies has made great gains in many schools, so that now even middling-sized colleges may have several writing specialists, most with Ph.D.s in writing and rhetoric from real graduate programs. New graduate programs in writing and rhetoric are springing up everywhere, and more and more students are coming to us wanting courses, certificate programs, M.A.s, and Ph.D.s. And as this volume testifies, we're developing undergraduate courses and even undergraduate majors in various facets of writing studies. We—writing studies and its specialists—have found our place in the academic pantheon.

So why am I nervous?

I'm nervous because our well-intentioned desire to expand our programs from graduate to undergraduate study may have effects we don't intend. The writers in this volume see undergraduate writing curricula as having two inter-acting goals: to prepare students for careers as writers (technical, computer, creative, or other) and to prepare them to participate in the civic life of their communities. These are wonderful goals, and if the programs achieve these goals, they will prepare students for satisfying work that needs to be done, and done well. However, we have examples aplenty of programs—creative writ-ing, mostly—that appear to exist to prepare writers only for graduate programs in creative writing. We have many literature programs that appear to have as their goal the preparing of students only for graduate study in literature. How often do we hear our colleagues urge excellent students to consider graduate school, to think about a career as a scholar, to *become like me?*

I'm nervous because I see "us," the profession of writing studies, behav-ing in ways I'd found disquieting and morally suspect in English departments: creating programs that prepare teachers of college-level writing in the absence of need, making programs larger despite dismal employment prospects for our graduates, focusing on self-aggrandizement (often phrased in terms of "respect for us as professionals with a field") rather than on being of use to students. How many of us—and I include myself, my hopelessly compromised and hypo-critical self, in this "us"—welcome and even entice students into writing stud-ies, because it's personally satisfying to teach good students who are interested in what we're interested in? How many of us take satisfaction from comman-deering, for a required rhetoric course, a course requirement for the English major once reserved for literature, or feel smug when students elect the comp/rhet M.A. program instead of the one in lit? How many of us, because we're committed to what we do and care deeply about it, desire to share that commit-ment and caring with others and do so in the only way we know how: through developing and expanding courses and programs and then inviting students into them?

I know I'd have to raise my hand if these questions were asked, and that makes me uneasy. I fear that I could be judged by the same rules I use for judg-ing literature professors, and I want to resist temporizing: I want to resist the urge to say, "Well, I was young and harsh then; now I've learned that things are more complicated than that."

The fact is, I'm a tenured full professor with a comfortable income, a nice house, and a decent academic reputation. I've got a small but real amount of power in my university, and if some of the TAs and lecturers call me "Boss," I smile, tell them not to call me that, but feel a small shiver of pleasure despite the echoes of James Sledd's term for WPAs, "Boss Compositionist." The fact is, I've benefitted greatly from being a WPA in an English department, and I've done so through helping graduate students become good teachers of writ-ing, and so freeing other tenure-line faculty from teaching first-year comp; through selecting and working with a wonderful group of lecturers (faculty who teach nine courses each year, not seven like the tenure-line folks; who share offices, unlike the tenure-line folks; who teach mostly first-year comp far better than the tenure-line folks; and who do it for thousands of dollars less);

and representing the writing programs in the department and university, all with great success—if a writing-across-the-curriculum (WAC) program, two graduate concentrations, two certificate programs, and a large, well-established writing center are indicators of success. We've got a darned good writing program in place here at Wright State University (Dayton) and our graduates compete well with M.A.s from schools across the country, schools with more fame and prestige. We do good work here.

The trouble is, we do too much of it. Each year we graduate into a very limited job market several people with M.A.s and aspirations of becoming writing teachers who too often end up coming back to teach for us, two courses per quarter, six per year, for $1,100 per course, victims of the syndrome Pauline Uchmanowicz (1997) rightly labels "hoop dreams." Until last year we had eight instructor-level faculty, who endured four-year limited-term contracts but whose turnover permitted us to hire one or two people with M.A.s each year, providing some salve for our consciences; but—trading one moral dilemma for another—we converted them all to lecturers with indefinitely renewable contracts, effectively ending our hiring of M.A.s until someone retires or resigns. Thank God we don't have a Ph.D. program, in which the moral conflicts make mine look paltry.

Undergraduate courses and programs in writing and rhetoric run the danger of participating in this same syndrome of enticement and abandonment, bait and switch. On the one hand, I want undergraduates, English majors especially, to know that writing and rhetoric exist. I want to teach courses that explore with undergraduate students various aspects of my field. I want to share my love of my work with them. But to what extent is my desire untowardly selfish? How many students will I entice into my field, extending hope that no attempts at tempering—by having them read the "Wyoming Resolution" (1987), for instance, or essays like James Slevin's "Depoliticizing and Politicizing Composition Studies" (1991)—will shake? The literature programs from which many of us earned our degrees acted irresponsibly, urging undergraduate students to begin graduate study with the lure of assistantships, packing their classrooms with full-time enrollments (FTE)–generating graduate students, and providing senior professors with ego-stroking advisees. Tendencies toward addictions run in families, and for many decades writing studies has been part of the family of English departments. Lisa Ede observes, "Simply by working in [academic] institutions . . . we become, whether we wish to or not, part of the complex and paradoxical story that they narrate" (1996, 119). With the best of intentions, we expand our offerings, broaden our appeal, and strive for curricular parity with other fields, but as we do we risk traveling down dangerous paths—creating stories with plots we cannot control and that look disturbingly similar to the ones from which we have striven to distance ourselves. I think we need to ask ourselves how much we want to expand our disciplines, not necessarily as a way of improving the education of students but as a way of gaining access to the same perquisites enjoyed by our literary parents and siblings.

Veni, Vedi, Vici?

And what do these perquisites entail? If the talk I hear at professional conferences is even partially true, one of those perquisites is—surprise, surprise!—release of writing specialists from teaching of, or even thinking about, first-year composition. Quoting John Trimbur, Nancy Welch notes,

> As writing takes "the social turn," Trimbur writes, teachers and researchers no longer locate their interests and questions in "students' reading and writing processes," but instead in "the cultural politics of literacy" (*College Composition and Communication* 1994, 109). With this shift, revision, understood as a late stage in a generic composing process, gets left behind, outdated as words like *prewriting* or *planning*. (1997, 24)

In his volume of essays promoting the "New Abolitionist" movement, Joseph Petraglia summarizes the "intellectual fragility" of first-year composition, which is "manifested in several ways: in the *persistently low status of writing as a study both within and outside of English departments,* in professional journal articles and conference presentations that are growing both in theoretical sophistication and *irrelevance to the composition classroom,* and in the rhetoric and writing field's ever-increasing attention to *nontraditional sites of writing behavior*" (1995, xii, italics mine). There's no doubt that first-year composition has had low status within English departments, despite—or perhaps because of—its lucrativeness, both in tuition for the department and university and in work for armies of graduate students; yet we seem to have come a long way from both the separatist movement of the mid-eighties that saw the creation of several writing programs independent of English departments, and so no longer subject to their hierarchies, and the sentiments expressed by Toby Fulwiler in "Freshman English" (1986). The abolitionists give up first-year comp as a hopeless cause, an "ill-conceived and rotting pedagogical structure" (Goggin 1995, 43), and look instead to "nontraditional sites" and scholarly projects that, like Trimbur's cultural politics of literacy, are "irrelevan[t] to the composition classroom" (Petraglia 1995, xii). The dangers here go beyond sinking into the same mire that taints literature programs; there are also dangers for writing and rhetoric as a field as well.

Most importantly, we risk losing our power base. Despite those in our ranks who question the effectiveness of first-year composition programs, faculty and administrators outside our field do not: in a survey of first-year writing programs that William E. Smith and I conducted, we found that first-year writing courses are required in more than 98 percent of the colleges and universities that responded (Bullock 1998, 3). That figure only confirms what we all know: first-year comp is, as Sharon Crowley has labeled it, "the universal requirement" (1991, 156). With increasingly crowded curricula and with students taking an average of six years to graduate from college, the pressure on departments across the university to streamline their requirements is great. Yet everybody needs to take first-year composition.

This near-universal belief in the usefulness and value of the course affords writing a special place in university life and provides the writing program with allies among faculty and administrators, even those who might not value humanistic study—at least not when it competes for curricular space with their own majors' courses. As we professionalize, as we turn our attention away from first-year comp to more theoretical scholarly pursuits and advanced courses and major programs, we may indeed gain opportunities for enhanced respect, interested students, and varied teaching opportunities; we may also forfeit the power of our service role. Latin has been a respected major in many universities for many years; but how large is the classics department at your school?

Discipline . . . and Punish?

Am I declaring this volume and the project it promotes to be dangerous, ill-conceived, and perverse? Of course not. As I look through the contents, I grow excited about the wonderful creativity, the courses I want to teach, the courses I wish I could take. At my school, we have just taught for the first time an undergraduate introduction to rhetoric and writing studies, a new option in the English major. I don't believe we should remain static or, worse, return to the days when it was thought that "composition studies" encompassed only first-year comp and, maybe, basic writing courses. With Charles Bazerman, I believe that while first-year composition is central to our professional identity and professional reason for being, it should be considered "a major site of instruction and support, but not the only site" (1995, 258). The courses outlined here offer additional sites for the work of our field.

I wish only to outline the dangers of which we should be aware, the pressures to which we are subject as we grow and develop. Ede notes that *discipline* is not only a noun but also a verb: "disciplines are inherently conservative . . . they tend to discipline, rather than to encourage, progressive practices" (1996, 116). They form a center from which to draw a personal and institutional—and disciplinary—identity, and, as Kenneth Bruffee reminds us, "WPA-ing [and, I'll risk extending his metaphor, writing studies generally] is inherently a boundary-negotiating enterprise. . . . boundaries," he says, "are where the action is" (1999, 55–64). Professionalizing—institutionalizing through developing undergraduate majors as well as graduate programs—is risky business, and for us writing folk, the risk inheres in losing sight of our strengths—being pragmatic, student-centered, experimental, even subversive—and taking on the weaknesses of others as we "discipline" ourselves.

Curriculum Development in Composition

Robert A. Schwegler

The widespread view that literature is a subject matter but that writing is a skill has tremendous ideological force, and this ideological force has created a curricular imbalance with direct and dire consequences for students, teachers, and the academy. What is needed now to build, or rebuild, our discipline is the ability to conceptualize writing courses as addressing fields of discursive, social activity. Such a reconceptualization will allow us to take a fundamental step toward developing worthwhile advanced courses that will provide opportunities for the practice and study of writing in its many manifestations.

For *ideology*, I have in mind the structures of belief, value, and practice that Pierre Bourdieu (1986) sees as shaping, reproducing, and determining the flow of capital and resources within fields of cultural and intellectual activity—what Terry Eagleton terms "the 'microstructures' of ideology" operating at the level of "'everyday life'" (1991, 158). During the last decades of the nineteenth century and the early twentieth century, the dominant academic view of literature was that it constituted a subject for study, analysis, interpretation, and research—this in contrast to other possibilities, such as an art of production or a vehicle for ethical discussion or personal growth (Graff 1987; Court 1992). The focus on literature as a subject had important consequences. The rapidly emerging collegiate academic departments and disciplines of the period largely developed around their objects of study, which were constructed as sites for analysis. Attention to performance, procedure, and production was relegated to institutions like conservatories, technical institutes, and schools of design and engineering, either as separate institutions or as distinct units within a university. Thus the view of literature as a subject matter was consistent with the structuring systems and values of its institutional context.

Many in the professoriat view curricula uncritically, simply as sets of courses, and curriculum development as the creation of a list of courses characterized by some kind of formal unity, achieved either through a theme, such as the study of American culture, or formal categories, such as historical periods, genres, and major figures. A curriculum, however, is a set of practices and material conditions: catalog descriptions and course proposals shepherded through often-contentious committees; catalog text and registration booklets promulgated widely, making binding and nonbinding promises and placing numbered course listings in the semblance of a coherent plan; teaching schedules and general education requirements stated according to course titles and numbers; the content of job announcements and tenure/promotion discussions; categories for distributing physical and monetary resources; part of the everyday language of students, instructors, administrators, and scholars; minds of bureaucrats and politicians using their recollections of college to formulate educational policy and funding. Curricular formation is competitive: the allocation of curricular space involves the distribution and reallocation of funding, time, and prestige, as well as of faculty and student bodies.

From the end of the nineteenth century through most of the twentieth, the definition of literary study as a subject matter acted as an expansive ideology, encouraging division and development and enabling literary study to occupy considerable curricular space. In contrast, the definition of writing as a skill that is largely impervious to scholarly analysis led to the restriction of its curricular development (Crowley 1998; Graff 1987).

Because literature was regarded as a distinct subject, it needed to be studied in courses and have a curriculum specifically devoted to it, not be part of history courses or courses devoted to multiple arts of expression. Mid-twentieth-century efforts to distinguish sharply between literary and ordinary or expository language further strengthened this position. Because literary texts displayed considerable complexity, they needed to be studied beyond introductory courses. The demand for more advanced and specialized courses grew as research revealed more complexity in texts and in literary interpretation and at the same time added to the subject matter: newly discovered or rediscovered texts, biographical and contextual information, and fresh critical and interpretive strategies (Graff 1987).

Perhaps the most important quality attributed to literature was variety, at least in terms of curricular consequences. Historical differences in texts justified the creation and proliferation of historical period courses; genre differences justified further subdivision and course proliferation. Emphasis on the uniqueness of each literary expression meant that courses and anthologies had to expand to include more and more texts, not just key exemplars. Increasingly crowded syllabi led to further subdivision: the one-semester English survey became two; the one-semester American survey underwent similar mitosis (Schwegler n.d.). Assertions about the value of literature and literary study, together with the rising prestige of the subject, justified an increasing allocation of resources and an expansion of curricular space.

In contrast, institutional, professional, and public discussions during the later nineteenth and early twentieth centuries defined writing as a skill and composition instruction as skills training (Connors 1997; Crowley 1998, 1990). This ideological frame still holds sway in many institutions, despite several decades of extensive research and attempts to erase the stigma of composition as a "course without a subject of its own." In curricular terms, it is much harder to divide a skill than a subject matter, except into stages. And the stages of composing have proven to be an unconvincing and unsuccessful rationale for course differentiation (Connors 1997, 210–56).

Frequently, writing was not even posited as a discrete skill that deserved curricular space of its own beyond a basic course. Thus efforts toward the development of advanced, variegated writing curricula often dissipated or were derailed by movements to make writing instruction a secondary element in courses denominated by some other subject matter, such as writing about literature, autobiographical writing, or writing across the curriculum (Russell 1991).

Because writing was regarded as a skill—a means to an end—it lacked, in contrast to literary study, both the variety and a principle of division that could lead to the creation of a curriculum that included numerous specialized courses. When I speak of writing as a skill, I do not, of course, mean anything like the complex cognitive processes outlined by process theorists or the culturally and socially grounded activities described by postprocess theorists. For much of this century, writing skill, in both theory and practice, has meant the skill to write an essay—perhaps the more appropriate term would be *theme*—in an appropriately academic style (Crowley 1998). It was defined as a unitary skill, more or less universal, and subject to only minor changes or adaptation based on task or context.

The basic unit of writing courses was, and remains, "the paper," that is, the various activities leading up to the production of a written text submitted for a grade. Thus writing as course content came to be regarded as centering on a structured and structuring unit, "the paper," as in "I'm working on a paper" or "This course requires five papers, each one of which will include extensive revision and peer critique" or "College Composition . . . Emphasis on writing six expository and argumentative papers." So widespread and widely accepted was this design principle that, I want to argue, it limited the variety of courses that one might imagine as part of a writing curriculum. It excluded, for example, courses that might provide important knowledge for writers, such as a history or survey of rhetorical theory, and also those developing forms of expertise, such as stylistics or document design (Crowley 1998; Adams 1993; Brereton 1988). Even today, the importance of "the paper" as a structuring unit is such that many attempts to develop an advanced undergraduate writing curriculum have been limited to the construction of a curriculum of writing courses rather than a writing curriculum of courses designed to develop expertise and knowledge important to writers.

Moreover, since most instructors regarded the composing of a paper as a structured, unitary activity, they resisted attempts to divide it and develop a curriculum of courses focusing, for example, on revision or editing or on constituent elements of the finished product, such as paragraphs (Connors 1997). In the early years of this century, courses based on divisions of the composing process appeared and disappeared quickly (Connors 1997; Brereton 1988). Even today it is hard to imagine a curriculum based on such a principle of division, though it is possible to envision courses focused on editing and copyediting, which are also fields of professional activity, or on style, which is at once part of the skill of composing and a textual constituent.

If writing is a skill that does not vary in substantive ways from context to context, then it becomes difficult to argue for a variety of writing courses, either in coverage or level: once students have "mastered" the skill of writing in a first-year composition course, they do not require further instruction. Such a view undoubtedly motivates many attempts to limit direct writing instruction to first-year composition, to first-year seminars accompanied by a liberal dose of general education, especially in the humanities, or to writing-across-the-curriculum programs (Russell 1991). Though assumptions of this sort have limited the development of varied and advanced writing curricula for most of this century, they did not preclude the development of advanced composition courses based on differing levels of student skills and abilities. Indeed, the rationale offered for many intermediate and advanced composition courses has often been that they are necessitated by differences in student ability (Adams 1993). And all too often the result has been a handful of courses offering more of the same, sustained by the need for practice, but at a higher level, justified by differing levels of ability.

The practice of treating issues of curricular complexity, variety, and level not as consequences of the subject of study or of the activity focus of a course but as justified simply by talent and time—student ability and the need for practice—dovetailed with one of the key assumptions of liberal humanism: that beyond a basic skill level, writing could not be taught, though it might be developed in the small, select group of people possessing the necessary talent and imagination. While this assumption—promulgated in professional discussions, in influential texts like Foerster and Steadman's *Writing and Thinking* (1931), and by the attitudes fostered in elite colleges and graduate programs (Crowley 1998)—encouraged the development of some advanced composition courses, it also limited the development of writing as a subject area, especially because the prestige of literary study drew students instead to "creative writing."

I am not arguing that the skills ideology was ubiquitous or uniform in its consequences. Yet it was certainly widespread, and alternative views of the writing curriculum rooted in the diversity or complexity of the subject matter had little influence. For example, modal theory, advanced by Alexander Bain and others, emphasized cognitive differences in the composing of narrative, descriptive, expository, argumentative, and poetic text, giving rise in the early twentieth century to courses and texts focusing on single modes. These soon disappeared, however, replaced by first-year courses covering several modes and by multimodal texts (Connors 1997).

Courses built around genres of writing provided another alternative in the early decades of the twentieth century, though there was little agreement from institution to institution on the kinds of writing that deserved curricular space (Adams 1993)—in contrast, for example, to the widespread agreement over the constituents of the literature curriculum. From mid-century on, courses in technical and business communication appeared, with considerable professional agreement on their coverage and goals (Lay, this volume; Adams 1993). Nonetheless, these courses were generally singletons, not part of growing writing curricula, and they were often offered by departments other than English, because most English faculty were unwilling to accord them anything but practical value—a clearly secondary position in departments of literary study grounded in an imaginative/practical binary.

There are probably many reasons that division according to subject matter failed with regard to writing courses while succeeding with literature courses. I want to argue that ideology played an important role, specifically, the lack of a set of beliefs attributing value and complexity to the act of composing and to the "nonliterary" kinds of discourse attended to in writing courses. But the times have changed. Extensive work in fields such as discourse analysis, cultural studies, and social theory provides both intellectual and institutional justification, as does the scholarly sophistication of modern rhetorical theory, along with cognitive, sociocognitive, and cultural perspectives on composing. Cultural and institutional change provide additional impetus for reform.

Most important, however, is the growing sense that the things that should be studied and practiced in writing courses—the processes of composing; discourse genres; contexts; readers; media; links among texts, knowledge, power, and action—form clusters distinct enough to deserve courses of their own, yet related enough to constitute a discipline and a curriculum. In practice and in theory, we are beginning to focus and conceptualize our professional and pedagogical activities according to fields of activity.

This concept of activity fields has strong curricular potential. It provides us with a principle of divisibility and with grounds for curricular presence and space. Yet it does not require the abandonment of a focus on skills development as an essential element of writing instruction. An activity field, or activity system, is, as David Russell defines it,

> . . . any ongoing, object-directed, historically conditioned, dialectically structured, tool-mediated human interaction. Some examples are a family, a religious organization, an advocacy group, a political movement, a course of study, a school, a discipline, a research laboratory, and a profession. These activity systems are mutually (re)constructed by participants historically, using certain tools and not others, including discursive tools such as speech sounds and inscriptions. The activity system is the basic unit of analysis for both groups' and individuals' behavior, in that it analyzes the way concrete tools are used to mediate the motive (direction, trajectory) and the object (the problem space or the focus) of behavior and changes in it. . . . (1997, 510)

Russell additionally argues that the concept of activity systems can be productively applied to text- and genre-mediated systems—what we might call discursive fields—and to learning to write within such fields.

A curriculum divided into courses focusing on different fields of activity, or discursive fields, has the advantage of acting as one divided according to subject matter—a powerful strategy in the struggle for departmental presence, curricular space, and allocation of institutional resources. At the same time, it retains an emphasis on writing skill, though it might be better to talk of expertise or kinds of expertise to avoid the universal and elementary connotations of the term *skill*.

Admittedly, the fit between courses and activity fields is not likely to be all that tight. Technical communication is not an activity field, but software documentation and technical documentation for computer hardware manufacturing are; at least, they are discursive activities characteristic of two different, though related fields: software engineering and hardware engineering. But a technical writing course can be designed to help students identify different activity systems and the discursive practices characteristic of them and can even include a focus on one or more specific systems. Or technical writing instruction can be divided into courses with specific focus on writing for the computer industry, writing in the health sciences, or even writing for mechanical and civil engineering. Such courses may seem rather narrow in coverage, but it is important to remember that for years English departments have followed the logic of subdivision, creating not simply courses focusing on Renaissance or nineteenth-century literature but also offerings like Renaissance 1: Sixteenth Century and Renaissance 2: Seventeenth Century or Romantic and Early Nineteenth Century as well as Victorian and Later Nineteenth Century. Most important is that the concept of activity fields provides a principle of division that can serve student need and faculty resources.

Courses on editing and publishing as professional activities (Miles, this volume), legal writing (Fulkerson, this volume), writing for community organizations, or media and political writing could be built around the recognition that, as Russell puts it, "organizations as well as individuals have writing processes and that analyzing the various writing processes of different networks of human activity—variously theorized as social or discursive practices, communities of practice, or discourse communities—can help us understand how writing works and people work with writing, individually and collectively" (1997, 81). Courses focused on activity fields would investigate recurring textual and discursive practices; relationships of textual knowledge, resources, and power; and systems of representation—all while stressing discursive participation in a field and offering opportunities for practice and response.

Activity theory provides a way of articulating the rationale for an advanced writing curriculum as distinct from both the text-centered, interpretive focus of literary study and the analytical, interpretive focus of cultural anthropology. Activity theory also provides a framework for viewing the subject matter of writing studies as varied and divisible, although inevitably subject to negotiation, consensus formation, and local conditions. Many of the courses outlined in this volume are steps in such a process, analogous to canon formation in literary studies.

The concept of activity fields, or activity systems, provides a framework for highlighting the complexity of each field and in so doing helps justify a curriculum of varied, specialized courses. And to the extent that the activities in a specific field are valued academically or culturally—the negotiation of power, knowledge, and actions in scientific, political, or economic domains, for example—specific courses are likely to become common components in writing curricula. The same forces are also likely to shape research agendas that will, in turn, affect curricular presence.

It would be hard to argue for a course hierarchy or sequence based solely on differences among fields, yet notions of activity and expertise that are essential to understanding the operation of discursive fields offer a student-centered justification for course levels: What kinds of knowledge and expertise will students need to bring to a course? What kinds of intellectual and social experience or development will the field and the mode of instruction presume? An activity-focused curriculum entails assumed goals for instruction, chief among them the ability to function as a writing agent either in one field or in a variety of fields (see Shamoon, this volume). The breadth or narrowness of this goal can help guide decisions of curricular scope and sequence.

I do not believe, however, that a curriculum built around activity fields alone will be either coherent or satisfactory. Some kinds of knowledge and expertise are common to many activity fields, and subject courses such as rhetorical theory or graphic design are certainly important for a writing curriculum. Such courses need not be "writing" courses in a narrow sense. A writing curriculum, as opposed to a collection of writing courses, allows for and may even require courses that do not fit current definitions of a composition course.

There is also a role for skills-focused courses in a curriculum built around fields of activity: attention to revision, invention, stylistics, or correctness, for example, is important when the instruction is rhetorically centered and sensitive to differing communities of writers and readers.

The notion of activity fields enables us to envision writing curricula that attend to the complexity and variety of writing activities and written texts, focusing on production and action rather than reading, interpretation, and criticism. This vision is ideological in a double sense: it gives structure to emerging practices and helps envision their structuring effects. It will likely have unintended consequences, too, but those are for a different time.

Rhetoric Within and Without Composition

Reimagining the Civic

Thomas P. Miller

Rhetoric and composition have been peculiarly fixated with freshmen (*sic*?). Physics 101 and History 1A are unlikely to be the subject of scholarly articles, let alone entire journals and graduate programs. This peculiarity has been noted by commentators, including those who propose eliminating the first-year requirement as a way to expand the discipline and reduce the exploitation of part-time teachers (Crowley 1998). Such proposals underline the fact that our area of study is curiously bifurcated between first-year and graduate programs, with only a smattering of composition courses between them. As David Fleming has noted, within English departments "rhetoric is featured prominently at the two extremes of higher education: at one end, a fifteen-week course on writing for incoming freshmen; at the other, a multi-year program of advanced study for Ph.D. students. Between the two, there is little or nothing" (1998, 173). This gap is being bridged by new undergraduate courses and majors that call us back to the oldest of rhetorical questions: If rhetoric is a discipline, what is its subject? This ancient question resurfaces from time to time, as when reforms of general education advocate replacing "skills" courses with writing instruction in "content" courses. When composition is reduced to skills, rhetoric tends to be reduced to theories of how to write, as is often assumed in the yoking of rhetoric and composition.

The traditional confines of English departments are being reassessed in response to internal and external pressures for change. In her 1998 presidential address, "Regeneration," the president of Modern Language Association (MLA), Elaine Showalter, argued for expanding graduate studies in English to stress "teaching and communications" (1999, 324). Service work and administration should be valued, and students should be prepared to write in nonacademic jobs and serve as community organizers. Quoting from the Woodrow Wilson Foundation Report *Unleashing the Humanities*, Showalter advocates preparing students to work in the media, nonprofit foundations, government agencies, and corporations—"careers that will allow humanistically trained scholars the opportunity to play public roles in a 'democratic society' dependent on the 'collective thought and imagination of its citizens'" (1999, 320). These innovations are of course quite familiar to those of us who work in rhetoric and composition. Showalter has to reenvision a civic perspective on workplace writing and public affairs because rhetoric and composition are all but invisible from her vantage point on the field. After all, she teaches at Princeton, which has no composition program and has not had a rhetorician on the faculty since W. S. Howell retired. Nonetheless, it is helpful for a president of MLA to call for such reforms because her position lends credibility to the changes that have already been instituted in some graduate programs and need to be implemented at the undergraduate level to redress the national decline in English majors. As we reassess the confines of the discipline, we need to review how English studies ever became reduced to literary studies in the first place.

Reviewing how English studies was first reduced to literary studies can help remind us of rhetoric's broader frame of reference. The subordination of rhetorics to poetics is a product of the Enlightenment.[1] Reception has been valued over composition ever since college English classes were first introduced in the middle of the eighteenth century. The transition from classical to modern cultural studies that established college English studies is useful to review because one could argue that English departments are moving toward a cultural position that is similar to that which the classical tradition occupied in previous centuries. The canonical texts and modes of response enshrined within English departments have held a classical authority among the educated, but this cultural capital is losing its currency as a result of technological and social changes in the political economy of literacy. As bastions of the culture of the book, English departments may well become the classics departments of the twenty-first century, especially if they continue to define themselves by literary rather than literacy studies. On the other hand, English departments are beginning to realize that they have been overproducing Ph.D.s in literature for more than twenty years, and new undergraduate majors and courses of study are beginning to expand the field of study. A review of the history of rhetoric can help us realize the potentials of these institutional reforms and the historical changes to which they are responding.

Professorships dedicated to teaching English literature, composition, and rhetoric were established almost simultaneously throughout the British cultural provinces in the latter half of the eighteenth century—a century earlier than at the educational centers of English culture. The transition from the ancients to the moderns turned on rhetoric and moral philosophy's shared concern for public discourse and popular values. Some of the first professors to teach English—most notably Adam Smith and John Witherspoon—taught rhetoric and moral philosophy. Moral philosophers began lecturing on the "sciences of man," including psychology, sociology, political economy, and cultural anthropology, while rhetoric moved away from the civic tradition to subordinate the composition of public discourse to commentaries on tasteful responses. These trends were shaped by the transformation of the reading public by cheap print

---

1. Before the eighteenth century, according to Ong, "poetry enjoyed no particular status as an independent academic discipline whereas rhetoric enjoyed enormous academic prestige" (1971, 6).

literacy, which expanded the numbers of readers who needed general education in taste and usage. This need was felt most pressingly by those at the boundaries of the educated culture—by Scots, Irish, Americans, and Dissenters, with the latter excluded by law from Oxbridge. It is not difficult to understand why professors who had to teach themselves English were the first to profess it, but this fact has profound implications for how we understand changes in education and related changes in the educated public, as I will discuss in the next section of this essay (see also Miller 1997).

The civic relations of rhetoric and moral philosophy are useful to review as we reflect upon the possibilities of the current situation. To reimagine the civic, we need to move beyond nostalgia for the civic virtues of the "good man speaking well." That ideology served, in part, to distinguish citizens from women, the uneducated, and others who lacked public authority. The civic tradition was concerned with exercising power through discourse, and a revaluation of the civic can empower rhetoric to become more than a how-to theory of composition. By beginning with personal experiences and ending with academic conventions, composition courses have valorized personal expression while doing the institutional work of teaching students how to pass by conforming to the status quo. Formalist approaches to academic discourse naturalize the dynamic process of translating experience into discursive conventions that arouse and fulfill shared expectations. In opposition to such formalist tendencies, civic rhetoricians have been concerned with the political art of negotiating received beliefs against changing situations to advance shared purposes. This concern for the dialectical relations of audiences, situations, and purposes has too often been reduced to accommodation strategies for writers. A civic philosophy of rhetoric can enable us to bring our work with service learning, new technologies, and political controversies into a unified project that challenges the hierarchy of research, teaching, and service that limits the social implications of academic work and devalues the work of the humanities.

Political Economies and Literary Technologies

Histories of college English tend to focus on the history of ideas contained within the discipline, adopting a trickle-down model of change that assumes that reforms of teaching follow upon theories advanced in elite universities. The history of college English is more like the history of English than we have recognized, as becomes evident when we look beyond the establishment of the scholarly discipline at Harvard or Oxford. English was first formalized and taught in the British provinces because people who lived in contact zones did not acquire educated tastes as part of their natural upbringing and thus had to be formally taught to distinguish the conventions of the educated from the dialectical differences of common people (Pratt 1992). Print spread a dialectical awareness of cultural conventions among audiences who had been excluded by the learned culture when it had been contained within expensive folios and ancient languages. The periodical press grew from 2.25 million in 1711 to 7 million at mid-century and more than 12 million a quarter century later (Williams 1961, 185). Much of the growth came outside the metropolitan centers, with the number of presses in the provinces tripling in the latter half of the century (Colley 1986, 101). This expanding awareness of cultural differences gave rise to efforts to make English as uniform as print. While only two English grammars were published before 1700, thirty-five appeared in the next fifty years, and five times more were published by the end of the century (see Alston 1965–72).

In addition to transforming the political economy of literacy, print also changed how knowledge was created and communicated. The "new learning" involved fundamental changes in the technologies of knowledge. Knowledge was no longer to be acquired by deductively reasoning from traditional assumptions but by inductively generalizing from the individual experience. In a departure from the highly figured forms of Ciceronian rhetoric, knowledge was to be communicated in a plain style that could serve as a window on experience. As learned languages ceased to be the definitive markers of the educated, educated discourse had to be distinguished from the language of common people. Two of the first professors of English, George Campbell and Joseph Priestley, were the leading advocates of correcting English by inductive generalizations from the usage of educated people. They were also influential proponents of the "new" logic and rhetoric. In fact, all the "new" rhetoricians and logicians identified by W. S. Howell's *Eighteenth-Century British Logic and Rhetoric* (1971) were Scots, Irish, Americans, or Dissenters. Thus the logical, rhetorical, and grammatical conventions of educated discourse were systematically reformulated not at the educational centers of the dominant culture but in the provinces. Following upon changes in the political economy of literacy, this reconception of the trivium redefined the technologies of knowledge that defined education and the educated.

As part of this development, political economy and other social sciences became formalized. The "sciences of man" were first formally taught by moral philosophers in the eighteenth-century British provinces. Political economy and psychology provided models for the circulation and internalization of discourse within the reading public. In his courses on rhetoric and moral philosophy at Glasgow from 1751 to 1763, Adam Smith lectured on the sentiments of the responsive auditor and the workings of the market. To formalize the natural laws governing the human psyche and the body politic, Smith's *Theory of Moral Sentiments* (1987b) published in 1759 and *Inquiry into the Nature and Causes of the Wealth of Nations* (1987a) published in 1776 invoke the "Newtonian method" to represent "human society" as "an immense machine" (Smith 1987b, 316). The stance of the disinterested observer was personified by the "impartial spectator." This "demigod within the breast" is internalized as a second self who stands aloof from conflicts in order to make a disinterested judgment (Smith 1987b, 131). Students internalized tasteful self-restraint by imitating the style and stance of belletristic essays such as those of *The Spectator*, which may have been the source of Smith's term (1987b, 15n). From this stance, one could see that self-refinement, the Protestant work ethic, and the "laws" of supply and demand were parts of a Providential order that worked for the good of the whole, even if it left most people illiterate and hungry. The impartial spectator aptly represented the political dislocation and fractured consciousness of educated provincials who had to monitor every word and thought to ensure their correctness, and it served to instill respect for the authority of disinterested social scientists and belletristic critics.

Revaluing the Civic

As an outsider who had to learn English tastes and morals consciously, Smith understood the dialectical processes involved in the social construction and psychological internalization of conventions. As an advocate of tasteful self-restraint, he helped establish college English studies as a means of teaching provincials how to refine a dialectical consciousness into a cultured sensibility. Smith set the position of the dispassionate critic in opposition to the rhetorical stance of the political agent who must determine how best to act in the heat of the moment. According to Smith, "the real, revered, and impartial spectator . . . is upon no occasion at a greater distance than amidst the violence and rage of contending parties" (1987b, 155–56). While Smith's moral philosophy recognized the dialectical possibilities of viewing moral issues and social interactions from multiple standpoints, he ended up valorizing the enlightened ideal of disinterested rationality, in part because he did not view public debate as a means of generating knowledge.

The civic potentials and limitations of Smith's moral philosophy are important because he was not just one of the first professors of English, he was also one of the first major theorists of modern society. The civic tradition in rhetoric and moral philosophy that dates back to Isocrates, Aristotle, and Cicero was still influential in Smith's period, not just in classical sources but also in the works of Machiavelli and Smith's contemporaries Adam Ferguson and John Witherspoon. Within this tradition, engaging in public debate helps the citizen know what is best. Purposeful practical action is a means to realize the potentials of situations, which cannot be determined in the abstract or from a distance. It is in the public sphere that shared values are debated against changing political needs, a debate that advances the common good. As Britain became a world empire and English a world language, what was shared or common could no longer be assumed, and Smith set out to develop sociological and psychological explanations of moral conventions that were consistent with his understanding of political relations. As an advocate of laissez-faire, he assumed that "the economy" was governed by natural laws that should be left to work without intervention, and this assumption devalued the public sphere as a domain for collaboration and purposeful action. In contrast with the ancients, modern society was defined as "commercial society," a consumer society in which "the interest of the producer ought to be attended to, only so far as it may be necessary for promoting that of the consumer" (Smith 1987a, 660). In these ways, Smith helped map out the discursive domain in which English first became established as an object of formal study, most notably by subordinating production to consumption, or rather reception.[2]

Such hierarchies no longer seem to be a natural part of the field of study, and it is time to reassess how English studies became reduced to literary studies. According to Habermas, the "modern concept of literary criticism is closely tied to the rise of the liberal, bourgeois public sphere," for the modern public sphere developed out of the eighteenth-century conception of the "public" as "the critics of art and literature" (1989, 10, 32). In Smith's era, "literature" continued to be used in the now "obsolescent" sense of "letters or books; polite or humane learning; literary culture," but it was becoming limited to the modern sense of nonfactual, nonutilitarian discourse and to a "profession" of literary writers whose works had special value because of their pleasing "emotional effect" (*Oxford English Dictionary* 1971). The spread of reading and writing threatened to popularize literature, and critics met this threat by carefully distinguishing the polite from the popular. Appropriate responses were modeled and used to canonize texts that evoked finer feelings. As Eagleton has discussed, "the birth of aesthetics as an intellectual discourse coincides with the period when cultural production is beginning to suffer the miseries and indignities of commodification" (1990, 64). The basic distinction into the arts and sciences only emerged in the eighteenth century (see the *Oxford English Dictionary* 1971), but in the next century, that distinction evolved into two separate educational cultures. Because it was too calculatedly purposeful to be an art or a science, *modern rhetoric* became an oxymoron for most academics. Only with the disintegration of the ideal of disinterestedness has rhetoric reemerged within the humanities, and then only in broad-based American English departments pressed to mediate changes in literacy by offering "remedial" instruction in the language of the learned—academic English.

Within the civic tradition, rhetoric and moral philosophy have been concerned with political debates, epideictic celebrations, and judicial negotiations of traditional values against changing situations. This dialectical engagement with the social construction of shared beliefs is fundamental to the civic tradition. The eighteenth-century emergence of the social sciences out of moral philosophy has not been written into the history of rhetoric, but the sophists are a

2. The civic is translated into the economic in the lectures on jurisprudence that Smith delivered while he was teaching one of the first university courses on English composition, literature, and rhetoric. Laying out the terms of capitalist political economy, Smith noted that the "foundation" of the "disposition to barter, which is the cause of the division of labor," is "that principle to perswade which so much prevails in human nature." This "power of perswasion" need not be taught because it is part of human nature and is exercised whenever we persuade people to do business with us by appeals to their self-interest (Smith 1978, 493; see also Smith 1987a, 27).

well-recognized case of the same historical dialectic. Like the Scots and Dissenters of the eighteenth century, the sophists were outsiders—non-Athenians who traveled among the Greek city-states as itinerant teachers. From their travels, sophists concluded that established belief systems were founded on custom rather than nature, and this comparative awareness was used to justify teaching people how to debate accepted beliefs. In the eighteenth century, relativism was checked by empiricism, for the "science of man" offered a stable point of reference and reliable methodology for instilling self-control and other enlightened virtues. As the world of print expanded, accounts of cultural differences proliferated, and people were taught to read them as "experiments" that demonstrated "that the untutored Indian and the civilized European have acted upon the same principles" (Millar 1773, iii). Nonetheless, in two of the most dynamic eras of its historical development, rhetoric was dialectically involved with accounting for cultural differences, formalizing social conventions, and translating shared beliefs into practical action. This ethnographic dimension is vital if the civic tradition in rhetoric and moral philosophy is to be more than a source of nostalgia for lost republican virtue.

Civic Literacy

As postmoderns, we are comfortable with all things rhetorical. It is not rhetoric but moral philosophy that seems anachronistic.[3] *Moral* is not a common term in academic parlance, and few of us would use "civic virtue" outside quotation marks other than as a historical reference. The classical ideal of the citizen speaking purposefully for the public interest contains too many problematic assumptions about how reasonable people can transcend differences to achieve the common good. We need a sense of the civic that treats differences as a productive part of collaborative action. In my own work, I have represented traditions as arguments about the means and ends that define a historical group. From this admittedly simplistic perspective, one can see that a tradition needs to value differences if it is to expand its shared sense of what is possible in this situation. A tradition stagnates if it gets locked into disabling dualisms that exclude alternatives and thereby limit the group's abilities to respond effectively to change, as in our own tradition, creative writing was set in opposition to popular and utilitarian forms. A tradition does well—and good if Alasdair

---

3. Moral philosophy has historically been too unsystematic and exhortative—too rhetorical—to be readily accommodated within the academic discipline of philosophy. For example, in the popular *Encyclopedia of Philosophy* at *moral philosophy,* one is referred to *ethics,* and that entry begins by dismissing practical ethics and instead concentrating on the history of metaethics. In this way, the political and social concerns of moral philosophy are reduced to individual ethics, with that in turn reduced to a domain of theoretical speculation. Such popular reference works map out domains of discourse in ways that should become part of our field of study as we move beyond a functionalist approach to academic discourse and take up the work of critiquing the value systems that define economies and technologies of knowledge.

MacIntyre is right—by elaborating fuller and more dynamic explanations of its historical experience, while a tradition can be evaluated as rhetorically static and morally unproductive when its values limit its ability to imagine and achieve its potentials. This model of practical morality exploits a dialectical sense of moral—one founded on the interplay of values and mores as an ongoing rhetorical process of translating shared beliefs into social action.[4]

This model of practical morality values rhetoric's civic engagement with political debates, judicial negotiations, and celebrations of popular values. Rhetoric has been most vital when it has been dynamically engaged with the domain that lies between what is up for debate and what is beyond question. This civic domain is the field of study that I hope rhetoric will reclaim as it expands its frame of reference beyond first-year composition courses. Embracing our tradition as practical moralists can help us position ourselves at sites of controversy where established assumptions are called into question in disciplinary debates, political conflicts, and changes in popular mores. The civic tradition provides strategies and concepts that can enable us to make productive use of such controversies. Too often the rhetorical triad of author, audience, and referent has been reduced to formalist categories for analyzing *ethos*, *pathos*, and *logos*. However, the rhetorical triangle can also serve as a frame for examining the positions of authority, modes of response, and representations of knowledge that constitute a discursive domain. This framework shifts the focus from the individual rhetor responding to a rhetorical situation to an examination of the discursive conventions that define who gets to speak with whom about what. Working with this easily learned heuristic, a student can research the contexts of a text to situate it within the social histories, ideological systems, and generic conventions that give it meaning and power.

Such traditional rhetorical categories can help us expand our frame of reference to include the political economies of literacy and the technologies of knowledge. As we know from our study of writing, such heuristics can help students think critically about how experiences become formalized in conventions that arouse and fulfill shared expectations. A critical awareness of the process of constructing shared beliefs is essential to a civic philosophy of rhetoric that makes sense of what we value. The contradictions contained within this process mark the sites of controversy that can evoke a dialectical awareness of the negotiation of morals and mores. As students examine what is up for debate, how it was called into question, and why it is useful to view the debate from multiple standpoints, they can learn to value critical reflection as a means

---

4. According to the *Oxford Latin Dictionary*, *moral* comes from *moralis*, which was coined by Cicero in *De Oratore* to distinguish practical philosophy from speculative philosophy, with Plato blamed for having made the distinction between abstract speculation and reflection on civic life (1967, 3:19). Like *ethikos*, *moralis* contained a dialectical sense of morals and mores that is still operative in common usage today, as when we discuss "the business ethic" or the "corporate ethos" to refer not to virtues but to the values that characterize a group.

to practical action, rather than as an end in itself. Students can develop this rhetorical stance by reflecting on their expectations about a text and its expectations about them, the experiences that validate and challenge those expectations, and the codifications of those experiences in discursive, moral, and social conventions. In other words, students can learn to question what is assumed, where those assumptions come from, and what gives them authority. If these are to be rhetorical questions, their answers must include actions. Critical judgment is generally understood to be the end of inquiry within English departments, as elsewhere in the academy—which is, after all, a product of the Enlightenment—but our own tradition treats critical thinking as a prelude to practical action. This rhetorical stance is regaining currency with the disintegration of disinterestedness as the unifying ideal of the arts and sciences. The technological, institutional, and cultural changes that face us make this a truly rhetorical moment.

We are confronted with a digital revolution in literacy, the collapse of disciplinary boundaries, and broad-based debates over whether universities should be state apparatuses, private corporations, or public institutions. Faced with such changes in the technologies and political economies of knowledge, we may be looking at the emergence of a "new learning" as far-reaching as that which prompted the transition from classical to modern cultural studies and established the research university. I am too nearsighted to play visionary, but I hope that this review can help expand our historical vision of the possibilities that open up to us here and now, in this book, in our classrooms, and in the communities that open out from them. We have other resources, of course. Readily at hand, we have the work of Paulo Freire to model a rhetorical stance on civic literacy. Freire understood literacy as a dialectical praxis that involved action on the world and reflection on the self for the purpose of realizing the human potentials of existential situations. He represented this model as

> Action   \
>   — word = work = praxis
> Reflection /
> Sacrifice of action = verbalism
> Sacrifice of reflection = activism (1970, 68n)

This model represents what I value in civic humanism, for Freire's writings combine the moral and the sociological into a rich understanding of the work of becoming human—a process of critical reflection and rhetorical action concerned with realizing social justice.

Claiming Freire as a civic rhetorician may be a stretch. However, to resituate rhetoric within its traditional relationship to moral philosophy is to help rhetoric, politics, and ethics regain the close links that were broken by the subordination of rhetorics to poetics. Critical ethnography of the sort that Freire applied to work on literacy is part of what can be reclaimed as we look past moral philosophy's evolution into the social sciences in order to revalue work

on practical morality. Moral philosophers taught courses such as Christian De-
fenses that were too didactic—too rhetorical—to be valued by those who
stand on the other side of the division of political science and political philosophy. Of course they were conservatives, even in their own time, and any attempt to apply their values to ours would be reactionary. However, a critical re-
assessment of their positions might help us value the work that could have been
and can be done with civic literacy. Perhaps a critical revaluation of the civic
possibilities of rhetoric and moral philosophy can help us relate what we have
learned to the work we need to be doing on the ethnographies of other traditions. Perhaps the work of folklorists, historians of rhetoric, and teachers of literacy are not as removed from one another as they may have seemed from
within the confines of departments that have functioned as bastions of the book.

It may be that the history of college English is more like the history of English than we have imagined. If so, what are we to do about the fact that our language is changing faster than it has since it was codified by print and taught by
the first professors of English—professors who worked in broad-based institutions that were more accessible to the public than those institutions at the center of the educated culture? Obviously, this is a rhetorical question. Then as
now, professors from elite institutions who gained prominence working with
the classics are not likely to recognize, let alone value, what lies beyond the
realm of their traditional expertise. Many of us have met their resistance to our
proposals for new majors, courses, and requirements. After receiving such reactions, some of us are moving out to establish new departments and interdisciplinary programs in rhetoric and writing. Such moves make sense when one
is confronted with departments that resolutely define themselves by the classics. However, as we develop rhetoric and writing into a subject of study, we
need to reassess the modern distinction between the arts and sciences that un-
derlies the reduction of literature to nonutilitarian, nonfactual discourse. Critical literacy begins with the ability to imagine alternatives, and one way to foster the civic imagination is to teach literature that challenges expectations,
makes other experiences knowable, and thereby calls established conventions
into question. Valuing the civic imagination is crucial if we are to resist the
functionalist tendencies in composition studies. These tendencies will increase
as we expand our field of study, because they follow from the reigning political economy and from the technologies of knowledge that do its work. The
civic imagination is vital if we are to realize the civic potentials of cyberspace,
service learning, and classroom inquiries into public controversies that challenge the options that the media represent for us. Being able to imagine the possibilities presented by differences is what enables a tradition to do well, and
perhaps even good. The dialectical possibilities of the civic imagination are
part of what our tradition has to teach us. By valuing it, we may learn to teach
not just rhetoric but rhetorically. Such learning could not be more timely.

The Academic Effacement of a Career: "Writer"

Linda K. Shamoon

Each year, thousands of high school students begin their college application process by consulting *Peterson's Guide to Four Year Colleges*, in which they find descriptions of approximately one thousand institutions of higher learning as well as an inventory of the major programs of study they offer. High school seniors interested in engineering, for example, will find in the guide's list of programs the broad category of engineering as well as the usual engineering subspecialties, such as chemical, civil, and electrical engineering. *Peterson's* substantial listing of academic specialties also includes less-traditional majors, such as ecology, sociobiology, restaurant science, hospitality, and even programs in wood and paper products. Interestingly, however, students wishing to pursue a major in writing will find no help in *Peterson's*; no entry exists for "writing" in the 1998 edition. As far as *Peterson's* is concerned, no such major exists in American higher education.

To be sure, students who have a strong interest in writing may search further into the inventory of available majors to find a few possible subcategories: creative writing, technical writing, and journalism, to name the most obvious examples. Nevertheless, the absence in *Peterson's* of the broad category "writing" represents a highly revealing elision in the academic landscape. As Robert A. Schwegler suggests in this volume, a lack of presence in the university's curriculum makes a serious statement about the generally perceived value or "currency" of an area of academic study. If there is no curricular presence, explains Schwegler, there seems to be nothing of substance to study, little to separate the area's activities as distinctive, few skills to be learned, and little expertise to be mastered. In the case of writing, the presence of a few subspecialties does not disrupt the general impression regarding an empty core. Instead, the few available specializations hold in place the narrowest conception of writing as an area without a base—or more accurately, as a set of practical techniques that may engender a few courses although their core content is in another area. Thus students who want to become writers should study something else, such as literature, engineering, or business. An education for writing as a career is not conceivable in academia.

Yet we know that some people make careers of writing in various and complex ways. Case studies by scholars of composition as well as portraits in the mass media tell us a lot about the careers of technical writers, novelists, and others who make a living by working within the standard categories. However, if we are to fully understand writing as a profession, we must also look closely at those writers who do not fit into official categories. Their career experiences, professional knowledge, skills, and practices will help us fill in the gaps and fully articulate the field of writing, broadly construed, as a profession and thus will help us reformulate the advanced undergraduate writing curriculum.

Toward this end, I have interviewed twelve people who call themselves writers or who, as one source said, make their living "by working with words." In this essay I offer thumbnail sketches of five of them: a freelance writer, a textbook writer, a poet-publisher-business-technical writer, and two romance novel-academic-business writers. Their careers are typical of the others whom I interviewed, especially in terms of the diversity of their writing activities and their overall insistence that their true occupational identity is that of "writer." In addition to these sketches, I shall reflect upon specific common elements among these writers, especially their self-designated professional identity and their broad expertise, and I argue that the lifework of these individuals offers important counterpoints to the prevailing narrow conceptions of writing as a profession. In fact, the careers of these individuals point to new, compelling directions in the advanced writing curriculum and to the need for courses that address the history, the variegated expertise, the public roles, and the ethics of writing as a profession.

The Five Interviews

Terry Vaughn

"My business card says, 'Freelance Writer: Print–Broadcast.'" These are the words of Terry Vaughn,[5] an author who contributes columns and features on economics and on international travel to a major national newspaper and to a national radio news network. Thus when Vaughn talks about his current work, he focuses on journalistic tasks, such as coming up with story ideas, following leads, tracking news, interviewing people, and producing radio tapes. When he talks about his lifework, however, he focuses on his writing. Vaughn explains that he "fell into journalism by default. Someone was paying me to do what I was doing all along: writing."

Vaughn's vita shows a long and varied list of publications. He has written three nonfiction books, one derived from New England lore and legends and two for a reference series on notable writers. Earlier in his career, Vaughn wrote stories and features for local and regional magazines and then recycled these pieces for thematically related magazines that reached different audiences. As Vaughn explains it, "I could see that I could write an article for a local New England magazine on an interesting annual event, for example, and then rewrite the article for a national magazine that focuses on travel and leisure. I

5. By request of the interviewees, all names used in this essay are pseudonyms.

could refocus the story yet again for a conservation magazine, and with a final twist I could develop the story into an essay for an ecology magazine." Even today in his journalistic work, Vaughn says, "I aim to sell a story three times. I know how to write for several genres, outlets, and audiences. I can write a feature for a magazine, shrink it down for a news article, and then find another outlet. This is how I can make my time pay." Even as a fledgling reporter for a monthly newspaper, Vaughn had wanted to be a fiction writer. He wrote short stories, publishing some every few years, and "when I got enough money," he says, "I took time to write a novel." "I got an agent to handle it, but it didn't sell." Then, returning to the present, he says, "I've got to get back to my writing. . . ." He is working on an idea he had picked up from a corporate press release: "Maybe from there I can develop it into a script for a travel show, and it has potential to become an essay on . . ."

Judith Adams and Katherine Daley

Both Judith Adams and Katherine Daley began their writing careers in similar situations: as editorial assistants in major publishing houses. Their professional experiences have taken them in very different directions. Both are writers.

Today, Adams is the author of three textbooks, each of which is in multiple editions and compact spin-offs, but she did not start her career as a writer of textbooks. Her lifework in publishing gradually trained her for this career. Starting with a degree in English, she went straight into the publishing industry as a production assistant, gradually learning to copyedit, which included tracking manuscripts, checking references, line-by-line editing, and proofreading, as well as reading for consistency and correctness of grammar, voice, and tone. "As a copyeditor I had to learn to recognize and live with the author's style. A bad copyeditor is one who can't get into the author's head or hear the author's voice." She then moved into production editing, coordinating the work of other editors, artists, graphic artists, typesetters, and printers, guiding the way books took shape from simple manuscript to final product. Her career grew more complicated. Publishing houses established development groups that would gather market data, conceptualize salable texts, and then solicit manuscripts. Adams became part of a concept-development team, and this work gave her a better sense of how to shape a text for an audience. Eventually, the original authors of the texts stopped writing subsequent editions, and, says Adams, "I became the authors—sometimes acknowledged in the book, sometimes not." On a typical day now, Adams may be working up new explanatory passages for one of the three texts, revising technical sections, reconsidering the page spread, or improving the page layout. "People in my family are impressed that I am revising and then making more money off the new editions. They think it's easy, just change a few words. Actually, it's hard and complicated work." And she adds: "I am a writer. I write all day."

Katherine Daley began as Adams did, as a copyeditor with a large publisher, but her career developed quite differently. Daley chose to leave the New York City office to work independently. For the next eleven years, she worked as a freelance editor from 8 A.M. to 2 P.M., and then from 2 P.M. into the evening she worked on her own poetry. At the same time, she began publishing an alternative literary magazine "to provide a venue for people who are doing short prose," which is now in its seventeenth edition, even though it is not financially self-sustaining. "At some point," explains Daley, "I had to accept the fact that the bills could no longer be ignored. I needed a more steady income, benefits, that sort of thing." Eventually, she answered a tiny ad in the "Help Wanted" column: "Technical Writer—Automotive." A local automotive mechanic needed a writer to translate his notes into five-page reports that could be understood by both laypeople and insurance adjusters. After five years of this kind of technical writing, Daley joined a public relations agency. Now she conducts case studies of engineers and others who use software applications, and she develops her observations into articles for trade magazines in the information technology industry. Throughout these years, writing poetry has also remained part of Daley's life work, along with editing, publishing, technical writing, public relations writing, the teaching of writing and editing, and networking with other writers. Amidst these professional activities, Daley returned to graduate school, earning a masters degree in creative writing, and receiving a major prize from her collegiate institution for a collection of her poems. Like Adams, then, Daley was once an editor, and she is a technical writer, a business writer, a poet. But as she says, "there are a thousand different ways to be a writer."

John Mills and Nell Mills

The afternoon I interviewed John Mills, he had just returned home after resigning his tenured position as a professor in a college English department. John Mills was ready to write full time. More accurately, his nonacademic career had developed to the point where it could support him and his wife—his coauthor—as writers.

Mills and his wife met while he was completing his doctoral thesis on sixteenth-century Scottish literature and she was finishing her undergraduate engineering degree. Several years later, on a whim, they collaborated on a short story, which they entered in an annual writing contest sponsored by a local chamber of commerce. They won two prizes: their story earned second place, and they discovered that they liked writing collaboratively. That success motivated them to try a more ambitious project, a novel. Using material from Mills' doctoral thesis, they worked up a plot, elaborated the characters, and developed every line collaboratively. By the time they finished, Mills and Mills had written a historical romance set in sixteenth-century Scotland, a novel that was picked up by a major publisher. Within the next three years, the same house published five more of their historical romances, with three more on the way. Mills and Mills' daily writing tasks are not all romance, however. On any given day they work on scenes for their next book, write proposals for new projects, create publicity for booksellers and their agent, answer fan mail and e-mail, supply texts and pictures for their e-mail and website, and currently are at work on a film script. In addition, they participate in the Romance Writers Association, writing newsletters, conducting workshops, and publishing articles on the craft of writing romance and historical novels. They also present papers at other national conferences, such as the Popular Culture Conference, and they recently received an award from the New Museum of Scotland for their work on telling the story of Scotland. "We are working seven days a week. We are never not working on our writing. We put in twelve to sixteen hours a day between us. But it is a pleasure," John Mills says.

To paste the label of "romance writer" onto Mills and Mills is to diminish their work. If asked, John Mills will say insistently, "I am a writer," and this is so, in the broadest sense of that term.

Reflections upon These Interviews

My interviews persuade me that *writing,* broadly construed, is the most accurate term for the careers of these individuals. Furthermore, I find at least four important common characteristics among them. First, they all engage in multiple forms of professional writing activities; second, they define their professional identity as "writer"; third, they ascribe to themselves certain kinds of distinctive expertise; and fourth, their professional activities position them in ways similar to one other, economically and institutionally.

These four commonalties gain even more meaning when they are integrated with information from the scholarly literature about the sociology of the occupations and professions. Ronald Pavalko, in his review of the scholarly literature, finds that sociologists agree on a cluster of attributes that mark certain occupations as professional, including the development of special expertise and the creation of a professional identity (1985, 19–29). In the analysis that follows, I draw upon the sociological attributes of the professions and upon the processes of professionalization to illuminate the lifework of these people and to suggest directions we educators ought to follow once we acknowledge the existence of a career called "writer."

Career Paths and Identity

The most striking commonality among the people I interviewed is that their career paths defied the narrow categories ascribed by academia and the public to the occupational activities of "writer." Each person I interviewed does not work solely as a creative, technical/scientific, or business/professional writer; rather, each overflows conventional boundaries. The different kinds of writing they do have a natural, generative relationship with one another. For the freelance writer, feature stories become news articles that become in-depth essays. More interestingly, John Mills indicates that the writing of romance novels entails communicating with a complex social network of readers, publishers, editors, businesspeople, and other writers. His novels are read by at least three audiences: a mass readership, writers of romance novels, and publishers of romance novels. In order to communicate with each of these audiences, he engages in a wide range of writing activities and produces many different kinds of writing. Thus Mills and many of the other individuals I interviewed routinely write in a number of supposedly exclusive categories, and they see this "border crossing" as natural to their careers.

All the people I interviewed identify themselves as writers—positively and emphatically. Three identify themselves as "writer" or as "freelance writer" on their business cards. John Mills in particular was emphatic about being a writer in the broadest sense, and Adams was amused by her family's misunderstanding of the nature of her work as somehow categorically different from that of her fiction-writing relatives. In addition, Adams is on the alert for public forms and documents that allow her to check off her identity as a "writer." She explains that on most official forms, she finds the academic and popularly inscribed categories of technical writer, publicity writer, reporter, and so on, but she would prefer to check off "writer." All of the people I interviewed saw themselves as working on texts that may differ in emphasis or details but that are in many ways similar in materials and processes, thus reinforcing Daley's statement "There are a thousand ways to be a writer."

Self Identity Versus Social Recognition

Identifying oneself as a member of an occupational group is fine, but according to Pavalko, full occupational identity entails a commitment to a community of people who work in similar ways and the granting of membership by them (1985, 27–28). Commitment and membership also arise out of shared values, training, language, and other factors crucial to creating a sense of specialness. In other words, one must seek and receive recognition of one's occupational identity.

Most of the people I interviewed fulfilled Pavalko's terms. Daley's explanation was typical: "It is crucial for me to keep in touch with others in the profession. It prompts me to keep developing and keeps me in touch with what others are doing, where we are headed." Similarly, Mills and Mills gained entry to the "world" of romance writers by becoming active in its professional association, to which they are now fully committed as part of their new full-time identities as writers. On the flip side, the interviewees—especially those in the publishing industry—who had little link to a professional association or to a community of writers and publishers expressed the least sense of their work as special, skilled, or of social value.

Pavalko points out that value claims are important for occupational identity because they attract new practitioners who want to be part of a community
dedicated to them (1985, 23). Unfortunately, the public and social value claims
for the written word are not widely understood or appreciated except when they
are questioned, such as when journalists plagiarize, newspapers and books are
poorly edited, or rock lyrics offend. This does not mean, however, that important social values and ethics do not exist or that they could not serve as a
motive for professional identification. In fact, whether writing becomes more
widely recognized as a profession may be tied in part to widespread clarification and more direct articulation of its value to a democratic society—a
clarification that could be prompted by reforming the education of writers as
professionals into one that emphasizes the writer's role in society.

Training, Knowledge, Expertise, and the Professions

Identity, common activities, shared values and concerns—these traits are important in creating any occupational category, but among the professions, the
claims to special knowledge, extensive training, and special expertise are
among the most crucial distinctions (Pavalko 1985, 22–23). In this regard,
writers as professionals face special issues. In our society, every literate citizen is supposed to have enough skill to write basic social documents; in academia, new college students are presumed ready to write beyond a high school
level. Writing is recognized as a diffused, widely held skill that grants no broad
professional expertise to those who choose it as a vocation. Is this popular
conception an accurate characterization? Did the people I interviewed possess
expertise?

All of the interviewees identify a common core of skills and knowledge
underlying their work as writers, including an understanding of audience; the
identification, researching, and analysis of subject matter; the crafting of language; and a self-awareness about the writing process. They spoke of mastering
a variety of skills: developing a line of sustained inquiry; sensitivity to language, voice, tone, and nuance; drafting and reworking; researching information; and an operational knowledge of multiple genres. At the same time, each
gained more focused occupational/professional expertise, from textbook publication, to rattling off the steps in the production of a taped radio feature, to the
crafting and promotion of period romance novels. All have acquired special expertise that has elaborated itself as they have practiced within the profession.

Expertise and Public Recognition

According to Pavalko, expertise is not constituted entirely within a profession:
the public must also grant that there is special expertise to be learned (1985,
23). Moreover, much specialized knowledge is contested. For example, the
tasks traditionally associated with nursing or pharmacy may be made into a

routine that is easily learned, subject to general supervision, and split apart from the community and values that originally gave them occupational substance and status. In academia, such "deprofessionalization" has occurred for writing. But the reverse of this process is also possible, especially in a post-industrial, technology-driven, service-based economy, where the production and communication of information dominate large segments of the marketplace. This new economy provides an opportunity for our discipline to focus students' and the public's attention upon the complex expertise of writing as a career and to develop writing classes that address the history, the public roles, and the ethics of writing as a profession.

Patterns of Employment and Autonomy

Another crucial element of professionalism is the freedom to work autonomously. In fact, the struggle for autonomy is the most salient feature of the professionalization process, according to Pavalko (1985, 25). Establishing the freedom to work independently as a writer certainly was central to the lives of the individuals I interviewed. Vaughn gained the freedom to work as a freelancer when his wife's work provided their health and insurance benefits; John Mills and Adams negotiated autonomy from institutional supervision through their contracts; Daley's career is best seen as a blend of these accommodations. While all five have found particularly productive ways to work within and against the predominant economy in order to control their time and their writing activities, they all spoke eloquently about the very difficult working conditions that pervade their occupational world, especially in the publishing industries, where outsourcing of line editing, graphic design, artwork, book development, interior design, and printing are common. These alternate labor conditions are worth considering closely, for they dramatize the process of deprofessionalization in the marketplace and point to several factors that help maintain the invisibility of writing as a profession.

For Adams and Daley, for example, copyediting had been a way into the profession of writing. Their first jobs had been as assistants to editors, and in the office setting they had the guidance of more skilled editors, as well as exposure to other aspects of publishing and book development. By contrast today, most freelance copyeditors work apart from other contributors such as editors, authors, or book designers. They read, correct, or annotate a manuscript usually without being involved in the project, often without any feedback and with minimal supervision. They are paid by the hour and in relation to the amount of copy reviewed; thus they are always under pressure to work faster and increase their "productivity." If they are not rehired, they have no indication as to why and no guidance as to how to improve. One of those interviewed but not featured above explained, "Freelancers are usually women. They are low-paid, without benefits, doing work in a manner that resembles factory piecework. They stay with the work because of the flexible schedule and the ability to work at home. But it is horribly abusive, nonetheless." In these circumstances, copy-editing has become standardized, routinized, and reduced to piecework. Copy-editing was once part of the profession of writing; now it is a low-skill job.

The important message here is not to mourn these conditions or to expect a reversal, but to understand what is at stake. First, as so often happens, the inevitable changes and continuing pressures of a capitalistic system conspire with other institutional forces, including academia, to deprofessionalize an occupation. Second, many of the intellectual resources needed by professionals to keep pace with such circumstances must be located in their education. In the case of writing-related occupations, however, these resources are missing. A professional education must nurture a lifetime commitment to keeping abreast of changing technologies and the ongoing development of expertise. In the profession of writing, this education must also include a full exploration of the socially contested areas of professional writing practices, such as the historical challenge to intellectual property rights and the very conception of writing as a profession. Direct education in such issues enables individuals to use the history and social circumstances of their profession as frames for anticipating and coping with future changes and developments in their careers. It is this kind of education that we in rhetoric and composition must put in place.

"Writing" as a Career and the Role of Education

In *Professionalism Reborn,* Eliot Friedson explains the educational tasks that are crucial to creating and sustaining a profession in its best formulation (1994, 177–78). According to Friedson's conception, educators and scholars must not work in isolation from day-to-day practitioners. Instead, they need to help create and extend disciplinary knowledge. They must critique current practices and ideology, and, extending Friedson's concepts, they must articulate the historical formulations of the profession and its practices while promulgating its societal value.

With Friedson's guidelines in mind, I want to close by articulating the kind of curriculum that acknowledges writing as a profession. This curriculum includes, of course, the specialty courses already available at many institutions, such as technical and creative writing. However, the best education for the profession must also include a more conscious awareness of the broad-based expertise of the writing professional; active knowledge of the historical foundations of the profession along with an array of critical approaches with which to encounter the always-changing economic and technical conditions of production; an ongoing engagement with the profession's value claims; and guided practice in the public and social roles of the writer as an agent for good in society. This education, then, has three focuses: expertise, history and critique, and the role of the writer in society.

Courses that address expertise help students write within and across categories of writing. Thus students should probably study both genre theory and style. Also, they should encounter an array of courses that present frames for understanding rhetoric and for participating in various discourse communities. Given the recent changes in the technologies of writing, students should also achieve a functional level of visual literacy and an awareness of how the technologies of writing affect both the processes and products of writing. Finally, a true preprofessional education will start students on their journey toward expertise in areas that the public, almost unconsciously, cedes to writers, including a functional and articulate knowledge of the grammars of our language within specific writing contexts; a knowledge of the methods and processes of writing, composing, and editing; and a knowledge of the English language and of literate action in a variety of contexts. We educators have routinely pushed such expertise onto "lower" levels of study, but it cannot be mastered in those venues. The preprofessional curriculum ought to help our preprofessional students embrace such knowledge, not flee from it.

The second area of preprofessional education must take account of the economic, social, and material conditions of the profession itself. Academicians cannot change the powerful forces driving our economy, but they can provide conceptual frameworks for understanding, critiquing, and maintaining professionalism in the face of such forces. Knowledge of histories of authorship, the book, and intellectual property rights—to name just a few subjects—both illuminate the past and frame expectations about the future.

The third leg of this tripartite education must address the societal role of writers. The importance of the written word in our democratic society must be more consciously promulgated through all writing classes but most particularly in the advanced curriculum. At the same time, we need to help formulate codes of professional ethics that will be continually revised and revisited. We must insist that our students learn to remain engaged in the public sphere. In a diverse, complex, and massive democratic society, we cannot afford to profess that the best or true role of the writer is to go off alone, write in isolation, and send back poetry of personal angst. Instead, we need individuals whose education in the profession of writing motivates them to participate actively in the public life of our country and to use their critical perspectives and rhetorical knowledge as a force for good in society.

Part Two

Considering Options for Core Courses in Advanced Writing

Histories of Writing and Contemporary Authorship

Andrea Abernethy Lunsford

Like almost all of the courses I have developed, this one grew out of a sense of my own inadequacies and out of the work on collaboration and collaborative writing I have pursued for what now seems like forever. As I read and studied more about the ideology attendant on notions of solitary writers/writing, I inevitably began to focus more on writing itself. To be sure, I had studied the history of the English language. I'd studied the history of texts. But to my chagrin, I realized that I knew very little about the history of our subject, *writing*. When I had an opportunity to present my chair's address to the 1989 Conference on College Composition and Communication (CCCC) meeting, I spoke at length of this lack of understanding and knowledge:

> We need to view writing from a variety of perspectives and throughout history. . . . In particular, we need to realize the extent to which writing was necessary for the invention of the "self." . . . [W]e need to realize the ways in which writing is itself a technology, a material technology. And again, we teachers of writing tend to know little about the evolution of that technology. . . . What we think of today as technology—machines mostly—are often simply extensions of the technology which is writing, though the new technologies are certainly affecting that writing—blurring writing and reading and speech and hence changing the relationship between the spoken and written word. (1990, 73)

Taking my own advice to heart, I had been learning what I could about the history of writing in the Western world. (I am still only a beginning student of the history of writing in Eastern cultures.) And the more I read and learned, the more I felt that I wanted to teach these histories to advanced undergraduate students. Thus during the mid-1980s, I began to develop two models for an undergraduate major's course that we still call Histories and Theories of Writing (English 574). The first time I taught this class, we read I. J. Gelb (1963), Walter Ong (1982), Jacques Derrida (1974), Michel Foucault ([1980] 1998), John deFrancis (1989), Elizabeth Eisenstein (1979), Albertine Gauer (1984), Eric Havelock (1986), Ivan Illich and Barry Sanders (1988), and almost always started with Kenneth Burke's essay on "Terministic Screens" (1966) and Plato's *Phaedrus* (1995), with its description of writing. Students were initially bewildered and, I feared, even a bit bored, having hardly ever thought of writing in more

55

than highly instrumentalist ways. Before midterm, however, class discussions became more lively; and they got livelier as students identified topics for research essays ("Where Do Dictionaries Come From?" "Are Rappers a Distant Descendant of Greek Rhapsodes?" "Is Sign Language 'True' Writing?"). This was a "standard" course based on "standard" sources, and it told a story, for the most part, of writing as hero—though, as Derrida insists, a violent hero at that.

I was not satisfied. Surely there were ways to start pulling at the seams of this fabric. Crucial to my attempts to do so was one startling moment forever etched in my memory. I was teaching the course during a summer term to a group of teachers. On the first day of class, we went around the circle, introducing ourselves and saying what had brought us to the course and what our special interests were. When we came to a teacher from Alaska, a Up'ik storyteller of note, she said what I remember as, "I wanted to take this class to find out what it is you people see in writing. Why you want to write everything down. What the big deal about writing is." And she continued to ask this question every day of the term, challenging all of the traditional assumptions I and most other students had brought to the course. I began to think about this course as, in some ways, a response to this powerful and provocative question. So I began to focus on the intense struggles over the basic definition of the term *writing* and struggles over the relationships between writing and thought, between writing and ideology, between writing and politics, between writing and gender, between writing and writer—and to explore these tensions. Most natural to me, given my own research on and commitment to collaboration, with its necessary linking of talking and writing, was focusing in a new and more intense way on the so-called "great divide" between orality and literacy, as well as on the production of writing in ways that would challenge reliance on the solitary, autonomous writer. Readings and materials on collaborative/collective forms of writing, including ghostwriting, corporate authorship, computer-generated writing, and so on, and on cultural constructions of authorship and various "crimes" of reading and writing such as piracy, plagiarism, and musical sampling piqued my own as well as students' interest, as did historical materials on women's (often secret) writing systems and on current debates over the gendered (or nongendered) nature of writing.

As I became increasingly engaged in theories and practices associated with the newest technologies of writing, I added related works, shifting the weight of the course more to the present. As a result, while my own latest version of the course still proceeded in chronological order and included Plato and essays on the history of Western alphabetic systems of writing, it also included readings on nonalphabetic—especially MesoAmerican—scripts as well as works such as Michael Joyce's *Of Two Minds* (1995); Christina Haas' *Writing Technology* (1996); and Sherry Turkle's *Life on the Screen* (1995). In future versions I will almost certainly include part of Ellen Ullman's *Close to the Machine* (1997). Indeed, I have taught one version of this course that focused entirely on digital literacies, as has another of my colleagues. Of the more recent works

I've added, most provocative to students has been the work of MIT psychologist Sherry Turkle, whose *Wired* essay "Who Am We?" (1996) always generates thoughtful and intense response; I would now pair her work with Burke's "Terministic Screens," which undergraduate students really "get" and which helps them in numerous ways to think about the ways they are written by their own and other discourses, along with *Phaedrus* as "must-reads" for this course.

Over the years, however, I have found myself wanting to modify more than the readings or content of the original course. In shaping assignments, for example, I have moved well beyond the concept of a researched term essay on some aspect of the history of writing. Students in my earlier versions of the course helped by alerting me to the high interest they had in tracing their own participation in writing and its systems and by prompting me to include a writing history assignment early in the term. For this early "unit" of the course, we now begin by reading several personal histories of writing: excerpts from St. Augustine's *Confessions* (1997), *The Book of Margery Kempe* (Butler-Bowden 1944), *The Autobiography of Malcolm X* (1965), and *Narrative of the Life of Frederick Douglass, an American Slave* ([1846] 1993); Michelle Cliff's "If I Could Write This in Fire, I Would Write This in Fire" (1988); bell hooks' "Narratives of Struggle" (1991); and sometimes a related piece such as John Lofty's essay "Time to Write" (1992). Since class size is likely to range from twenty-five to forty-five, depending on the term and on other offerings, I must always make adjustments. For smaller classes, we often proceed by bringing in individually written "conversation starters," brief pieces of writing for the assignment, and working on them together, usually for half of the class period, which is two hours long; for larger classes, we do most of that response work in small groups. Student responses to this assignment, which takes about two weeks to prepare for and carry out, vary widely, from annotated scrapbooks, to letters to friends and family members, to straightforward chronologies, to websites, to at least one play, to an essay written in columns by a Hopi student in order to differentiate the four voices out of which she weaves her writing self. We usually conclude this unit of the course by sharing our literacy histories and by going back to examine the very earliest readings in the course—Plato's *Phaedrus* (1995), along with excerpts from Eric Havelock's *Muse Learns to Write* (1986), and Mary Louise Pratt's *Imperial Eyes* (1992). Having investigated their own histories of writing technologies, students come to the charges against and claims about writing made by Plato, Havelock, and Pratt with new insights and new attention to detail.

For another assignment, students prepare a collaboratively conceived and written piece—an extended definition of the term *writing*, for example, that includes a reflection on the salient features of collaboratively produced texts. I can always count on this assignment to bring forward discussions not only of workload and what I call the "martyr syndrome"—in any group, the idea held by each member that he or she is actually doing all the work—but also of how to assign credit and how to take ownership of the joint property of the text. In-

deed, this particular assignment often leads to the research-based term project
I still ask all students to carry out. Now, however, I describe the project in ways
that invite field as well as library research and that might result in a website, a
PowerPoint presentation, or a poster to accompany an oral presentation. In
short, students now experiment with presentations and projects in which writ-
ing/print text is not the sole or transparent medium of expression.

In the Ohio State University English curriculum, English 574 is an "advanced" course in several senses. First, it is one of a long series of courses designed for students in their third and fourth years of undergraduate education
and specifically for English majors. In addition, this course is one of several
that follow from First-Year and Second-Year Writing, the introductory and intermediate writing courses all students at Ohio State take. Finally, this course
is part of a series of specialized courses in the theory and practice of rhetoric
and composition, including Rhetorical Theory and the Analysis of Discourse;
Writing and Learning (a Writing Center seminar, including tutoring and case-
study research and writing); Professional and Technical Writing; Grant Writing; Rhetoric and Community Service; and an advanced honors seminar currently under development that will allow for various courses under the general
heading of Studies in Rhetoric and Writing. Given their particular interests, undergraduate students develop a cluster of courses that becomes an important
part of their major programs in English. Prospective teachers will usually build
clusters around courses that call for hands-on work, such as the Writing Center seminar. Those interested in graduate school in the field lean more toward
the theory-heavy courses, and those intending to go into some writing-related
field such as publishing, journalism, sales and marketing, and so on, focus on
the courses on professional discourse. In addition, creative writing students often augment their studies with one or more of these courses, as do many students whose primary interests are in the study of literature.

I advise students in all wings of English study to take this course, for it
seems to me to be crucial to understanding our place in the history of textual-
ity that is changing even as this book is in preparation. A course in the history of writing and authorship asks students to think seriously about, and to enter, a discussion of questions that may well hold one of the keys to our future:
What is writing, where does it come from, and what does it mean—on many
levels—to write? How can writing work to both oppress and liberate people?
How is writing imbricated in personal as well as legal, social, political, economic, and spiritual journeys? What rights and duties accompany various acts
of writing? What is the relationship of writing and language, and in what ways
can they and can't they be the objects of possessive ownership?

For writing, to paraphrase bell hooks, is almost always a "place of struggle."
As students struggle with their own writing in terms of these questions, applying them to their own lives, to their own progress of education, they have an opportunity to practice the kind of rhetorically sensitive, carefully situated critical
thinking that higher education has frequently promised but less often delivered.

Theories of Composing

Sandra Jamieson

Composition tends to be taught predominantly at the first-year undergraduate level (FYC), while writing theory and practice tend to be taught at the graduate level to those who are or will probably be teaching writing to first-year undergraduates in the future. Sometimes writing theory is taught as part of a tutor training, service-learning, or literacy education program, either as part of weekly inservice meetings or as a discrete course. It is less common to teach writing theory to undergraduates *as theory*. Yet what the study of writing theory brings to the advanced writing curriculum is the lens through which students may view their own writing and the writing process itself. When writing theory is taught as a mechanism to further one's understanding of how writing works, it invites students to step back from their experience of writing and to theorize it, thereby theorizing about language itself—the ways it constructs us as subjects and the way we try out identities through it.

As an introductory course, Theories of Composing prepares students to theorize about things they take for granted, such as the fact that some people find writing "easier" than others. It also invites them to challenge their assumptions about the relationship between language and thought, language and identity, and the creative process. Such preparation serves them well for the rest of their undergraduate curriculum, especially if they follow it with courses that invite them to apply the theories learned in this course. Taken at the end of the program of advanced writing classes, Theories of Composing invites students to rethink the concepts they have learned. They may consider how their own writing has changed throughout their program of study, how the writing they have done has helped them learn, and how they have used writing to create meaning and enter into a dialogue with their fellow students. In either case, this course leads students to an intense focus on the act of writing, both as a personal act and as a social act, thereby adding another layer to the material they learn throughout the writing curriculum.

I first considered teaching Theories of Composition to undergraduates as an option when an undergraduate student, Jillian, asked if she could enroll in my graduate writing theory class. I agreed, with some hesitation, but quickly realized that she had a different and deeper level of engagement with the material than the graduate students. In a journal entry she expressed her frustration that her classmates were approaching the material as something they could *use* in order to become better teachers, whereas to her the primary interest was what this material made her realize about her own composing processes and writing in general. To be fair, many of her classmates were thinking about themselves as writers as well as writing teachers, but their career plans made the course a very different experience for them. By the end of the term, Jillian was sharing the readings with friends who weren't in the class, and the course had a "shadow enrollment" among the undergraduate population. When an e-mail message from a former undergraduate—a sociology major—included the phrase "well, it's just like Paulo Freire said in that essay you gave to your graduate class last year," I knew I had to design an undergraduate class.

Some people have reacted to this idea with hesitation. Would the material be too difficult? To what would the students apply the theory if not to teaching? In a literary theory course, students apply literary theory to literature. In graduate writing theory courses, the students apply writing theory to their teaching or draw on it to design assignments and syllabi that they might later use as teachers. How would it work to teach a class that invited students simply to apply writing theory to the act of composing? How much of the class would focus on the students' own writing? *And wouldn't the material be too difficult?* Experience reassures me. Undergraduates can read the most difficult theory if the teacher guides them through it. And once students understand, the world they took for granted changes. Jillian and her friends had been perfectly able to grasp the material I had taught in the graduate course, but they approached it from the context of their own writing. Like students in any writing class, they applied what they learned to their own writing processes. Like students in the graduate class, they also theorized the writing process and grappled with developing their own theory of composing based on their readings.

Theories of Composing has four goals: that students develop a deeper understanding of the writing process in general; that they realize the complexity of literacy and writing; that they come to a deeper comprehension of their own writing process; and that they become more conscious of the rhetorical choices that writers make in different writing situations. A class like this will tend to attract a wide variety of students and must find ways to speak to them all. Some of them may be tutors in the college writing center; others may be tutors, note takers, or study partners in various courses and programs throughout the college; some may be literacy or ESOL volunteers off campus, in college-supported programs, or as private volunteers; and still others may be enrolled in the education certification program. Another group may be involved with the school newspaper or other journalistic enterprises. Not all students will be English majors or writing minors, and several will be there solely to strengthen their own writing skills in preparation for the GRE, LSAT, MCAT, and other such examinations or because a professor somewhere told them they had to improve their writing. The course must respond to the various needs of its audience but also move that audience to the location it must occupy in order to meet the goals of the class.

To this end, the students need to apply the theories they read about first to the writing and composing practices of others, then to their own writing and composing practices, and finally to a larger writing situation of which they are a part. Before they apply theory, though, the students need to engage with that theory *as theory* and explore their reactions to it from within their larger epistemological frameworks. In most cases, they will come to articulate—and sometimes modify—those frameworks throughout the investigation. I believe that it is essential for the students in this class to understand how theory, pedagogy, and the writing process itself develop from the values we hold and the belief system that drives those values. When they do this they will understand the structures behind their classes and conversations about writing. The moment when Jillian asked me whether a former high school teacher taught the way he did because he was an expressivist and described his pedagogy in terms of his assignments was the moment that I realized on how many levels this theory can operate. Her analysis of his theoretical position helped her to see why she had had a difficult time with the writing assignments for that class. Once they have articulated for themselves what they value in writing, what their peers value, what society values, and how these values interact with other values, students from this class will be ready to approach any writing situation critically and creatively, whether that situation is another writing class, a workplace, or the public realm. This course also has the potential to transform students' experiences of courses outside of the writing program. Understanding the ways in which what is valued in writing stems from larger values and epistemologies will help students comprehend what is required for writing in any discipline, preprofessional course, or extracurricular activity. Understanding their own beliefs and values with regard to writing will help students respond to those requirements—or articulate their resistance to them! Whether students who understand writing theory write the remainder of their college papers in English literature or biology, those students are more likely to write papers that represent a conversation about an issue with a real audience and context rather than simply responding to an assignment from within the traditional hierarchy of teacher as possessor of knowledge and student as demonstrator of good study habits.

It is my experience that *which* writing theories are taught matters less than *that* writing theory is taught, so readers trying to imagine their own version of this course should not do so on the basis of which textbook and articles I use but rather should determine how a variety of theories might best be presented to their particular student population. While I initially imagined using a collection of articles from books and *College Composition and Communication*, the publication of Victor Villanueva's *Cross-Talk in Comp Theory* (1997) and Mark Wiley and others' *Composition in Four Keys* (1996) offered practical alternatives. Although I am delighted by the range of articles offered in both of these texts, I prefer to organize the purely theoretical part of the course according to the same format as my graduate class, using the conceptual categories of current traditionalism, expressivism, cognitivism, and social constructionism and essays that represent each of these theoretical orientations. It is my hope that the students will find a way inside each theory we study and will try to see through the lens of that theory. I want them to explore writing and the composing process from within each theory in the firm belief that one theory will make more sense to them than the others and that this, in turn, will help them locate themselves and their own behavior and values.

I do not see each theory as necessarily mutually exclusive, but there are two mutually exclusive epistemologies to be found in this course, and these are whether "good" writing can be taught or whether it cannot. While we tend to like to find compromise positions, this version of the old nature/nurture debate should be allowed to surface as many times as it needs to, and it probably will surface again and again—with different people on each side. When such shifting positions emerge in the classroom, I take them as a sign that the students are really grappling with theory and its larger implications, and I stifle a contented smile at each groan of frustration, while I encourage my students to "write that down, try to articulate exactly how you are feeling right now and why." In order to provoke such angst, the course follows the structure below, which works for classes that meet once or twice a week:

Week 1: An introduction to the course, texts, and each other. Sign up for presentations. Brief writing workshop. A history of composition instruction in America.

Week 2: An overview of writing theory and the apparent need to classify, categorize, and perceive a Kuhnian paradigm shift.

Week 3: The end of Current Traditional Rhetoric and the rise of Process Theory.

Week 4: The Expressivist Movement.

Week 5: Cognitive Development Theory.

Week 6: Social Constructionism.

Week 7: The politics of literacy: race, class, and gender.

Week 8: Theorizing writing: Research into a writing situation—imagining and designing research projects.

Week 9: Seeing others as writers: Responding to other people's writing—style, grammar, and other debates.

Week 10: Seeing others as writers: Responding to other people's writing—talking about writing in context (audience, content, etc.).

Week 11: Seeing yourself as a writer: Responding to writing assignments and situations—including reports on student research projects.

Week 12: Seeing yourself as a writer: Developing your writing process.

Week 13: Last class—Full circle: A discussion of what has been learned, resisted, and lost in this course and an analysis of this class as a writing situation (student evaluations of the class).

At the end of each reading set—generally three articles—in Weeks 2–7, the students write a position paper responding to a series of questions. For example, in the first week they read an extract from Stephen North's *Making of Meaning in Composition* (1987), James Berlin's "Contemporary Composition" (1982), and Richard Fulkerson's "Four Philosophies of Composition" (1979) (all are included in *Four Keys*; only Berlin is in *Cross-Talk*), and write a response to the following prompt.

These articles offer several different ways of categorizing writing.

> Summarize the various categories offered and try to make connections. If you can, try to come up with your own categories based on these; if not, decide which one seems to make the most sense and explain why. Consider the following questions as you prepare to write your position paper (you may use your answer to any of them as the position for the paper, or you may come up with a different position): Why do you think these theorists put so much effort into designing categories? What purpose do you think these categories might serve? Do the different categories make sense to you? What does all of this tell you about the field you will spend this semester exploring?

This first discussion is the hardest. The essays assume a knowledge of the field that the students don't yet possess and speak to an audience they have not yet become. The material *is* difficult, and it is important to reassure students that theory is difficult, that they may not "get it" the first time, but that the more they read, the more they will understand. At this point I introduce the concept of discourse communities, discuss the role of background knowledge, introduce the importance of perseverance, and set the stage for the discussions of literacy in Week 7. As outsiders, or newcomers, to the discourse community for which the essays were written, the students lack the background knowledge the essays assume. It can be very useful to refer back to these essays in subsequent class discussions, articulating the outsider feeling and comparing students' informed discussion late in the course with their initial reactions at the beginning.

The next six weeks follow the same structure, with a group of three to five students assigned to begin class discussion by asking questions about the readings and risking assertions that their peers might challenge. In the second half of the course, students begin to apply what they have learned to the writing of other students, thinking of ways to speak to the writer from within the theoretical framework each student is developing and justifying what they say in terms of the beliefs and values we have discussed. Here we discuss controversial issues such as grammar, style, structure, dialect, and slang, in addition to audience, purpose, tone, and voice—focusing on the reasons these topics *are* controversial and the ways readers might respond to them in a variety of different texts and genres. Extracts from listerservs such as WPA-l (listserv@asu.edu) on these topics both inform and intrigue the students as they realize that they really are entering a conversation *about* writing rather than simply receiving agreed "facts" and rules.

Finally, they apply those same theories to themselves, critiquing a piece of their own writing from another class, analyzing the ways they respond to writing assignments, and studying their own writing practice through protocols and double-entry notebooks. For their final project, students reflect on a "writing situation" of their choice. Situations may include literacy education, cross-cultural writing, gender and writing, tutoring, computers and writing, writing in the disciplines, Ebonics, academic writing, collaboration, writers with learning disabilities, or the composing practices of group X, which may or may not include the student writer. Their task in this project is to think about the writing situation in terms of one of the theories or theorists we have discussed and in terms of the class's overall discussion of values and assumptions. The resulting papers might propose revisions to a program with which the student is familiar, offer analysis of why a program functions as it does or why a specific writing situation unfolded as it did, or explore the case of one specific writing moment or process, which could range from a failed chemistry laboratory report to how to explain the organization of college papers to a student with learning disabilities using computer programming as a model. The audience will range from the director of the program the student is discussing to a fellow student, but it will rarely be "the professor." In some cases the project will require substantial additional reading, while in others that reading might be minimal. This is not a research assignment in the traditional sense but rather an opportunity for students to apply theory to practice and their own experience. As such, it requires them to meet the goals of the course in a paper that represents a conversation about an issue with a real audience and context—the kind of paper they came to college to learn how to write.

This course could, of course, be focused in many different ways. As I said before, I think the significant thing is that students are reading theory and coming to understand the need to theorize. One could teach this course using the kind of subject breakdowns in *Four Keys* or *Cross-Talk*, or one could select other readings from other sources or collections, for example, the *Landmark Essays* series. Regardless of the approach, it is helpful to present a range of theories, to invite students to "try them on," and to take it as slowly as the students need to go. This latter may be the most important thing, although a close second would be to design the course with sufficient flexibility to allow students to explore their own concerns and apply the theories to issues that matter to them. Once they have learned to see writing as the subject of study rather than simply as a means to record what one has learned, the students are ready for any and every other class they take. And they will never view the act or processes of writing in the same way again.

Texts That May Be Considered for This Course

Villanueva, V., Jr., ed. 1997. *Cross-Talk in Comp Theory: A Reader*. Urbana, IL: NCTE.

Wiley, M., B. Gleason, & L. W. Phelps, eds. 1996. *Composition in Four Keys: Inquiring into the Field*. Mountain View, CA: Mayfield.

Discourse Studies

Gail Stygall

Contemporary linguists have chosen to confine their work to areas of
language study that are susceptible to mathematical or empirical val-
idation; until recently, they have shown little interest in moving beyond the study of the sentence. . . . Linguistics favors an extremely
narrow, noncontextual notion of what it means to be a user of language. Thus compositionists must recognize that linguistically based
pedagogies necessarily operate as though texts are constructed in a
cultural vacuum.

—Sharon Crowley, 1989

The notion of social practice usually implies a broader social dimension of discourse than these various acts (e.g., conversation) accomplished by language users in interpersonal interaction. For instance,
an interaction between doctor and patient, between teacher and student, as well as a parliamentary debate or a courtroom session, are
not only complex forms of institutional dialogue. They constitute,
or are inherent parts of, the more complex discursive and social
practices of teaching, providing health case, legislation, and "doing"
justice.

—Teun van Dijk, 1998b

Although the relationship between writing and linguistics has alternated between proximity and distance, the rise of discourse studies in the 1980s and
1990s has provided a different avenue for successful collaboration between
the two areas of study. While the "linguistics" described by Sharon Crowley
above accurately characterizes North American Chomskyan linguistics of the
last half century, it does not describe discourse analysis or discourse studies
as practiced in the United Kingdom, Western Europe, and Australia–New
Zealand. Contextually sensitive and oriented to actual language use, discourse
studies of the type described by Teun van Dijk above—a discourse analysis
of social practice—offers a range of perspectives on contemporary problems
in rhetoric and composition that are sufficiently useful to justify the role of
discourse studies in the advanced undergraduate curriculum in writing and

rhetoric. Some of the most exciting work being done today in rhetorical studies and writing research makes extensive use of discourse analysis. Discourse studies includes a wide range of sites for consideration of the interactions of language and society: the analysis of talk in writing groups; studies of discourse patterns in student writing and features indicating language variety; the analysis of how standard language is deployed in public debates about race and ethnicity; the intricacies of legal textual practices; genre analysis; and the study of second language writing. As discursive practices, those boundary activities of naming, allowing, excluding, and declaring truth and falsity are of vital interest to both discourse analysts and rhetoricians. In my experiences over the past decade in teaching discourse studies to undergraduates and graduates, I have found that for many students, the way to understanding the importance of rhetoric is through discourse studies.

What is the place of discourse analysis in the advanced undergraduate curriculum in rhetoric and writing? For me, the answer is that it should be well integrated into that undergraduate curriculum. It provides students specific tools with which to analyze aspects of larger rhetorical approaches. It allows them additional means of analyzing the contextual and pragmatic aspects of crafting their own spoken and written language strategically. It provides students with the means to identify the subject positions to which they have been assigned and to examine their alternatives. And to the occasional dismay of their family and friends, their teachers, and sometimes their employers, it helps them become acute observers of the discourse practices of others and accordingly, better rhetoricians themselves.

Designing the discourse studies course typically presents teachers with two organizational options: arrange the course by discourse phenomena or theoretical construct (e.g., discourse markers, speech acts, conversational analysis, pragmatics) or by topic (discourse and gender, discourse and politics). Most available textbooks and reference handbooks—Evelyn Hatch's *Discourse and Language Education* (1992), Deborah Schiffrin's *Approaches to Discourse* (1994), or van Dijk's four-volume series, *Handbook of Discourse Analysis* (1985) and his more recent two-volume *Discourse Studies* (1998)—are arranged by one of these two patterns. Neither approach seems to work well by itself. And much of what the traditional textbooks do is better located in the graduate than undergraduate classroom in terms of length, variety of topics, and expectations of knowledge about the various disciplines involved. So instead of selecting one or the other, I build the course around students' movement from concrete collection of data, to constructing a repertoire of analytical tools, to discourse theory, and finally to full analysis.

At the heart of my decision to lead with concrete collection of data is the idea that the students' desire to analyze and theorize arises from the need to explain data in which they already have an investment. A student who wonders why her writing group members always interrupt one of the group members or one who wants to know why her writing in history seems so different from her writing in English already has a vital discourse question at hand. Another student observes that members of underrepresented groups speak little in public meetings, and he notices that the women seem to speak even less often than the men. Another notices that the talk in mixed-sex groups differs from single-sex conversations. Yet another wonders what parts and features of his papers his teachers actually have responded to in their written commentary. Without beginning with concrete discourse problems, students typically will not find much to interest them in abstract discussions of discourse features and phenomena. Part of the reason that an abstract presentation is less effective may also have to do with the traditional presentation of linguistics in English departments, in which students are asked to take on faith that the linguistic concepts they learn—phones, phonemes, morphemes, constituents—have some use outside the examples their textbooks give. Most of us learn better with clear stakes in the outcomes of our learning.

The movement of the syllabus from concrete data to full analysis takes place through a series of writing assignments. The first asks that students collect some preliminary data from a discourse area they propose to study, explaining their reasons for selecting the site or situation and what they think is possible to learn from an analysis. These proposals are shared among class members, and as I'll describe below, they take place as the class is learning about the tools available to analyze discourse.

The second assignment requires students to read two articles from scholarly journals on the site or situation they propose to analyze. Each student then prepares a two- to three-page summary and evaluation of a relevant article to be compiled into a class collection. Because students come to the course with varying levels of knowledge about discourse and about linguistics more generally, they may need to sample a number of journals before they find accessible work. Journals that students have found useful include *Discourse Processes*, *Journal of Narrative and Life History* (now *Narrative Inquiry*), *Discourse and Society*, *Text*, *Language in Society*, *Linguistics and Education*, *Journal of Pragmatics*, *Women and Language*, *Written Communication*, *English for Specific Purposes*, *System*, and *TESOL Quarterly*.

In the third assignment, students work in theory groups to outline an approach to their language analysis, to clarify assumptions embedded in the approach, and to understand what problems each approach entails. In this assignment, one group of students might be working on explaining M. A. K. Halliday's earlier work in *Language as Social Semiotic* (1978), while another might be describing and examining quantitative sociolinguistics while collecting the criticisms made of that approach—say, reading some of William Labov's work (1966, 1973, 1972), with Norbert Dittmar's early critique (1976) and Ben Rampton's (1992) or Glyn Williams' (1992) more recent ones. Another group might focus on conversational analysis, both as linguists understand it and as communication studies scholars use it, while another focuses on critical discourse analysis. All of the groups consider the implications of collecting "empirical" data in a postmodern, post-structural framework. Groups write a collective report and make it available to the class.

The final writing assignment is a report on a discourse project. The current version of the assignment describes the general requirements in the following way:

> The last project of the quarter will be a paper in which you present an argument or claim based on the empirical discourse data you collect. By empirical, I mean data collected by audio- or videotaping of naturally occurring language in conversations, lectures, group discussions, debates, radio or television talk shows, or an analysis of a set of collected written texts, including transcripts of electronic communication as well as the more typical newspapers, letters, instructions, scholarly articles, and the like. You will also be required to apply your knowledge developed in your Theory Group to the analysis you complete here, including the strengths and limitations of the theory and method you have chosen. You will also need to place your work in the ongoing conversation about discourse analysis. You may include parts of your journal article reports here, as well as additional references.

Students have chosen a wide variety of projects. Analyses of local crime reporting in the newspapers, the discourse markers present in a professor's lectures, terms of address in various social settings, discourse patterns of African American vernacular English present in hip-hop lyrics, and the discourse analysis of the documents of a public school have all been term projects presented both to me and to the class.

With the structure of the course based on a progression of activities and writing assignments, the readings can be quite flexible. Because conversational analysis is relatively unknown to most students, I often lead with both a brief exercise and a reading in that area. I have often used Deborah Tannen's (1984) early work on conversations to display what aspects of conversation we take for granted, and I have also used Deborah Schiffrin's (1994) interviews in Philadelphia as well. Issues of language and gender, though, are often the most provocative and a means of opening up how we think about the social aspects of how we talk and write. Recently, I have drawn on two collections for examples to complicate students' ideas about discourse and gender, Kira Hall and Mary Bucholtz's *Gender Articulated* (1995) and Anna Livia and Kira Hall's *Queerly Phrased* (1997). Students often come to this course with an ideologically driven notion of the conversational "floor," that is, who gets to speak and when. In this conventional wisdom, women talk too much, men must fight to be heard, and everyone has a fair shot at speaking in public arenas. That some students don't speak in class is often assumed to mean that their silence is a choice. How gender, race, ethnicity, and class interact with fairness, choice, and conversational "turns" becomes an issue for research. In my current version of the course, the readings extend and enrich this discussion by including Laurel Black on student-teacher conferencing (1998), Marty Nystrand on writing groups (1997), the Sadkers (1994) and David Graddol and Joan Swann (1989) on gender in large-group classroom discussions, and Susan Herring on academic, electronic discussions (1996). Students then conduct their own brief conversational analysis, in another classroom, perhaps by counting the number of students who actually speak in class or perhaps by timing the length of turns in a personal conversation.

The next reading students do provides them with the linguistics and discourse tools of analysis. We do work with the classic linguistic "levels" but focus on those that have prominence at the discourse level. Thus we spend some brief time on phonetics, phonology, morphology, and syntax but then move to discourse markers, evidentials, cohesion, deixis, modality, and transitivity, working primarily from photocopied exercises and spending about two weeks on these concepts. Wallace Chafe's work on the writing and speech of academics provides a set of readings that allows students to see some of these aspects at work and to see that the analysis applies to both speech and writing. At this point, students are ready to engage in a wider selection of reading and do so through their summary and evaluation of scholarly articles. I provide examples to work through in class and turn to Ellen Barton on evidentials and metadiscourse, Linda Brodkey on critical analysis, Valerie Balester, Arnetha Ball, and Lisa Green on African American discourse, and Jim Tollefson on language policy for continuing to extend the range of possible discourse analyses. In the final section before students finish their projects, I provide brief overviews of a number of theoretical perspectives and then work with each of the Theory Groups to help them compile a brief reading list, depending on their selection.

Thus the writing and rhetoric student leaving the Discourse Studies course has a new repertoire for the analysis of talk, text, and the contexts of both. At the end of the course, students understand that rhetoric and discourse analysis interact in ways that are productive for both. If rhetoric retains some aspects of its classical sense of persuasion, then discourse analysis provides powerful analytical tools with which to describe audience, context, and goals, whether used for spoken or written texts. And discourse analysis allows the rhetorical analyst to bring a finer discrimination to bear on contexts not typically thought to be overtly persuasive, such as ordinary conversation, the classroom conversational "floor," and student-teacher conferencing. Discourse analysis is, to my mind, the linguistic arm of rhetoric.

Contrastive Rhetoric/Comparative Rhetoric

Yameng Liu

Two General Curricular Objectives

As a scholarly discipline, contrastive rhetoric undertakes to compare rhetorical patterns, norms, and values across linguistic and cultural boundaries. An introduction to the discipline serves two crucial purposes within the curricular framework of advanced writing. It prepares the writing majors for functioning professionally in a world that is becoming increasingly multicultural and globalized. And it helps students develop specific skills of critical thinking that are indispensable to their understanding of and participation in communication across all kinds of boundaries.

A contrastive study of rhetorics would necessarily sharpen the students' awareness of the rhetorical dimension of cross-cultural interactions. Successful communication across cultural or linguistic divides, as the students are likely to find out through this course, is by no means merely a matter of being able to understand one another's languages. A knowledge of and a sensitivity to one's own and one's interlocutor's culture-specific rhetorical norms are just as instrumental. The study would also enhance the students' competence in interpreting, analyzing, and critiquing intercultural communication. Since it necessarily directs attention to all those theoretical and practical difficulties one encounters in efforts to go beyond one's own cultural parameters, the course also encourages the students to reflect on and to rethink the complicated and charged relationships among self, other, culture, community, language, meaning, and knowledge. Serious reflections on these issues would place the students in a better position to understand and make informed judgments on any cross-cultural communicative action that they would be performing or be involved in. Since cross-addressing, cross-arguing, or cross-persuading has become all but routine in our time, it is difficult to imagine how a professional writer can perform her duties without the above-said awareness and competence.

Three Sets of Issues

The course, however, is as valuable to the writing curriculum as it is difficult to design. Some of the difficulties are inherent in the discipline of contrastive rhetoric itself. The need to describe, interpret, or otherwise represent different

71

rhetorical practices for comparison or contrast, for example, poses thorny epistemological issues about whether or how someone situated and inscribed in one cultural context can adequately understand and characterize complex practices in another culture or in a different system of signification. The conventional approach tends to make, as its enabling conditions, four assumptions: that there are "rhetorical universals"; that the set of theoretical concepts, categories, and presuppositions comparative rhetoricians typically apply are culturally neutral; that the representation of the "other" rhetoric resulting from the application of these interpretive tools is basically accurate; and that it is possible to formulate a "general theory" of rhetoric that will apply in all societies. None of these is free from controversies.

The same need also gives rise to sensitive political and ethical issues. Cultural or international politics are necessarily involved, even only as a backgrounded presence, in any effort to compare across boundaries. And the problems are rendered much more complicated, intense, and urgent by the currently prevalent postmodern theoretical ethos, especially by the dominant intellectual concern with the self-other relationship and the emerging consensus among political philosophers that the most potent form of power is the power to control the concepts in which reality is constructed for a people or to define the interests, values, and preferences for that people. Whether we like it or not, the question of how practitioners of contrastive rhetoric situate themselves vis-á-vis the cultural Other, negotiate the power relations within which they are entangled, and strive to achieve representational justice will insist itself and demand attention from students of contrastive rhetoric.

Then there are the methodological issues that often turn out to be no less troubling. Even though contrastive rhetoric is evolving into an open, interdisciplinary inquiry, it has yet to outgrow its historically formed special relationship with applied/text linguistics and, in particular, with the concern over the teaching of second-language (L2) writing. To instructors of contrastive rhetoric as an advanced writing course, this deeply rooted association poses a number of questions about what methodology they ought to be adopting, of which three stand out as deserving special attention.

First, are we going to focus primarily on identifying and comparing textual features as the basis for generalizing about differences in rhetorical behaviors across cultural boundaries, or must we rather endeavor to go beyond the text per se, and concentrate our attention instead on the way the text is embedded in, authorized by, and functioning within its broadly defined cultural context? Second, should linguistic concerns and categories continue to enjoy a privileged status in the structuring of this course (e.g., comparing "cohesion devices" or modes of paragraph development), often at the expense of what have been more unmistakably established as rhetorical concepts and interests (e.g., the interest in how the "rhetorical situations" in question compare with one another, how "cultural ethos" is projected in each case, or how "coherence effects" are created on the basis of different presuppositions about the dynamics of speaker/audience interaction)? And third, should contrastive rhetoric be oriented toward making broad generalizations about culture-specific rhetorical preferences or tendencies (e.g., "native speakers of Japanese tend to be less direct in expression than those of English"), or must its practitioners strive for more particular and finer-grained comparisons (e.g., "under what specific circumstances are Japanese politicians more likely to resort to indirection than their American counterparts")?

One Possible Approach

The need to engage and address these issues determines that to be pedagogically productive, the teaching of contrastive rhetoric ought to center on opening up the discipline as a site of contention among differing perspectives, interests, and purposes, over the as-yet unsettled and unsettling relationship between culture and rhetoric. Since it is unlikely that many of the students are literate in languages other than English, the best point of departure for the course may be a close look into the English-based, diverse sets of rhetorical values and expectations associated with different cocultures in American society.

The course may be divided into three phases of more or less equal length. Phase I offers an extended, comprehensive introduction so that students who have otherwise very little idea about the field of inquiry may become initially acquainted with its scope of inquiry, its purposes, and its motivating concerns and issues. Applying the conceptual framework that this introduction sets up, in Phase II the class then examines what has been done in the name of contrastive rhetoric and intercultural communication, the two main disciplinary sites where comparative studies of rhetoric have been conducted. This critical survey enables the students to gain a heightened awareness of the theoretical presuppositions, interpretive tools, and methodological principles currently constitutive of the field. The acquisition of this awareness makes it possible to switch to Phase III of the course, where attention is focused on one or two very specifically defined topical areas (e.g., "the representation of the Japanese mode of communication" or "silence as/v. eloquence across cultures") for an in-depth investigation into the possibilities the discipline offers and the challenges it poses.

Representative Episodes

To engage the students' interest, the instructor may want to consider using "representative episodes" from communication among cocultures to drive home the relevancy of contrastive rhetoric. One such episode is the 1996 controversy over NCTE's curriculum guidelines for teaching English.[1] Critics in

1. For a sample of opinions critical of NCTE's curriculum guidelines for teaching English, see "How Not to Write English" (1996); Klein (1996); and Cleveland (1996).

their op-ed pieces took the guide's authors to task for writing "in a tongue barely recognizable as English." Their accusations—for example, "vagueness," "inaccessible lexicon and syntax," "circumlocution"—throw light on a no-nonsense conflict between two markedly different sets of rhetorical norms. Textual evidence suggests, furthermore, that at the root of the attack was most likely to be an ideological conflict.

The controversy suggests the need to clarify the distinction between the conflicting norms in question and to sort out their relationship, which is necessarily caught up in a tangled web of issues. It calls for an understanding that the rhetorical practices that one finds deviant and offensive may be perfectly normative within another cultural context; for example, linguistic studies have shown that "strategic vagueness" is in fact a common rhetorical device employed by academic writers for the purpose of negotiating complex boundaries or mediating among conflicting interests. One of the insights that the case provides is that we can only identify, characterize, or define the rhetoric of any discourse (e.g., the academic discourse) comparatively, that is, through an often implicit comparison or contrast with its Other (e.g., nonacademic or "public" discourse). Comparison is an essential operation whereby identity is constructed. Careful analysis of episodes such as this makes it easy to introduce the students to the rationale, scope of inquiry, functions, strategies, and central issues of this field.

Theoretical Resources and Textbooks

In part because contrastive rhetoric as a discipline is still in its early stage of development, one often has to turn to other fields for theoretical resources. The self-reflections of comparative philosophers offer the much-needed conceptual tools for exploring the epistemological issues in contrastive rhetoric; the instructor might consider using, for example, *Interpreting Across Boundaries* (1988), by Larson and Deutsch. To cultural studies one turns for what is needed to address the political issues involved, for example, Stuart Hall's "Ideology and Communication Theory" (1989) and "The Local and the Global" (1991) on culture, identity, and globalization. And scholars working in the field of comparative communication studies have been contemplating on the methodological issues. Their discussions throw much light on problems associated with the selection of the right approach; for example, see *Comparatively Speaking* (1992), by Blumler, McLeod, and Rosengren.

For Phase II, Ulla Connor's (1996) recent overview of the field provides a framework for a critical survey of a key area of inquiry in this field, whereas useful readings in intercultural communication are conveniently found in popular undergraduate textbooks such as Samovar and Porter's *Intercultural Communication* (1997). Depending on the specific topic(s) for investigation in Phase III, one usually has to locate and collect suitable texts from a wide range of scholarly journals and other relevant publications.

Writing Projects

The relationship between culture and rhetoric, according to linguist Michael Clyne (1994), can be explored by (1) comparing native discourse across cultures, (2) examining the discourse of nonnative speakers in a second language, and (3) examining the ways people of different cultural and linguistic backgrounds interact with one another. In the case of an undergraduate advanced writing course on contrastive rhetoric, efforts must necessarily be focused on the last two approaches. Nonnative speakers' writings in English are easily available for rhetorical analysis and for comparison with what native speakers have written for similar purposes. As English is fast becoming the lingua franca of scholarship and more and more academic journals are taking a cross-cultural interest or are orienting themselves toward an international audience, one can easily find, for example, articles on similar topics by scholars of different cultural and linguistic backgrounds.

The World Wide Web allows easy access to English newspapers and journals published in many non-English-speaking countries, for example, *The St. Petersburg Times, The Asahi Shimbun*'s English Edition, and *China Daily.* A comparison over a period of time of the opinion pieces in these papers with those in the U.S. media, for example, could yield interesting findings about how modes of persuasion and argumentation differ from one culture to another. Of greater interest to many students are the mushrooming Internet chat rooms and discussion groups that have enabled people from around the world to interact with one another without actually coming together. Bringing the interests of contrastive rhetoric to bear on a reading of selected transcripts of such discussions could be another worthy project for the class. How the relentless process of globalization and the rise of English as the virtual world language have impacted the way people from different countries and cultures communicate with one another, and how this new situation ought to change the disciplinary practices of contrastive rhetoric, promises to become among the topics of the greatest interest to comparative rhetoricians. The instructor would do well to encourage the more sophisticated students to work in this direction.

Seeking the Good

A Course in Advanced Argument

John C. Bean

My course in advanced argument regularly evolves as I seek better ways to integrate competing goals. At least I think the goals compete. They are derived in part from my early experience as a teacher of argument, when I came under the influence of two powerful little textbooks: Kenneth Bruffee's *Short Course in Writing* (1980) and Richard Braddock's *Little Casebook in the Rhetoric of Writing* (1971). The differing philosophies of argument in these texts initiated for me a dialectic that many years later I am still trying to work into my advanced argument course. In the following pages, I will describe the terms of this dialectic as embodied in three course strands and then explain the assignments I use to integrate the strands into a coherent (I hope) course design.

Strand One: Bruffee and Thesis-Driven Argument

My first strand reflects Bruffee's early and profound influence on my teaching of argument. One of the ironies of our history as a profession is that in the early 1980s, when Bruffee was hailed for his pioneering advocacy of social construction and collaborative learning and when the five-paragraph theme was universally reviled for its muffin-tin reductionism, Bruffee himself taught writing through a series of three-paragraph essays he called "Two Reasons," "Nestorian Order," "Strawman," "Strawman and One Reason," and "Concession." Using prescribed forms heuristically, Bruffee's assignment sequence teaches the argumentative strategies of asserting a claim, developing supporting reasons and evidence, summarizing objections and opposing views, and responding to them through refutation or concession. My colleagues and I used Bruffee's text for several years in a first-year program, where I saw the power of these little assignments to teach purposeful and organized thought.

Teaching tightly structured claim/reasons/support arguments, therefore, constitutes one major strand of my course in advanced argumentation. I teach an advanced version of Bruffee's forms by using the generic structure of the conventional classical oration: *exordium, narratio, propositio, partitio, confirmatio, confutatio,* and *peration.* To help students generate substance for these arguments, I teach Toulmin analysis for its powerful focus on bringing

76

unstated assumptions to the surface and linking one's arguments to the values of the targeted audience. Another component of my Strand One instruction is stasis theory, in which I emphasize the stases of definition, cause, analogy, evaluation, and proposal. Throughout Strand One, I rely primarily on my own textbook, with John D. Ramage, *Writing Arguments* (1998).

I am reasonably satisfied with this strand as long as students write about local issues or address teacher-designed cases that don't have a long history of public debate. But I am often disappointed when students address big public issues like gun control, the destruction of rain forests, or legalization of drugs, because they tend simply to reproduce the issue's stock arguments. Their dutifully researched arguments—despite their smooth surfaces, their clear claims, their logical structures of reasons and evidence—seem uncompelling, predictable, and closed. As a consequence, much of my advanced argument course tries to work against the grain of these too-pat productions, aiming for a more complex and troubled discourse—for signs of struggle and discovery.

Strand Two: Braddock and Rhetoric/Persuasion

Another early influence on my teaching of argument was Richard Braddock's *Little Casebook,* which introduces students inductively to the persuasive strategies of language, including the complications of voice, audience, and perspective. "Instead of prescribing rules for good writing," says Braddock in his preface to students, "the book presents problems [and exercises] designed to help you develop . . . a modern theory of rhetoric" (1971, ix). Braddock's agenda is clear in his first assignment, which asks students to write two different descriptions of the same place by altering voices. Later assignments are called "A Paper with an Ironic Voice," "An Explanation for a Naïve Reader," "An Exploration of the Psychological Roots of Controversy," and "A Search for Credibility—the Writer."

My Strand Two assignments, inspired by Braddock's pedagogy for teaching "a theory of rhetoric," include analyses of style, in which students examine the rhetorical effect, for example, of switching information from a main clause to a subordinate clause, of selecting and arranging details in different ways, or of using different figures or tropes; of the rhetorical construction of statistical and numerical data, for example, the effect of raw numbers versus percentages; and of the persuasive strategies of visual images, for example, the effects of selection, perspective, and focus. Longer assignments in this strand include alternatives to the thesis-first arguments of Strand One: restructuring arguments for different audiences, using narrative and Rogerian strategies, or transforming arguments from a linear print format to flyers, billboards, or advertisements. Although I am not yet skilled enough with hypertext to ask students to create advocacy websites, this is the direction toward which Strand Two of my course may evolve in the future. Whereas Strand One of my course tends to promote a positivist confidence in the writer's authority and the transparency of truth, Strand Two tends to promote a postmodern, rhetorical view of the world, where truth is perspectival and evidence is constructed.

Strand Three: Seeking the Good

The juxtaposition of Strands One and Two initiates a dialectic leading to Strand Three, which I think of as my "seeking the good" strand, in which I try to find some sort of epistemological middle ground between certainty and perspectivism. I don't want students to think of argument as either a pro/con game or an endless kaleidoscope of perspectives. I want them to see argument as a serious enterprise with serious consequences, as a principled search for the best solution to complex problems, solutions that must take into account alternative perspectives and points of view. At root, I hope for the same kind of world that Deborah Tannen seeks in *The Argument Culture* (1998), a world where people argue passionately but where they also listen empathically and are willing to change their views in light of better knowledge or more fully examined and considered values. The need to argue draws us into the world to understand it better and into ourselves to forge or discover consistent and articulable values. It often draws us too, I think, into what Tannen calls the complex and muddled middle rather than the simple extremes on any issue. Drawing students into complexity is my goal in Strand Three.

What I dislike about my students' too-pat position papers in Strand One is that the writer's stance isn't troubled; the writer's thesis hasn't been *earned*. Consider, for example, a predictable stock move in an argument about rain forests: "We should preserve tropical rain forests," a student will argue, "because the rain forests can provide new cures for cancer or other diseases." This reason will be supported with testimonial quotations, often from an advocacy website, about scientists researching medicines derived from rain forest plants or tree bark. The writer then moves to the next stock argument: "Another reason we should preserve rain forests is that they are essential for combating global warming." Nothing ruffles the surface of this writer's world. Who, we might ask, is the imperial "we" in the writer's claim? Who decides whether rain forests live or die? What questions has this confident writer not asked about tropical economies, about Brazilian land ownership, about the plight of Brazilian poor, or about our own complicity in the economic forces that make it profitable to cut down rain forests?

My Strand Three strategy is to create assignments that delay closure by rewarding question asking. My most successful assignment is an exploratory paper written to the following prompt:

> Choose a public policy issue on which you are currently unable to take a stand. Explain why the issue both interests and perplexes you. Then write a first-person, chronologically organized account of your thinking process as you investigate your issue through research and your own critical thinking.

Writing expressively rather than persuasively, students tell the story of their own wrestling with an issue. They are rewarded for delaying closure, for researching multiple perspectives, for investigating substantive and conflicted questions about the subject, and for examining their own often divided and contradictory values. This assignment often produces the writing that most deeply satisfies me in my whole course.

Another closure-delaying assignment that I am developing is inspired by the discussion of research problems in Booth, Colomb, and Williams' *Craft of Research* (1995). The authors point out that beginning researchers often try to solve huge practical problems in the real world, such as homelessness or acid rain, instead of focusing on some smaller, lesser-known concern embedded within a larger issue. "So write your paper," they advise the beginning researcher, "not to solve the problem of acid rain, but to solve the problem that *there is something about acid rain that we don't know or understand,* something that we need to know before we can deal with it" (55). This insight has led me to refocus major research assignments on a small aspect of a big issue: not "Should we preserve rain forests?" but "What social and economic factors in Brazil lead to deforestation?" If some economic problem in Brazil could be addressed, perhaps its solution could help solve the larger problem of preserving the rain forests. A student's goal is to find and support a claim inside the subissue, letting the larger issue frame the smaller.

My Course Design

In designing my course—which is a 300-level, five-credit, quarter-system course—I struggle mightily to interweave the three strands so that they don't appear as discreet modules but as different emphases inside an integrated whole. I build my course around a sequence of argumentative projects. The first project uses a course pack of readings on a public issue, which provides a common subject matter for class discussions of Toulmin, stasis theory, and rhetorical analysis. Students write several short arguments on this common topic to practice the skills needed for the major course assignments.

My second course project is a practical proposal to solve a local problem. The required argument has a tight, Strand One structure; it must clearly address the value system of the decision maker who has the power to enact the proposal—a Strand Two rhetorical/persuasive focus; and it requires extensive research into the local causes of the problem, the constraints against solving it, and the costs and benefits of the proposed solution—a Strand Three seeking-the-good focus).

A third course project results in two extended pieces of writing and a speech. Here students are asked to research an issue of public policy or value that truly perplexes them at the beginning of the course. First they must write an exploratory research paper written to the prompt described above under Strand Three. This paper is due about halfway through the course. Next they must take a stand on their issue and write an argument that they imagine to be published in a print magazine or newspaper of their choice. Finally, students must give a five-minute persuasive speech on the same issue, supplementing the speech with a poster or flyer that mixes visual and written elements. This project integrates all three strands of the course.

Conclusion

Although I have yet to produce a course design that fully meets my goals, I am satisfied that my course deepens students' appreciation for the complexity and importance of argument. It prepares them for further work in rhetorical theory and for writing in different genres for different purposes. And because it raises students' awareness of epistemology as a philosophical problem, it helps them see what is at issue in the ancient debate between Socrates and the Sophists or in postmodern variations of the same conversation.

The History of Rhetoric

Richard Leo Enos

There are clear signs, both direct and indirect, that reveal the importance of including the history of rhetoric in the advanced writing curriculum. Studying the history of rhetoric has long been a feature of graduate writing programs. A survey conducted by Thomas Miller of the University of Arizona and published in *Rhetoric Review* (1993) shows that the vast majority of doctoral programs in rhetoric offer at least one course in the history of rhetoric. This study, which concentrated on graduate education, does not even begin to account for the numerous undergraduate courses offered throughout the United States and abroad. Tangentially, the emergence of publications that stress the history of rhetoric, such as *Rhetorica: A Journal of the History of Rhetoric* and *Advances in the History of Rhetoric,* are further, albeit indirect, registers of the academic value of such an area of study.

The benefits of the history of rhetoric to graduate education and scholarly research extend, in very important ways, into the undergraduate curriculum. The History of Rhetoric course introduces writing students to the ways that meaning is made and shared with others. The importance of sharing meaning is endemic to every effort of communication—oral, written, electronic—so much so that each culture has sought to explain and refine the process of expressing thoughts and sentiments. Recent works, such as George Kennedy's *Comparative Rhetoric* (1999), reveal the breadth and variations of rhetoric across time and cultures. Our own Western heritage of rhetoric is European in origin. This course concentrates on presenting the way in which rhetoric has been a dimension of our history. Understanding the history of rhetoric not only provides students with a more sensitive knowledge of our past, but (as will be discussed below) it indirectly sharpens analytical skills and examines many systems that advance useful heuristics for expressing our thoughts and sentiments.

Five features of this course enhance the education of undergraduate writing majors. First, studying the history of rhetoric enables students to understand how language operates in social interaction. By its very nature, expression is a social activity. A historical course allows students to view these processes in a way that dramatizes how people of different cultures and periods have different values, perspectives, and methods of expression. Second, this course reveals the relationship among three components of English departments: literature, creative writing, and rhetoric. Many students recognize these three components as part of the curriculum but often assume they are autonomous. This course,

as discussed below, helps students understand the intellectual relationships that
have existed for centuries and that serve as the conceptual foundations for English studies. Third, students are tempted to think of history as "telling a story"
that is whole, complete, and unified. This course enables students to see that the
act of composing the history of rhetoric is itself an argument. Students begin to
realize that the choice, selection, and presentation of "data" are ways of vali-
dating the historian's interpretation of that material. In short, historiography is
inherently an argumentative process and therefore a rhetorical act. Fourth, the
history of rhetoric is fraught with problems. Sources often appear to be incompatible. Accounts often seem inconsistent or, at the least, to rival other interpretations. This course provides students with the opportunity to see the history
of rhetoric as a problem-solving process that sharpens critical-thinking skills.
Fifth and finally, studying the history of rhetoric gives students the opportunity
to practice their own abilities in rhetoric through exercises that require them
not only to analyze historical problems but also to use the heuristics of rhetoric
to express analyses in clear, lucid prose. The following perspectives and objectives elaborate on the features that The History of Rhetoric offers.

Perspectives and Objectives

The History of Rhetoric as a Site of Discourse Contexts

The History of Rhetoric offers undergraduate students the opportunity to understand the impact of rhetoric on Western thought. One of the underlying assumptions of the course is that students will benefit from an understanding of
the founding, and foundation, of their discipline. Some students assume that
this foundation is little more than a chronicling of events and a reporting of the
activities of individuals. One of the primary objectives of the course is to illus-
trate that the opposite is the case. The History of Rhetoric provides the opportunity to understand how influential discourse is in shaping the mentalities of
not only luminaries but entire societies. Much of our grounding in the study of
rhetoric stresses the relationship between cognition and expression in various
social contexts—that is, how meaning is made and expressed to others. In most
cases, the practice of rhetoric is intended to gain adherence or resolve problems
that can be remedied by discourse. Discourse is composed rhetorically in order
to provide and share a view of reality. Rhetors often structure language in order to establish with readers and auditors what is meaningful and thereby construct a basis for understanding and agreement. Correspondingly, theories of
rhetoric seek to explain why rhetoric operates in various ways, as well as how
auditors and readers respond. Such theoretical explanations, in turn, help us to
adjudicate the appropriateness of rhetorical techniques. The history of rhetoric
provides the opportunity to study rhetorical practices and evaluate rhetorical
theories across cultures and through time. From such an examination, students
become sensitive to various heuristics or inventive strategies.

Integrating The History of Rhetoric into the Curriculum

The History of Rhetoric can serve the students and department in several ways. First, as an advanced undergraduate course, it can be directed toward students who have declared English as a major. English departments typically have three major concentrations: literature, creative writing, and rhetoric and composition. The History of Rhetoric course can serve as a foundation for the department by demonstrating to students the long and close ties that rhetoric has had with literature and poetics, the classical term for creative discourse. The primary emphasis in the course is on the rhetorical tradition, but efforts are constantly made to align rhetoric with the prevailing status of literature and poetics. For example, Plato's dialogue on Homer and epic poetry in general, the *Ion,* can be discussed along with readings from the *Iliad* and *Odyssey.* Aristotle's *Rhetoric* can be compared and contrasted with his *Poetics.* Cicero's *De Oratore* can be used to view the persuasion inherent in Vergil's *Aeneid,* Livy's *Ab Urbe Condita,* and Horace's *Roman Odes.* In each instance the basis and emphasis is rhetoric, but comparing the prevailing views of rhetoric will contextualize its relationship with literature and poetics. In some instances the basis of comparison will be theory, at other times criticism, and at other times orality and literacy. This approach allows students to have a much more integrated view of the field and, indirectly, helps them see the ties that bind most English departments. The following is a list of possible topics that are intended to foster integration while teaching the history of rhetoric.

Week 1: The Greek Oral Tradition

Week 2: The Alphabet and the Emergence of Craft Literacy

Week 3: Homeric Literature and the Oral Tradition of Rhapsodes

Week 4: Plato's Views on Rhetoric and Poetics

Week 5: Isocrates, the Sophists, and the Rhetorical *Paideia*

Week 6: Aristotle: Mimetic and Non-Mimetic Literature

Week 7: Roman Notions of Rhetoric, Literature, and Poetry

Week 8: Rhetoric and Poetics in the Augustan Principate

Week 9: Quintilian and the Classical Tradition of Education

Week 10: St. Augustine: Pagan Rhetoric and Christian Literature

Week 11: The Three Medieval Arts of Rhetoric

Week 12: Scholasticism, Humanism, and Renaissance Rhetoric and Poetics

Week 13: The Literary Arts and the Rise of the Vernacular

Week 14: British Rhetorical Theory: The Criticism of Taste

Week 15: American Rhetoric and the Development of English Departments

The History of Rhetoric as an Argument

Students learn that not only the history of rhetoric, but all history, is an argument. That is, history is both a recording and an accounting of events. The choice and selection of what to record and account for is an act of preference on the part of the historian, who makes decisions about what is or is not important for the subject under examination. When we see such collections as *The Rhetorical Tradition* (Bizzell and Herzberg 1990), we need to remember that the choice and selection of entries are based on multiple criteria, some of which include the availability of primary sources, the length of entries, and perhaps even copyright permission! In this sense, the activity of "making" history is itself rhetorical. The historian is, in effect, marshaling an argument about what events mean and how these events ought to be interpreted. Thus students come to understand that the history of rhetoric has several dimensions. History is simultaneously an accounting and an argument that justifies the validity of a particular interpretation. For example, one of the questions that historians of rhetoric must face is "Who should be included in the history of rhetoric?" Until recently, the emphasis in the history of rhetoric had been upon prominent males, with an orientation toward political events. Recently, arguments have been made that such an orientation neglects, and by default, devalues other important social dimensions and groups in our history. Current efforts in the history of rhetoric have broadened the scope of study by including women. Good examples of such histories are Andrea A. Lunsford's edited volume *Reclaiming Rhetorica* (1995) and Cheryl Glenn's *Rhetoric Retold* (1997). These two works, as well as the Kennedy volume mentioned earlier, are fine examples of how historians of rhetoric can argue for expanding or even reconceptualizing the rhetorical tradition.

The History of Rhetoric as
Problem Solving and Critical Thinking

The History of Rhetoric provides students with the opportunity to study the ways in which rhetoric can be used as a resource for solving—and for judging solutions to—problems. Rhetorical theories are often developed to explain how and why judgments are made. In one respect, the history of rhetoric can be viewed as an interpretation of how individuals and groups have dealt with social issues. For example, from the beginning of the course, students confront serious problems that challenged ancient Greeks. We can frame some of these problems into such questions as "Is rhetoric valuable enough to warrant attention as a serious discipline?" or "Are the merits of effective rhetoric judged only on the standard of popular approval and not the tests of rationality?" Such questions prompt students to examine the nature and intent of education itself and the function of rhetoric in the curriculum. Students, in turn, may also be self-reflexive and examine their own educational values by asking such questions about their own personal goals. To nurture problem-solving skills, students are asked to respond to issues that grow out of weekly readings, lectures, and discussion. By generating a large quantity of ideas from diverse perspectives, such exercises encourage students to develop creativity, and they also encourage students to advance distinctive responses, to elaborate on initial ideas, and to weigh ideas for their saliency and appropriateness. In the early stages of the course, the instructor provides highly defined problems, often with rival positions that are matched in strength. As students progress through the semester, the weekly "problems" become increasingly vague and ill-defined. Students learn that part of the exercise is to understand what the salient issues are and how to express these issues clearly. Generally, such assignments facilitate the basic features of creativity through problem solving: fluency, flexibility, originality, elaboration, and evaluation. Specifically, students learn to argue for an accounting of what historical problems exist and how they can be resolved. They also learn to select heuristics that are the most sensitive methods of analyzing these problems. Finally, students sharpen their own writing skills by expressing their interpretations in written prose.

The History of Rhetoric as Skill Enhancement: Analysis, Synthesis, and Expression

Through weekly writing, students learn that the choice and selection of issues, the presentation of facts, and the interpretation of those facts are themselves rhetorical acts inherent in the history of rhetoric and the rhetorical tradition. They begin to realize that the history of rhetoric is not only the reporting of events but also a rhetorical act in which meaning is argued and shared between writer and reader. These short, defined assignments assist students in analysis in important but limited ways. In a more extensive assignment in The History of Rhetoric, students dilate these skills into longer research papers in which they resolve more complex problems. Because The History of Rhetoric is often presented as a survey course, the value is placed on coverage, where a substantial amount of material is read and discussed. Yet developing skills in ways that teach methods of historiography aids students in sharpening analytical skills and enhancing expression, and it also provides an appreciation for the rhetorical dimensions of research. To meet this latter objective, teachers often consider requiring a paper on a specialized topic. Two objects thereby come into apparent conflict. On the one hand, coverage is mandated by the nature of the course. Yet refining research skills in historical methods is a natural opportunity and a necessary skill. One resolution to this apparent dilemma is to require extensive reading for approximately the first two-thirds of the course. This reading can be monitored weekly by short problem-solving assignments that focus on various discrete but related skills. In the latter third of the course, students may declare their own topics for a "micropaper" written in the standard format of a research paper, with its components condensed to six to eight pages. This length limitation makes the assignment close enough to the two-page weekly responses that the task and methods are related. There are, however, salient differences between the short assignments and the micropaper. As is apparent from the above description, the short assignments are constructed and directed by the instructor. The micropaper requires students to choose their own problem, structure a clearly expressed thesis, justify why the method of analysis will best meet the objectives, and project the possible implications of such a study. These two types of assignments facilitate analysis, synthesis, and expression.

The advanced undergraduate course in the history of rhetoric just described has the potential to introduce students not only to rhetoric but also to the field of English. Emphasizing problem-solving and analytical skills facilitates student engagement in issues central to their education while also offering heuristics that develop writing skills.

More Than a Matter of Form

Genre and Writing

Kathleen Blake Yancey

When I was asked to teach University of North Carolina–Charlotte's version of advanced comp, Expository Writing, I was both pleased and puzzled. Pleased for the obvious reasons: I like to teach writing, I welcomed the opportunity to work with advanced writers, and I thought I could develop an interesting curriculum for this course. Which, of course, is the puzzle: what would such an interesting curriculum look like?

In part, this text narrates one segment of that curriculum. In part, this text explores what happened when students encountered that curriculum. In part, this text theorizes the curriculum.

In whole, this text speaks to the roles that two key concepts can play in advanced undergraduate writing instruction: rhetorical situation and genre. Although separate, each is implicated in the other. They work together collectively. Pragmatically, they provide structure and conventions for a writer. Theoretically, they provide a language with which we can talk about the texts we write and about the authors we compose in and through those texts.

*   *   *

An Expository Writing classroom: a computer-based writing studio. An Expository Writing class workshop: a series of focused quickwrites, introduced one at a time.

- The first task: In fifteen minutes, explain World War II to an audience of college students.

- The second task: In fifteen minutes, explain World War II to an audience of American six-year-olds.

- The third task: In fifteen minutes, explain World War II to an audience of Japanese middle school kids.

- The fourth and final task: In fifteen minutes, explain World War II from the perspective of someone who was involved in the experience. Use whatever form suits: dramatic monologue, dialogue, letter. Use whatever desktop publishing features are appropriate: font size and style, italics, boldfacing, white space—all those elements that constitute the rhetoric of the page.

*   *   *

Here's what happened:

The first task: In fifteen minutes, explain World War II to an audience of college students.

OK, they say. *Not too tough.* (*Not too interesting.*) Working from a World War II data sheet, they work together, talking, writing, keyboarding in a reportlike account. When did it start? How long did it last? Who were the leaders? How many dead?

The second task: In fifteen minutes, explain World War II to an audience of American six-year-olds.

Oh no, they say, groaning. *How to do this? What to include?* they inquire. *Your call,* I say. *Think like a six-year-old.* Slowly, working from the same material and from their own reading and writing experiences, they begin to create another account that wanders into something else, into another genre. Sometimes, it's account-qua-fairy tale: "Once upon a time. . . ." Sometimes it's account-qua-morality play: "When bullies get out of control. . . ."

The third task: In fifteen minutes, explain World War II to an audience of Japanese middle school kids.

Oh no, they say, groaning, only this time they mean it.

The fourth and final task: In fifteen minutes, explain World War II from the perspective of someone who was involved in the experience. Use whatever form suits: dramatic monologue, dialogue, letter. Use whatever desktop publishing features are appropriate: font size and style, italics, boldfacing, white space—all those elements that constitute the rhetoric of the page.

Oh my, they say. *This could be interesting.*

*   *   *

World War II officially started in 1939 when Adolf Hitler, leading Nazi Germany, invaded Poland. Germany's conquest of Europe was soon joined by Japan and Italy to form the Axis powers. Japan was focused on conquering China and the South Pacific, while Italy's efforts were mostly in North Africa.

All three were very successful until Japan made the mistake of bombing Pearl Harbor on December 7 of 1941. This brought the U.S. into the war. . . .

Over the course of the next three years, the Allies were able to retake North Africa and Europe, while it was primarily the U.S. that defeated Japan in the Pacific. The war in Europe ended with the fall of Berlin, while the war in the Pacific ended with the U.S. dropping bombs over the cities of Nagasaki and Hiroshima in Japan.

Many times people become angry at other people, just like you become angry with your brother/sister, or friend, etc. But that kind of anger is nothing compared to a war. In a war, people actually use guns and other weapons to kill each other. In 1939, a world war began. That means that several different countries were fighting against each other. The leader of Germany, one of the countries, was Adolf Hitler. He was very evil and he wanted to take control of the world and tell everyone what to do. He did not like other people who were different from him, so he had them killed.

At first the United States was not in the war. One day Japan flew an airplane over a place in Hawaii where the United States kept a lot of their ships. Japan dropped a bomb, which is an exploding device similar to very powerful fireworks, destroying all of the ships and killing many people. After this, the United States entered the war. This war lasted 5 years, and it ended when the United States dropped two bombs on two cities in Japan.

When we were writing for the 6-year-olds, we were in a completely different genre than when we were writing for non-American readers. Our voice had to be different because of the audience. This is important to remember when you are writing. The audience you are writing for makes a difference in the way you write and how you present the material.

* * *

Another set of sequenced tasks, same intent:

- For an audience of college students, tell the story of Lyndon Baines Johnson.

- For an audience of six-year-olds, tell the story of Lyndon Baines Johnson.

- Write a patterned piece—one using the white space of the page—to tell a "creative" story about LBJ.

* * *

I, Lyndon Baines Johnson, was born in 1908 in a hardscrabble area of Texas.
I was born on a farm in Iowa.
I was a teacher.
I am barely out of high school.
I started my political career in 1948 as a Senator.
I didn't get a chance to start a career.
I am married and have two beautiful daughters.
I am engaged to be married to my high school sweetheart.
I initiated federal aid for education, HUD, and Medicare.
I created the "Great Society" and the "War on Poverty."
I was drafted into the war in Vietnam.
I accelerated the war in Vietnam. I am watching race riots in my cities.
I am watching my friends die day after day.

I died January 22nd, 1973, 5 days after the war ended.
I was the last American soldier to die. I died January 21st, 1973.

> The purpose of this writing . . . was to give a biography of LBJ's life in a creative way. We chose to show his life parallel to the last American soldier to die in Vietnam. We changed the font sizes to show the strengths and weaknesses in both of their lives.

* * *

Like their analogues in other arts—finger exercises on the piano, for example, and sketches on a drawing pad—these *writings-as-design* function as rehearsals of a sort. In this exercise, the tasks also include working with others, working from the intuitive, theorizing what was just written. That theorizing is the student writing the curriculum—as only he or she can, based on experience plural: on generalized writing experiences, on specific reading experiences, on rehearsals such as these. The tasks here, based in genre and rhetorical situation and the rhetoric of the page, provide experiences that can then be reflected upon and theorized.

That the tasks are multiple is a key part of the curricular design. The materiality—the story of the LBJ who created civil rights legislation and who is the same LBJ who, it is claimed, stole his first election and took such pleasure in showing his appendectomy scar—doesn't change. What changes is how we work with that materiality and how our understanding changes as a function of such work.

* * *

> The LBJ exercise really made me think about the use of language when we had to make an informative report from a series of . . . sentences. When we had to create the report for American college students, the concern was to chronologically get the material right. The focus changed when we had to design the report for the Japanese. As an American, it was a real struggle to pretend I didn't know anything about LBJ or the English language.

* * *

Another day: Student work is posted around the room, as in an art gallery. We walk through the gallery, reading the work of multiple genres, the multiple lenses through which we understand an event. Students nominate their favorites and explain why. Writing in one genre, the review, they comment on the role of genre in how we read and react and understand.

> I picked number five [a letter] for the one that I liked best. I love to read letters anyway. The letter was easy to read and follow. I guess for me I liked it because my Dad went to Vietnam and I have often heard stories from my Nana. . . . The letter made me feel sad, and somewhat emotional. Why? Well, because the thought of being in a war and leaving behind your life is rather scary. . . . The letter sounds real.

Why does a letter recounting an event sound more real than a research report? I'm not certain that it must. I am certain that, in part, it's a matter of genre, that the language of genre helps define the question.

* * *

Expository Writing is not a course in writing history, as my account seems to suggest. This segment on writing history for others fits with other segments—one on reviews, another on author's choice, for instance, where considerations of genre are very much a part of the planning of the text.

Still, history is a good choice for these tasks: it connects to narrative, the most popular genre among my students, at the same time that it stretches what for them are the boundaries of narrative. History, it is said, is the story of the victors: does that matter? Upon what genres does it rely? And what is the relationship between history and truth?

* * *

The historian will write history from the viewpoint of his country and culture. Take for instance the Revolutionary War. If you live in the United States, you learn that the thirteen colonies, after numerous attempts, rightfully declared their independence from Great Britain. They were being treated wrongly and the British refused to correct their actions. . . . However, if you live in Great Britain, you learn that the thirteen ungrateful colonies unlawfully declared their independence. They didn't want to pay their war debts; they didn't want to pay their taxes. . . . Could both stories be true?

* * *

When I began teaching this course, I didn't think in terms of genre: I thought in terms of voice, convinced that one aim of an advanced undergraduate writing course should be to help students create and work with and work in diverse voices. Voice as metaphor, but always in context: hence the role of rhetorical situation. With rhetorical situation comes text, or more precisely kind of text: genre. The idea here was to avoid the problem of school genres as described by David Jolliffe:

Here's what I see happening in too many writing courses: We say we want students to write essays, but we really expect them to write themes. Sometimes we want students to write editorial columns or reviews, but we still call them essays, and then we penalize students because they write themes and not editorial columns or reviews. And only rarely do we show students actual models of the kinds of papers we want them to write. (1996, 226)

The exercises outlined above invite students to work both within the constraints of genre and beyond them, to engage with material in an experimental way and then to reflect upon that experimentation. Readers of Donald Schon (1987) will no doubt recognize this approach as well: work in context with others, then review, reflect, and theorize. Such a methodology, located in the specifics of a particular situation, makes for good practice.

I begin with history for a couple of reasons. For one, it works from lots of different kinds of documents—the personal (letters, diaries) as well as the public (records, transcripts). In this range of documents, genre is made visible. Private documents are identified differently than public, and yet public is known in terms of private. For another, in spite of the emphasis on primary documentation and a presumption of objectivity, we see historical accounts changing as their authors do. The student authors see this themselves. I don't have to explain or persuade; the experience does both.

This approach, like all the curricula I know, doesn't produce a universal effect. (*Alas.*) It does provide a set of practices and, perhaps more importantly, a language that helps some students—though never all—theorize what they do so that they might write in a more intelligent, informed, and self-aware way.

*   *   *

In their words, students explain—to us, and thus to themselves—how the lens of genre works.

In those explanations, I see very different accounts, each accurate and truthful even in its own way. It's in exploring those ways that I begin to understand. Understanding is itself, of course, a rhetorical act.

> The genre I was most inclined to use was the narrative essay. Most of my emails used this format. I did not like the argument or research genres. I assumed that argument meant confrontation and research meant boring. I now realize that I mis-read the . . . quality of those styles.

> Besides just learning a definition for voice and genre, I learned about these concepts and their applications to writing. I now see writing as a complete process that is not dictated by rules and a ticking clock, but rather as an empty page. . . . I see writing as beginning with planning including questioning my purpose and considering my reader so that I can create an appropriate voice. I no longer feel the need or desire to conform to genre, but see genre as a framework to build from, not necessarily within.

> I . . . know that my writing can achieve the same effects for me that my artwork did. My pen and paintbrush are the same. The words (voice) become my images. The final result is an arrangement of the objects (genre).

*   *   *

The end of the term: portfolios read, grades assigned. For most of these students, given that they are seniors, education concluded. Prompted "Describe the writer you will be one year from now," students provide differing answers. Holly *will still be evolving into a proficient and effective writer;* a graduating senior, she'll undertake that development out of school. Holly's unusual in that she has a plan for her *evolving*. In the context of teaching elementary school, she'll address letters to parents, author stories for children, compose advocacy texts about why teachers should be paid better wages. In contrast to Holly, most students: they're merely wishful, and I struggle to believe that the wishes are sincere. *I hope to continue on improving and hopefully.* . . . Sincere or not, they see what's likely: *I haven't the opportunity to practice the art of writing as much as I would like*. What's more: precisely because they are beginning to understand writing, they can sketch the general outlines of that *opportunity* that doesn't exist.

Describe the writer I will be one year from now?

> That question really scares me. Before this year, I never really cared about my writing. All of a sudden it matters to me that I like my writing and that others get the message that I am trying to send. . . . Practice alone is not enough. If you are a runner, you can only get so fast with practice every day. There is a reason you have a coach. The coach can take your physique and match it to a running that is most appropriate to you. The coach may see that your stride is not wide enough; the beginning or end of the run is a little slower. The coach can give specific exercises that can improve the runner's ability. . . . If I do not continue my education in English, I do not know that my writing will be any better in one year.

A traditional English major writing ten short days before graduating from college, Heidi knows exactly what she did not take as a major: writing.

*   *   *

How shall I understand this course?

It's called Expository Writing, this version of advanced comp.

But in its emphasis on genre and voice and poetic and rhetoric and rhetorical situation, it's expository writing plus, one venue among many.

Or: in the words of my student, it's about *the art of writing*.

In both catalog and classroom practice, Expository Writing is a senior-level course that students take as they put one foot out the university door. In a curricular and rhetorical parallel reality that overwrites the college catalog, however, this course doesn't conclude or culminate at all. Rather, it functions as an introduction: to ways of writing, ways of reflecting, ways of understanding, ways of theorizing. Taken together, these ways compose the outlines of a major that could be called writing studies.

Which, borrowing from my student, we might even call *the art of writing*.

Style, Race, Culture, Context

Rebecca Moore Howard

> The assured prescriptions of a Strunk and White seem woefully in-
> adequate when placed in the context of the provisional and contin-
> gent formulations of postcolonial criticism.
>
> —Alan Wright, 1998

At some point just beyond the mid-nineteenth century, style disappeared from the modern rhetorical canons. After the Renaissance years, in which style was the center of a rhetorical education, to the exclusion of the other canons; the Enlightenment years, in which all five canons were taught but style remained preeminent; and the Romantic and modernist years, in which style indexed the character of the author, the venerable canon of style suddenly vanished as an object of instruction. Just prior to that disappearance, stylisticians—among whom are numbered literary theorists, linguists, and a few rhetoricians—had prided themselves on objective, replicable analyses of texts. In accord with these textualist stylisticians, scholars of the new discipline of writing studies gave style a preponderance of their attention, devising pedagogies such as generative rhetoric and sentence combining that were designed to improve students' prose style—and their critical thinking, in the bargain.

But dissonant voices entered the conversation: Marxists pointed out that teaching style inevitably privileged middle-class white speech codes; multiculturalists celebrated the value of other codes and other styles; and poststructuralists asserted that the text on which textualist stylistics depended was too indeterminate and unstable to be studied in any sort of objective, replicable manner. After Stanley Fish's "What Is Stylistics and Why Are They Saying Such Terrible Things About It?" (1996), only the carcass of textualist stylistics remained. One of Fish's chief targets, Richard Ohmann, published very little about stylistics after 1973. Ironically, after a respected career in functionalist textualist stylistics, Ohmann offered, as one of his final statements on the subject, the *College English* article "Use Definite, Specific, Concrete Language" (1979), in which he derided some of the chief tenets upon which textualist composition pedagogy of style had been predicated. Together with the Conference on College Composition and Commmunication (CCCC) policy argument for

94

linguistic relativity, "Students' Right to Their Own Language" (CCCC 1974), Ohmann's 1979 article encouraged writing specialists to believe that style could not and should not be taught.

So the entire discipline of writing studies turned away from teaching style. A few textbooks survived—notably the Strunk and White chestnut,[1] as well as entries by Sheridan Baker, Joseph Williams, and others. And certainly a valorization of style persisted: both teachers and students of writing continue to prize good prose style, however that term is defined. Yet the discipline of writing studies has come to regard a pedagogy of style as colonial in its impulses and futile in its effects.

This amounts to a judgment against textualist stylistics. But textualist stylistics is only one branch of the field; scholars of writing have insufficiently explored the possibilities of a contextualist stylistics that attends to the mutual constitution of text and context and that celebrates the diversity of styles produced by cultural diversity and complexity. Adopting a contextualist perspective on style, an advanced undergraduate course could explore some of the possibilities identified in a fall 1998 Texas Christian University (TCU) doctoral seminar in stylistics.[2] These principles lend themselves to a pedagogy of style that exceeds the strictures of now-abandoned textualist stylistics.

Functions of Style

- Style can be a means of invention: as writers craft a style in a given text, they are discovering and developing their beliefs about their topic.

- Style can provide a focus for analysis of and response to texts: readers conducting stylistic analysis are discovering not only how an argument is constructed but also the means whereby the text affected them.

- Style can persuade: the reader is more favorably disposed toward a text written in a style of which the reader approves.

- Style can reveal the writer's sense of relationship to his or her audience, purpose, or topic.

- Style can help the writer establish, discover, or revise his or her individual identity and group allegiances.

- Style can index both writer's and readers' cultural codes.

1. The original edition of which is now available on-line: *http://www.cc.columbia.edu/acis/bartleby/strunk.*
2. Seminar members are Heidi Beierle, Dan Fredrick, Rebecca Moore Howard, Mark Noe, Melanie Peterson, Amy Rupiper, Kurt Schick, Patricia Tallakson, and Artist Thornton. Their work on style pedagogy will be explained in a chapter in the forthcoming *Composition Pedagogy in Perspective: Landmarks and Horizons, 1972–1999,* ed. Rob McDonald and Christina Russell McDonald, Portland, ME: Calendar Islands.

The Cultural Work of Style: a Sample Lesson

One inevitable component of any course in style is the discussion of levels of style, what sociolinguists (e.g., Trudgill 1983, 102–10) call "levels of formality" and Roman rhetoricians typically classified as "grand," "middle," or "plain" style. For the Romans, each of these levels matched a particular rhetorical situation; in modern usage (e.g., J. M. Williams 1999), plain style and its hallmark, clarity, are in all situations desirable. Provocatively implicated in the modern valorization of clarity is the modern notion of good usage—the usage of prominent, influential speakers and writers. This notion of usage governs the style labels attached to lexical entries in dictionaries, and the Good Users whose usage and opinions collectively determine those labels are commonly listed in the introductory apparatus to the dictionary. Clarity, in this complex calculus, can be expressed only in good usage.

Which means, of course, good usage is not vernacular, not slang. Students in the advanced style class will generally agree to these primary, unexamined tenets of the literacy representations of contemporary American education. But the teacher of style can introduce the class to a list of words that linguists hypothesize as being of African origins, words transmitted to American English through plantation creoles and their descendent, Ebonics. I provide a few examples in Figure 2–1; a fuller list appears (as does a list of etymological sources) in Figure 2–2 on page 101.

Of all the entries listed in the table, the one that most stirs me—and usually my students, as well—is the (mis)representation *uh-huh* and *uh-uh,* widely attested as the words of affirmation and negation in several West African languages. Robert Farris Thompson, for example, notes them in Yoruba. And they are today in widespread use in American English, by members of all social classes, despite the efforts of people like my grandmother. As I grew up in the Upper South, I was forbidden to use *uh-huh* and *uh-uh.* My grandmother explained, "Ladies don't grunt." (Instruction about what ladies did and didn't do was a significant feature of my upbringing, though much of it didn't "take.") Bigmother lost the battle with me and with society: today we all use *uh-huh* and *uh-uh* in spoken English as words of affirmation and negation. But in a sense she won the battle in the dictionaries, for there the words are listed, but not as words, not as adverbs (the part of speech with which *yes* and *no* are labeled), but as interjections. They are, according to our dictionaries, grunts.

What cultural work does one find style performing in these lexical entries? Good style is effected through good usage; good usage is determined by good users; good users determine what is "standard" usage and what is "vernacular"; words of African origin, common in Ebonics but also adopted into American English, are vernacular; hence the language of Ebonics cannot be the vehicle of good style. African contributions to the English lexicon are labeled "vernacular" (or as interjections) or are attributed to European sources. Africans cannot be good users; Europeans can. And sample lessons such as these demonstrate

Word attributed by linguist(s) to African origins	Etymology given in *American Heritage College* and *Random House College* dictionaries
banana (Holloway & Vass; Dalby)	*AH:* Portuguese & Spanish, from Wolof, Mandingo, and Fulani. *RH:* Spanish < Portuguese < West African.
boogie (Dalby)	*AH:* No etymology. *RH:* ?
chigger (Dillard revised by Marckwardt)	*AH:* French < Old French < Vulgar Latin. *RH:* Caribbean.
cola (Holloway & Vass; Dalby)	*AH:* West African. *RH:* Mandingo.
daddy (father) (Holloway & Vass)	*AH:* Prob. of baby-talk orig. *RH:* < *dad;* Childish alter.
dig (to understand) (Holloway & Vass; Dalby)	*AH:* Middle English; prob. akin to old French *digue.* *RH:* Middle English.
gorilla (Holloway & Vass)	*AH:* Neo-Latin < Greek, perhaps of African origin. *RH:* Neo-Latin < Greek.
jazz (Dillard revised by Marckwardt; Holloway & Vass; Dalby)	*AH:* ? *RH:* ?
mojo (Dillard revised by Marckwardt; Holloway & Vass)	*AH:* No entry. *RH:* No entry.
tango (Dalby)	*AH:* American Spanish, possibly of Niger-Congo origin. . . . *RH:* American Spanish < ?
uh-huh, uh-uh (Dalby; Thompson)	*AH:* No etymology. ("interjection") *RH:* No etymology. ("interjection")
you all (Schneider; Dalby)	*AH:* No etymology. *RH:* No etymology

Figure 2–1   Howard "Style, Race, Culture, Context"

to students of style how our cultural traditions—in this case, the methods whereby dictionaries determine the etymologies of words—accomplish cultural work that few people would consciously endorse yet that affects us all in our attitudes not just toward style and usage but toward ourselves and others.

Designing the Advanced
Undergraduate Course in Style

A contemporary pedagogy of style should be governed not just by a nostalgic retrieval of classical principles but also by an analysis of the cultural work accomplished by style and by its cultural valorization. Style is not just a means to clarity. And whether it can possibly mark an autonomous, inspired author is a hotly contested issue among theorists of authorship. What style can do, though, is provide a rich, close reading of texts—an approach that has the eloquent potential to bring writing and literature together; it can provide a means whereby writers can craft not just their textual personas but their own sense of personal identity; and it can establish a field on which writers negotiate with a target audience and discourse community.

To craft a course in contextualist style, the teacher must consider objectives. Will the course make students better readers of literature? Certainly an advanced style course can be used effectively to this purpose. When designing such a course, though, one should not fall back into the textualist stylistics that valorized a single style and that used prose style to extrapolate the character and genius of the author—the stylistics in which students were rendered colonized subjects, the passive admirers of master texts. Rather, students in the advanced course in style should be taught that the criteria for good style change according to audience, context, and purpose; that style is not only constructed by but also constructs the contexts in which it occurs; and that, far from being unitary or stable, style derives from a complex, shifting interplay of writer, purpose, audience, and context. The advanced course in style should put students in charge, making them not reproducers of conventions but analysts of those conventions and the cultures that produce them. It should invite students into the project of discovering why and how style is valued in contemporary Western letters.

These principles should, in fact, govern any pedagogy of style, and they certainly apply to the course that I will describe in greater detail. In this course, the term begins with students' gathering examples of style from a variety of media—not just printed texts but also fashion, film, music, and art. The class uses the collected texts to probe potential definitions of *style,* while recognizing that the term will persistently elude definition. The meaning of this exercise is in the process, not the product. In this early stage of the term, students' own written texts are *not* used for stylistic analysis; otherwise, students might be intimidated by the exercise, and the range of peer response could be constrained by students' efforts to protect fellow writers' feelings. Even advanced students need to be comfortable with one another and with stylistic analysis before they collectively apply what they are learning to one anothers' texts.

As the term gets under way, students engage in stylistic close reading of a variety of texts that come not just from canonical literature but also from public media—and in a variety of genres, with class members providing some of the texts to be analyzed. While analyzing texts, students identify what cultural work style is performing. Is it creating a provocative ambiguity? Is it conveying a strong sense of the individual author? Is it defining its audience? Is it offering inclusion or exclusion to its audience? Is it establishing the author as superior or inferior to the audience? Is it making membership overtures toward a target community? Is it facilitating ready comprehension of information? Is it providing entertainment? The class keeps an ongoing log of its discoveries about the cultural work of style.

While the students are analyzing texts, the teacher introduces them to pertinent sections of a textbook, such as Kolln's *Rhetorical Grammar* (1999) that provides a structured but nonprescriptive vocabulary for conducting stylistic analysis.[3] In this course, students need to apply some basic linguistic analyses that go beyond what is provided in the writers' handbooks adopted in the required composition sequence. A book like *Rhetorical Grammar* offers chapters on sentence structure, sentence rhythm, cohesion, "voice" (that contested category), and sentence length. I would not recommend, however, that students work through the Kolln chapters *before* they begin stylistic analysis. Rather, they should enter a source text, identifying its stylistic moments; then the teacher should guide them through pertinent chapters in Kolln. The class can work through those chapters, using them to answer questions raised by their prior reading of the source text. Then they can return to that source text, equipped with a more specific and sophisticated set of tools for analyzing it and explaining what, in the style of the text, is happening to them as readers. Such activities encourage students to notice the effects of style upon them as readers and to consider how those effects are generated.

Meanwhile the course should also involve students in stylistic exercises that allow them, in a preliminary way, to see how their own writing already engages and manipulates style. My favorite way of accomplishing this task is through the translation activities of summary writing. Zoltan Abadi-Nagy, a Hungarian scholar and translator of American literature, describes translation as an act of intensive close reading (1998). The dictionary, says Abadi-Nagy, is of little use in translation; what one needs instead is an encyclopedia—or actually, a whole set of encyclopedias—to aid in translating the spirit of the source language into the nuanced target language. The translator is always alive to the losses and changes that take place.

---

3. In preparing to teach the course, instructors will benefit from consulting Bradford (1997) and Weber (1996) but will probably not want to assign these to undergraduates.

In Abadi-Nagy's description, the formidable problems of translation all re-
volve around issues of style. Listening to him talk, I long for bilingual students
who could be guided through exercises in translation as a way of learning an
attention and sensitivity to style.

But even monolingual students can be engaged, at the advanced level, in
stylistically oriented translation. The "translation" in question would be the
translation that occurs in summary. Taught in introductory courses, summary
is a tool of reading comprehension and a genre of academic writing; taught at
the advanced level, it is a tool of stylistic analysis in close reading. In the advanced style class, not only do students write summaries, but they explicate
what is stylistically lost, changed, and gained in the translation.

Other useful exercises for the early part of the term are explained by
Kathleen Blake Yancey in this volume. Yancey's exercises in genre shifting
lend themselves very well to students' practice of stylistic options, constraints,
and effects.

As the students become comfortable with stylistic close reading and with
one another, they can undertake stylistic analysis of the texts that they themselves wrote early in the term. This analysis should focus on style as a means
whereby writers can discover new meaning and intention in their own texts; as
a means to craft a variety of rhetorical and personal subject-positions; and as a
means of identifying the limits of the rhetorical and personal subject-positions
available to writers.

Equipped with analytic language and tactics from the Kolln text and experienced in the stylistic shifts that occur in translation, students should be
ready, at approximately midterm, to begin working intensively on their own
prose style repertoires. First they work with their own writing samples from the
early part of the course, using these as objects of analysis.

But then they need to begin using their knowledge of stylistics to develop
the writing that they are doing at the moment. Ideally, this writing is not assigned in the style class but is instead the work they are doing outside that class,
for other courses they are taking, or for public or private writing tasks in which
they are already engaged. Peer-group pedagogy works well in this passage of
the syllabus—not so much for the purposes of improving the text at hand but
for helping the writer recognize the effects that the stylistic choices are having
upon readers and consider possible alternatives. Instead of prescribing what
students' style should look like or what it should endeavor to accomplish, the
advanced style course should invite students to discover and describe the options available to them. And the earlier lessons from the style text (e.g., Kolln)
should be reinforced throughout this part of the syllabus—lessons that tell students not what their style should look like but how to understand and manipu-
late their prose styles.

I offer a parting word of caution, one that I cannot overemphasize: The
style course should de-emphasize clarity as the goal of instruction. Because
composition scholarship on style has for the most part lain fallow for a quarter

century, the precepts that guide what remains of style pedagogy accord with critical perspectives of twenty-five years ago. Unfortunately, this means that in some of the leading textbooks, clarity is the primary or even sole goal of style. Thus the boundaries between style, grammar, and usage blur, and the term *style* comes to signal a really good mastery of grammar and usage. The beacon of clarity obscures other effects of style; it assumes that meaning precedes expression; and it ignores not only the ways in which criteria for style vary from one context to another but also the ways in which the writer's stylistic options are constrained by the relative distribution of power between writer and audience. At present, no style textbook accomplishes all these agenda. Still, textbook selection requires careful preview, for a textbook highlighting clarity will hamper a wide-ranging pedagogy of style. In this regard, a return to classical principles serves the teacher of style well, for ancient rhetoricians believed in adjusting style to audience, rhetor, purpose, and occasion, and they described it as an instrument not only of clarity and correctness but also of ornament, fullness of discussion, persuasion, presence, and fluency.

Word attributed by linguist(s) to African origin	**Etymology given in *American Heritage College* and *Random House College* dictionaries**
bad (very good) (Smitherman; Dalby)	*AH:* No etymology. *RH:* No entry.
bad-eye (threatening, hateful glance) (Dalby)	*AH:* No entry. *RH:* No entry.
bad mouth (Dillard revised by Marckwardt; Holloway & Vass; Dalby)	*AH:* No entry. *RH:* No etymology.
banana (Holloway & Vass; Dalby)	*AH:* Portuguese & Spanish, from Wolof, Mandingo, and Fulani. *RH:* Spanish < Portuguese < West African.
banjo (Holloway & Vass; Dalby)	*AH:* Akin to Jamaican E. *banja,* fiddle; prob. akin to Kimbundu, Tshiluba *mbanza.* *RH:* Spanish < Latin < Greek.

Figure 2–2   Appendix 1: Sample Desk Reference Dictionaries' Etymologies of Selected English Words Attributed by Linguists to African Origins

continued

be with it (Dillard revised by
  Marckwardt; Dalby)

AH: No entry.
RH: No entry.

bogus (Holloway & Vass; Dalby)

AH: English.
RH: ?

boogie (Dalby)

AH: No etymology.
RH: ?

bug (insect) (Holloway
  & Vass; Dalby)

AH: No etymology.
RH: Middle English.

bug (to bother or annoy) (Dalby)

AH: No etymology.
RH: Middle English.

cat (man, fellow) (Dillard revised
  by Marckwardt; Holloway
  & Vass; Dalby)

AH: Middle English.
RH: Middle English.

chick (female) (Dalby)

AH: Middle English.
RH: Middle English.

chigger (Dillard revised
  by Marckwardt)

AH: French < Old French < Vulgar
  Latin.
RH: Caribbean.

cola (Holloway & Vass; Dalby)

AH: West African.
RH: Mandingo.

daddy (father) (Holloway & Vass)

AH: Prob. of baby-talk orig.
RH: < *dad;* Childish alter.

dig (to understand) (Holloway
  & Vass; Dalby)

AH: Middle English; prob. akin to
  old French *digue.*
RH: Middle English.

dirt (earth) (Dalby)

AH: Middle English.
RH: Middle English.

do your thing (Dillard revised by
  Marckwardt; Dalby)

AH: Middle English.
RH: No entry.

elephant (Holloway & Vass)

AH: Middle English . . . < Greek.
RH: Middle English < Anglo
  French.

fuzz (police) (Holloway & Vass)

AH: Perhaps back-formation <
  Low German.
RH: cf Dutch *voos* spongy.

goober (Dillard revised by
  Marckwardt; Montgomery;
  Holloway & Vass; Dalby)

AH: Bantu.
RH: African origin; cf. Kimbudu
  nguba peanut.

Figure 2–2   *continued*

goose (to nudge someone in the anus) (Dalby)	*AH:* Middle English. *RH:* Middle English.
gorilla (Holloway & Vass)	*AH:* Neo-Latin < Greek, perhaps of African origin. *RH:* Neo-Latin < Greek.
gumbo (Dillard revised by Marckwardt; Montgomery; Holloway & Vass; Dalby)	*AH:* Louisiana French < Bantu. *RH:* Louisiana French < Bantu.
guy (fellow, person) (Dalby)	*AH:* Middle English and Low German. *RH:* British slang.
hear (to understand) (Dalby)	*AH:* Middle English. *RH:* Middle English.
hep cat (Holloway & Vass)	*AH:* No etymology. *RH:* No etymology.
hip (Dillard revised by Marckwardt; Holloway & Vass; Dalby)	*AH:* Perhaps Wolof. *RH:* ?
hippie (Holloway & Vass)	*AH:* < *hip.* *RH:* ?
honkie (pink white man) (Holloway & Vass; Dalby)	*AH:* Possible blend of Wolof *honq* . . . and *hunky.* *RH:* Origin uncertain.
jam (as in jam session) (Holloway & Vass; Dalby)	*AH:* No etymology. *RH:* Shortening of *jamboree* < ?
jamboree (Holloway & Vass)	*AH:* ? *RH:* ?
jazz (Dillard revised by Marckwardt; Holloway & Vass; Dalby)	*AH:* ? *RH:* ?
jitter (to tremble, shake < the jitters, jitterbug) (Dalby)	*AH:* Perhaps alternation of chitter (< Middle English). *RH:* Middle English.
jive (Holloway & Vass; Dalby)	*AH:* ? *RH:* ?
john (average man who can be taken in) (Dalby)	*AH:* < the name *John.* *RH:* No entry.

Figure 2–2   *continued*

juke (Montgomery)

AH: Prob. < Gullah . . . of West African origin; akin to Wolof *dzug* . . Mandingo (Bambara) *dzugu* . . . [An extensive "regional note" on Gullah follows.]

RH: Gullah.

kick the bucket (Holloway & Vass)

AH: Middle English.
RH: Middle English.

kill (to affect strongly, as in "you kill me") (Dalby)

AH: Old English.
RH: Middle English.

lam (to depart quickly) (Dalby)

AH: ?
RH: Scandinavian.

mojo (Dillard revised by Marckwardt; Holloway & Vass)

AH: No entry.
RH: No entry.

mumbo-jumbo (Holloway & Vass; Dalby)

AH: Perhaps of Mandingo origin.
RH: Mandingo.

oasis (Holloway & Vass)

AH: Late Latin < Greek, probably of Egyptian origin.
RH: Late Latin < Greek < ? Egypt.

okay/O.K. (Dillard revised by Marckwardt; Asante; Holloway & Vass; Dalby)

AH: Abbreviation of *oll korrect,* slang respelling of *all correct.*

RH: probably after the *O.K. Club,* formed in 1840 by partisans of Martin Van Buren, who allegedly named their organization in allusion to "Old Kinderhook," his birthplace being Kinderhook, New York; but cf. also the Bostonian phrase *all correct.*

okra (Dillard revised by Marckwardt; Asante; Holloway & Vass; Dalby)

AH: Of West African origin; akin to Akan (Twi) *nkruma.*
RH: A West African language.

phoney (Holloway & Vass; Dalby)

AH: Irish Gaelic.
RH: Irish.

poontang (Dalby)

AH: No entry.
RH: No entry.

poop (to defecate) (Dalby)

AH: Middle English.
RH: Middle English.

Figure 2–2   *continued*

rap (Holloway & Vass; Dalby)	*AH:* Possibly Middle English. *RH:* Middle English.
rumba (Dalby)	*AH:* American Spanish < Spanish. *RH:* Spanish, possibly of African origin.
samba (Dalby)	*AH:* Portuguese, possibly of African origin. *RH:* Portuguese < Africa.
sorcery (Holloway & Vass)	*AH:* Old French. *RH:* Middle English.
tango (Dalby)	*AH:* American Spanish, possibly of Niger-Congo origin. . . . *RH:* American Spanish < ?
tote (Montgomery; Holloway & Vass; Dalby)	*AH:* Perhaps (via Black West African English) of Bantu origin. . . . *RH:* ? < Angolese.
uh-huh, uh-uh (Dalby; Thompson)	*AH:* No etymology. ("interjection") *RH:* No etymology. ("interjection")
voodoo (Dillard revised by Marckwardt; Montgomery; Dalby)	*AH:* Louisiana French < Ewe *vodu* and Fon *vodun.* *RH:* Creole French < some West African tongue; cf. Ewe *vodu* demon.
yam (Montgomery; Dalby)	*AH:* < Portuguese and English Creole . . . of West African origin. . . . *RH:* Probably from Portuguese < West Africa; akin to Senegal *nyami* to eat.
you all (Schneider; Dalby)	*AH:* No etymology. *RH:* No etymology.
zombie (Dalby)	*AH:* Caribbean French and English Creole < Kimbundu. *RH:* West Africa.

Figure 2–2   *continued*

Theory of Visual Design

John Trimbur

The advanced rhetoric course I describe here, Theory of Visual Design, offers a partial answer to a larger problem that has preoccupied me lately, namely where and how visual literacy, visual communication, visual culture—whatever you want to call it—fits into writing instruction and rhetorical education. This question, of course, is not a new one. In many respects, it results from the unfortunate, to my mind at least, separation of composition and communication, marked institutionally by the walkout in 1913 of speech faculty from the National Council of Teachers of English (NCTE) and the subsequent development of media studies in communication departments, as well as by the failure in the late 1940s and early 1950s to unite composition and communication teaching in the Conference on College Composition and Communication (CCCC) (see Brantlinger 1976; George and Trimbur 1999).

My working assumption is that visual representation does indeed belong in the writing curriculum. For me, this assumption follows from my belief that writing instruction should be thoroughly grounded in rhetoric and that visual communication constitutes part of the available means of persuasion. Once we get rid of a "metaphysics of presence" that privileges voice in writing, it becomes possible to see that writing itself is a form of visible language, continuous with rather than the verbal opposite of the visual, and to think of matters of visual design, such as page layout, typography, and text/graphic integration, as fundamental to composing rather than a technical afterthought to an invisible cognitive process. From this perspective, the issue is how to incorporate visual design and visual communication into a sequence of writing and rhetoric courses.

To talk in terms of a sequence, of course, raises the problem of how we designate levels in writing instruction and rhetorical education. What organizing principles of curriculum design entitle us to say that a course is introductory or advanced? As you can see in the chart, the writing curriculum at Worcester Polytechnic Institute (WPI) begins with a general introduction to visual culture in Elements of Writing—there's no freshman composition, and this first course is an elective that enrolls mostly sophomores and juniors—and then moves on to more specialized issues of visual design and visual rhetoric in advanced courses. Now, you've probably also noticed that the chart's "claim"

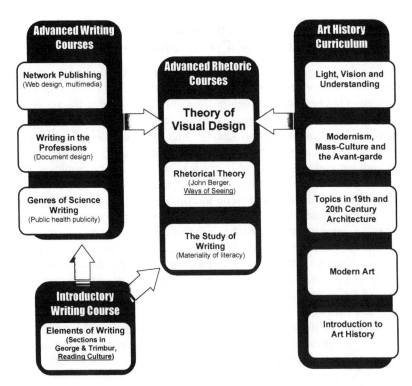

Figure 2–3 Theory of Visual Design
Thank you to Sarah Walkowiak for designing and producing the chart.

is that courses are "advanced" because they *come after* an introductory one. There's something to this argument—courses at least *seem* more advanced when students have already taken coursework in the field—but it's really more of a description than an explanation.

In contemporary writing instruction, there have been two main, but not mutually exclusive, approaches to incorporating visual literacy into the writing curriculum: (1) assign visual communication to advanced courses in professional writing (technical, business, scientific, public relations, journalism, and so on)—the applied vocational other of (a still residually belletristic) composition studies; and (2) use elements of visual culture—whether artworks, ads, television, films, graffiti, and so on—as topics to write about in introductory courses. Before I go any further attempting to explain what makes courses such as Theory of Visual Design advanced, I want to review these two approaches. Both have long histories; both appear in the writing and rhetoric sequence at WPI; but neither, in my view, gives a fully satisfactory answer to the problem of how to sequence visual representation in a writing and rhetoric curriculum.

Visual Communication
in Advanced Professional Writing

Taught either as an aspect of advanced professional writing courses or as a separate course in a professional communication sequence or major, visual communication has been placed—correctly, in my view—under the auspices of
delivery, the fifth canon of rhetoric, with an emphasis on document design, the
visual display of information, readability, and so on. Despite the salutary emphasis on students as producers, I worry that this approach too often reduces visual communication to handy, ready-made solutions to design problems. There
is, of course, a literature underwriting this approach, from usability research to
Edward Tufte's magisterial work on information design (1983, 1990, 1997).
Nonetheless, studies of, say, how readers scan documents or deal with old and
new information do not exhaust the rhetorical issues involved in visual design,
for these studies themselves are in general already committed to a rationalist
view that equates intelligibility with readability, separates the reception of information from the pleasures of seeing, and favors the grid over more open
forms of design (see, for example, Barton and Barton 1990; Bierut et al. 1994;
and Friedman 1973).

Assigning visual communication to advanced professional writing courses,
moreover, suggests that the visual display of information and the use of visual
design in persuasion are largely concerns of the workplace and thereby, in pedagogical and curricular terms, matters of vocational training. It's worth noting
that this view of visual communication as part of a preprofessional education
does offer a reason visual representation belongs in advanced professional
writing courses: these are courses for students who have already self-selected
themselves according to career interests, and it therefore makes sense to concentrate on the forms of visual representation characteristic of the professions
they seek to enter. The other, unstated side to this explanation is that students
who don't have such vocational goals don't really *need* coursework in visual
communication. The main problem here is that identifying visual communication as vocational or preprofessional work ignores the uses of visual representation as the available means of persuasion in other spheres. The revived interest
in public writing and civic rhetoric in particular would seem to draw attention
to genres formerly associated exclusively with professional writing, such as
flyers, newsletters, brochures, news briefs, posters, and so on as means of participation and influence in public forums.

Visual Culture in Introductory Composition

If advanced professional writing courses want to introduce students to the types
of visual representation characteristic of the workplace, the second approach
I've mentioned—using visual culture in the introductory writing classroom—
is surely more nebulous but, in certain respects, more revealing about what is

at stake in trying to think through the relations between visual and print literacy. Visual and media literacy, after all, have been a constant concern of English teachers, at least since F. R. Leavis and Denys Thompson's 1933 textbook *Culture and Environment* raised the idea that media education should be a primary responsibility of English studies. Since the National Education Association's (NEA) 1958 report *Mass Communication and Education,* with its emphasis on "the school's obligation . . . to help the student build a clear awareness of the capacity of the media of mass communication to alter, to falsify, to delude, and to misrepresent" (73), and the British National Union of Teachers 1960 conference "Popular Culture and Personal Responsibility" (for its Leavisite calls for "discrimination," see D. Thompson's collection *Discrimination and Popular Culture* [1964]), English teachers have worried about the effects of visual representation on the future of reading and the printed word, while at the same time trying to devise strategies, as Charles Paine (1997) puts it, to "inoculate" students against the epidemic of popular culture and mass communication.

The reason for incorporating visual culture in introductory courses, according to this approach, is to protect students against the visual so that they can learn print literacy in the essayist tradition, whether academic or bellelettristic. This approach comes from a deep-seated logocentric belief in the power of the word and an accompanying suspicion of the image. On one hand, visual representation figures as a developmental stage and a sign of intellectual immaturity, a prop that can be abandoned gradually as textbooks and other reading materials advance from grade to grade, relying less on pictures and more on print alone. On the other hand, the visual also figures in a more sinister way, not simply as a stage that can be outgrown but rather as a constant danger, whether a provocation to idolatry and graven images, as in the Hebrew Testament, or a contributing cause of the "eclipse of reason." An article in a special issue of *College English* on mass culture catches Stanley Aronowitz in a deeply pessimistic Frankfurt school mood, when he points to the "new illiteracy" and the crisis in cognition apparent in the "gradual but relentless growth of anti-intellectualism in American life . . . partially stemming from the rise of what I will call a *visual culture* that has increasingly replaced other types of communication, particularly the written and verbal forms" (1977, 769). Accordingly, in Aronowitz's view, composition teachers should lead students into an examination of the media that have colonized their life worlds, with the goal of removing the "safety valve of mass culture" so that the "intolerable" conditions of "ordinary existence" can come to light (1977, 773).

I don't want to sound altogether dismissive of such an approach. There is, after all, the need to approach visual culture from a critical perspective. At the same time, Aronowitz's approach is problematical in the way it represents students as unwitting victims of visual culture, with short attention spans, a predisposition toward the literal, and an inability to form concepts. Notice the visual here does the work it was once assumed orality did in erecting barriers to advanced literacy.

Not all media educators have polarized word and image in such striking ways. In the NCTE report *Television and the Teaching of English,* for example, Neil Postman urges English teachers to "avoid the temptation to pit television or any other medium against print" (1961, 13), which is, of course, what Postman himself has done in later works such as *Amusing Ourselves to Death* (1985). Stuart Hall and Paddy Whannel's guidebook for media education *The Popular Arts* (1964), despite its residual Leavisite inflections, refuses to set the "discrimination" strategy against the media. In their view, "in terms of actual quality . . . the struggle between what is good and worthwhile and what is shoddy and debased is not a struggle *against* the modern forms of communication, but a conflict *within* these media" (15). Hall and Whannel sought a compromise between Leavisite discrimination and Raymond Williams' stress on "ordinary culture" by acknowledging that "one of the central purposes of education is to train the ability to discriminate," while looking to the introduction of popular culture into the curriculum as "an extension of this basic aim to cover new and highly relevant areas of experience" (388–89).

Recent composition textbooks, inspired by the turn to cultural studies, such as Diana George and my own *Reading Culture,* which now includes in its third edition (1999) a "Visual Culture" section in each chapter; Maasik and Solomon's *Signs of Life in the USA* (1994); and Harris and Rosen's *Media Journal* (1995) follow Hall and Whannel's efforts to avoid reductive accounts of students as cultural dupes in need of correction and to validate their experience by casting students as participant-observers and budding critics within visual culture—a goal that seems to me quite fitting for introductory courses. But in an advanced course, I wanted to join the practical approach to visual communication in technical writing to the theoretical grounding and critical edge in these composition readers, to pose students as both critical participants in visual culture *and* designers of visual messages.

Designing Theory of Visual Design

For me, the main problem in designing Theory of Visual Design as an advanced course had to do with finding a way to combine criticism and production. I wanted to extend the emphasis on visual rhetoric introduced in Elements of Writing and developed further in the advanced theory courses The Study of Writing and Rhetorical Theory, while drawing on such practical matters as publicity design, document design, websites, and multimedia treated in the advanced professional writing courses, Genres of Science Writing, Writing in the Professions, and Network Publishing. In addition, because I teach in a humanities and arts department, I wanted the course to articulate in some useful way not only to the writing and rhetoric concentration but also to the art history concentration. In this sense, the design of the course was influenced, as course design tends to be, by local considerations.

The result is that Theory of Visual Design is very much a hybrid—and a kind of balancing act. The content of the course focuses on the social semi-

otics of visual design, the history of graphic design movements, and social reform documentary photography. The emphasis is on close reading, weekly papers, and a longer research project. At the same time, the course also includes
four design experiments. Now, I must admit that I am not qualified to teach a
studio course in graphic design or photography. But I felt strongly that students
needed to practice visual design as well as to read about it, to understand how
graphic designers pose design problems and invent solutions. So my compromise was to use an end-of-the-term portfolio system, for which I graded not the
technical quality of the four experiments—which ranged from professional
level to amateurish pen or pencil sketches—but the students' conceptualization of their work.

I organized the course around three main issues: how visual design is used
for purpose of identification (signs, trademarks, icons, logos, etc.), display of
information, and persuasion. Like all courses at WPI, Theory of Visual Design
met four hours a week for seven weeks.

Readings for the Course

- Gunther Kress and Theo van Leeuwen's *Reading Images: The Grammar of
  Visual Design* (1997) to develop a common vocabulary and close analysis
  of visual codes;

- Richard Hollis' *Graphic Design: A Concise History* (1994) to get a historical overview of design movements, national traditions, and the interaction among avant-gardes, politics, mass culture, and the market; and

- James Curtis' *Mind's Eye, Mind's Truth: FSA Photography Reconsidered*
  (1989) to locate documentary photography in relation to art photography
  and photojournalism and as a case study of propaganda for the New Deal
  and the ethics of social reform photographers' relation to their subjects,
  starting with Jacob Riis' "invasions" of the tenements in *How the Other
  Half Lives* ([1890] 1996) and Lewis Hine's child labor work (1998) and
  then moving to three documentary photo-essays from the 1930s, James
  Agee and Walker Evans' *Let Us Now Praise Famous Men* ([1939] 1980),
  Dorothea Lange and Paul S. Taylor's *American Exodus* (1939), and Mar-
  garet Bourke-White and Erskine Caldwell's *You Have Seen Their Faces*
  (1937).

Main Assignments for the Course

- Six short weekly papers of visual analysis, in which students apply the social semiotic terminology introduced in *Reading Images* to visual representations of their own choice. We read a chapter a week.

- One eight- to ten-page research paper. Examples: Tibor Kalman, Bolshe-
  vik posters, roadside signs, logos and corporate identity, Robert Frank's
  Americans ([1959] 1998), Jules Cheret and the Art Nouveau poster,

Bauhaus typography, ads from 1930s magazines, psychedelic posters, peace-punk graphic style, photomontage.

- Four design experiments (logo, infographic, collage or photomontage, visual narrative or photo essay), presented in a portfolio with introduction and commentary at the end of the term.

Results

I've taught the course three times, so the following findings should be considered preliminary.

Perhaps the most striking result is that students showed a remarkable willingness to do close readings of visual texts and work with Kress and van Leeuwen's social semiotic vocabulary. This varied dramatically from the WPI-normal resistance to close reading of literature, not to mention critical theory in general. Students talked repeatedly about how helpful theory could be, how it changed the way they looked at the world, as designed and composed, and how they became aware of visual codes they had taken for granted.

A corollary is that the class overcame very quickly the normal accuracy/inaccuracy polarity that haunts most discussions of representation at WPI. For example, students took seriously Kress and van Leeuwen's discussion of modality and their distinctions among different coding orientations and types of realism—conventional photographic naturalism, scientific/technological, abstract, hyper-real. I think this was the most successful I've been in trying to get students to see that the "real" is represented according to the truth value assigned to (in this case, visual) propositions.

Finally, a series of interesting design questions came up concerning legibility and readability, reading paths on magazine pages, subordination of word to image, debates for and against the grid and information bands, relation of photos and captions, and distortion in infographics, as well as issues in the history of graphic design, such as the modernist aspiration to end art and design for life, the role of visual design in forming national markets and cultures, the current devolution into niche markets and "hip consumerism," the use of graphic design, especially posters, photomontage, and photo essays, in politics and social reform movements, the relation of design and technology, and so on.

A Final Note on What's "Advanced"

I want to make sure that Theory of Visual Design comes across as work in progress and as an experimental response to the question I raise concerning the place and purpose of visual representation in writing instruction and rhetorical education. In terms of the larger question this volume of essays raises about what makes writing and rhetoric courses advanced, I can offer these observations. Part of the success of the course—and a key factor in making it seem "advanced"—is that in general the students who enroll bring with them a range of knowledges acquired in earlier courses, not only about, say, the materiality of literacy in The Study of Writing or the "male gaze" according to John Berger (1972), Laura Mulvey (1989), and Richard Leppert in Rhetorical Theory, but also about art history, computer science, and engineering graphics courses. In this sense, the level of the course must depend in a very real way on the preparation and sophistication of the students, and in certain respects you could say that Theory of Visual Design is advanced because of its position in the sequence of writing and rhetoric courses and because of the fact that students usually take it after other courses.

My main reservation in pressing this observation is the simple fact that students learn outside the curriculum as well as in it, and certainly a number of undergraduates with little or no coursework in writing and rhetoric have done very well in Theory of Visual Design. By the same token, I've observed students doing what I'd call advanced work on visual culture in the introductory course Elements of Writing. So I must admit that despite my seamless representation of it, the writing and rhetoric curriculum does not exactly operate like a Venn diagram, where you have to complete one step in the sequence in order to take the next. I think the visual design course takes on its advanced character or feeling not only because of its position in a sequence but also because of what it enables me to do, namely to pay undivided attention to visual representation—and its relation to verbal representation—without feeling guilty that I'm not teaching students how to write.

In writing instruction, we've found it pretty easy to justify "advanced" courses in specialized areas of writing—from the usual professional ones in scientific, technical, and business writing to the equally professional but not always acknowledged as such ones in memoir, travel writing, writing about the arts, and so on. The urgency here, I think, is to make these advanced writing courses critical and theoretically reflexive. On the other hand, the challenge of courses such as Theory of Visual Design is to explain why courses that don't take their primary aim as that of teaching writing—that instead want to *study* literacy, rhetorical theory, visual design, and a range of specialized topics we're just starting to imagine—have an equal claim to space in the writing curriculum.

Part Three:

Considering Options for Elective Courses in Advanced Writing

The Rhetoric of Gender as Advanced Writing

Mary R. Lamb

The Rhetoric of Gender enhances students' writing skills by fostering a "rhetorical conscience" applicable not only in academic and professional settings but in civic and social ones as well. While *gender* is replacing *feminist* in much current scholarship, emphasizing masculinity and gay/lesbian/bisexual/transsexual (GLBT) issues as well as feminist and women's studies, The Rhetoric of Gender nevertheless runs the risk of being narrowly perceived by students as feminist proselytizing or women's consciousness raising. Indeed, to its detractors, feminism is often characterized as "victim politics," in which women unfairly blame patriarchy for all their problems. The rhetorical effect of this hyperbole is that many men and women feel absolved of any responsibility for social change since they do not perceive themselves as victims or villains. As a challenge to such attitudes and fears, this course seeks to draw all students into a conversation about the rhetorical effect of gender in writing, moving away from polarization and blame to dialogue and responsibility, which consequently promotes a rhetorical conscience in students that fosters not only good writing and critical thinking but also social responsibility and a deeper and more theorized understanding of the role of language and rhetoric in our lives.

The full text of this essay appears on the enclosed CD-ROM.

Course Description

This course examines how gender is rhetorically constructed in cultural texts in order to foster in students a "rhetorical conscience" that will enhance their writing skills in professional, civic, and social contexts. Drawing on both feminist and rhetorical theory and history, we read a variety of rhetorical texts and analyze gendered claims and rhetorical situation. The first part of the course develops an awareness of students' gendered identity as writers, theorizes the relationship between language and gender, and locates gendered appeals in writing. In the last part of the course, students theorize the gendered binary and engage in cultural criticism.

Rhetorical Theory

Major Figures in the Aristotelian Tradition

Arthur E. Walzer and David Beard

Students are not initially attracted to theory. Opposing theory to both facts and application, most students tend to think of theory as an esoteric concern with little utility. These views need to be confronted early in the course in rhetorical theory. To begin to convince students that theory is not an esoteric concern of academics only, we stress that everyone has a theory of language but that for most, the theory remains unexamined. . . .

We also stress that people have a definition of *rhetoric,* and we ask students to provide their definitions. . . .

We stress that even at its end, the course will not provide a single definitive theory and that more important than identifying what rhetoric is or articulating a single theory is the creation of a set of statements about rhetoric that are consistent with one another. The goal of the course is an awareness that the way we think about rhetoric influences how we practice it and that, therefore, theoretical thinking is the basis for changing existing practice.

The full text of this essay appears on the enclosed CD-ROM.

Course Description

Is it right to appeal to the emotions? Would we be better off without arts of persuasion? These and similar questions were debated in ancient Greece and have been a subject of discussion ever since. This course traces how these concerns have been addressed in the most important rhetorical theories from ancient times until today.

What We Teach When We Teach the Postcolonial

Deepika Bahri

Like all cultural expression, postcolonial material demands that students pay attention to the context of production, its underlying cultural structure, and the choices made by the author. If postcolonial material seems to demand this more insistently than other, more mainstream writing, it is because its difference has become a naturalized expectation. The committed teacher will struggle to take this principle of difference and acquaint the student with the value of making all written expression *strange,* the better to study and understand it. The ultimate goal would be for students to learn the invaluable skill of defamiliarizing their own productions through the course of analyzing context, register, ideology, and culture. . . .

Concepts such as mimicry and subalternity, thoughtfully used, can prove very useful in addressing the politics of writing classrooms and the production of "educated" or "institutionalized" subjectivity. Beyond this, they are useful in studying the production of discourse in any of several situations where power conjoins with the production of knowledge but remains ambiguated by its own contradictions.

The full text of this essay appears on the enclosed CD-ROM.

Course Description

This course will focus on literature that demonstrates the complexity of growing up during and after colonization. Although the *bildungsroman, erziehungsroman*, and *kunstlerroman* are predominant types in such literature, the course will also include autobiography, poetry, drama, and essays that explore the theme of evolving consciousness under and after colonization. Background readings will acquaint us with the philosophy and ideology underlying educational policy in various cultural contexts. As we read and write about these selections, students will be expected to demonstrate an understanding of the relationship of language and writing to historical context and rhetorical exigency.

Literacy and Technology

Dennis Baron

This course seeks to provide students with a sense of how technologies affect the ways they read and write. Literacy has always been intimately tied to technology: we use tools to write, and technology mediates our reading. Writing itself is a technology. Students look at the history of literacy technologies, from the dawn of writing to the age of the computer, studying how the technologies of communication shape the manner and kind of writing and reading that get done. We look as well at who gets to read and write, since access to technology has always affected access to literacy. Finally, students examine the development of their own literacy practices reflectively in light of current writing technologies. Along the way, we explore such topics as the information glut; class, gender, and literacy; the apparent decline in literacy; the development of virtual genres; and the emergence of a transnational web culture.

The full text of this essay appears on the enclosed CD-ROM.

Course Description

In this course we will examine reading, writing, literacy, and technology from a historical point of view, from the dawn of writing to the age of the computer, exploring the different theories of orality and literacy and looking at the spread of literacy through various communities. We will look particularly at present-day literacy and how it is affected by the computer revolution, exploring such topics as the information glut; class, gender, and literacy; the apparent decline in literacy; the development of virtual genres; and the emergence of a transnational web culture.

Below the Surface

A True-to-Life Course in Editorial Practice

Chris M. Anson

Most conventions of language are not explained in terms of their social and textual histories. As a result, students never reconceive their dominant ideas about the nature and origins of rules; they leave our courses believing that even in the midst of so much that "depends" in writing, there is a single code of correctness. . . . This approach to error not only fails to motivate students to care about adherence to conventions in their prose, but it also misrepresents the truth about language and writing. . . . In an intellectually responsible course in editorial practice, students learn that errors lie on several different continua of severity . . . [and] that the conventions of language have social histories. . . . These intellectual goals do not, of course, diminish the need for students to learn how to work with texts and how to become successful editors of their own and other people's writing. In some ways, the course gives them a variety of new and interesting tools to increase their knowledge of certain conventions. But it also treats these conventions in an intellectually responsible way, elevating them to the status of other important fields of study—physics, astronomy, math, history, music—beyond whose basic levels of information lie whole realms of uncertainty, mystery, and continued investigation.

The full text of this essay appears on the enclosed CD-ROM.

Course Description

This course, designed for upper-level undergraduates or students in M.A. programs, focuses on the realm of editorial practice with special attention to the ways in which the conventions of written discourse are socially constructed and mediated. The course engages students in a variety of investigations while they learn how to work on texts in different genres and from different academic, professional, and public settings. Topics include the historical analysis of specific conventions or rules of discourse; the effects of violations on readers' processing or construction of the writer's persona; the relationship between content and error; and the study of editorial debates about existing practices or practices too new to have been judged by the editing profession.

Computers and Communication

Johndan Johnson-Eilola

The complex nature of on-line communication requires students to move among numerous disciplines and topics. The advanced communication course described below is organized around four "moments" in computers and communication: communication as articulation/connection, communication as the fluid blending of multiple media, on-line communication as a social activity, and technology as politics. . . . Communication, especially in postmodernist societies, is increasingly the articulation rather than the simple production of information: citizens and workers in information cultures depend not so much on their skills at producing raw, new text but instead on their abilities to find, filter, and arrange information in useful ways. . . . One of the key assumptions informing the course I describe here is that computers participate in, but do not necessarily cause, new patterns of symbolic work, patterns that are not adequately described by *writing*, with its reliance on alphanumeric text.

The full text of this essay appears on the enclosed CD-ROM.

Course Description

Covers critical aspects of computer-based communication from functional, social, and theoretical perspectives. Class activities include extensive discussion, both face-to-face and on-line; research essays; and real-world projects ranging from hypertext and multimedia through MOO.

Civic Literacy and Service Learning

Bruce Herzberg

Why would we wish to teach civic or public discourse in an advanced writing course? This may seem like a needless question. After all, it is by no means a novel practice to draw on the immediacy and relevance of public issues and the image of a real audience that comes with writing, say, a letter to the editor. More recently, too, we have seen in our journals a surge in historical and theoretical discussions of public discourse and the public sphere, driven by motives both political and pedagogical. And finally, those who teach service-learning courses, as I have been doing, are naturally impelled toward public discourse for the obvious reason that we are engaging in community issues and community action.

But these impulses to teach civic discourse do not, at least for me, explain adequately the motives and goals of such a focus. Before I moved my own writing course in this direction, I felt that I needed to understand the theoretical justification for doing so and particularly to understand the relationship of the civic discourse focus to the goals of teaching academic or professional discourses that are fundamental to the mission of our writing courses.

The full text of this essay appears on the enclosed CD-ROM.

Course Description

Rhetoric is the art of using language persuasively. In college and the professions, persuasiveness is closely tied to research. The persuasiveness of written or oral reports depends on your ability to find and evaluate information and ideas, to organize what you find around a pertinent central thesis, to argue effectively for your interpretation of the material, and to present it clearly and convincingly. Advanced Expository Writing is therefore designed to teach methods of research and persuasive writing.

Section 001

In this section, we will study and write about education in America. Our work will lead to a research paper as well as a general audience statement on a public-policy issue in education. A service-learning project is a required part of the course.

Political Rhetoric and the Media

Beverly Wall

As its own complex nexus of art and study, rhetoric spans thousands of years; hundreds of countries, cultures, and languages; and dozens of traditions, schools, periods, genres, major figures, and intellectual controversies. If we want students to achieve civic literacy in a multimedia public world, then we need the help of rhetoric to reweave its oral, visual, and deliberative threads into our teaching of writing and critical thinking. To teach the course, I find myself rethinking almost everything in terms of a reconceptualized contemporary rhetoric that draws from the classical tradition of the liberal or "free" arts, those essential civic arts needed by citizens in democratic societies. In this regard, Plato's provocative questions still challenge us; and Aristotle, Isocrates, and Cicero still offer important insights for the contemporary teaching of rhetoric. Many faculty who teach service-learning courses understand this perspective well. They have experienced what happens in a class when a teacher decides that language and logic are as important to students' active participation in society as they are to students' personal development or academic pursuits.

This class is part of the Intercollegiate Electronic Democracy Project (IEDP)—a grassroots teaching and learning collaborative for faculty interested in public writing, political debate and argumentation, and the civic traditions of rhetoric—and makes use of the multiclass networks for students available on its website (*http://www.trincoll.edu/depts/writcent/edproject.html*).

The full text of this essay appears on the enclosed CD-ROM.

Course Description

George Orwell called political language "the defense of the indefensible," yet democracies need a lively public culture of argument and debate in order to come to terms with complex issues, to define values, to make decisions, and to solve problems. This course will explore the contemporary state of political rhetoric in the United States, with a focus on the dynamic interactions of television, radio, print, and cyberspace. Students will participate in electronic discussions with peers across the country as they debate national issues.

Writing About Race and Ethnicity

Valerie Balester

I am usually uncomfortable talking about "race" to students. "Ethnicity" or "culture" I can handle, but "race" is a term fraught with danger, emotionally loaded, socially constructed in so many ways I cannot predict or even understand. When I use "race" in a classroom, I am never sure how I will be heard. Against every ounce of my will or intention, against every stirring of my heart, I have offended students, have been accused of being racist, or have been viewed as complicit in the oppressive military/industrial complex. Or I have been labeled a liberal, feminazi, lesbian do-gooder.

These reasons for caution are also the very same reasons we *should* talk about race in the advanced writing classroom. Pressing national concerns should be the stuff writers grapple with, at least sometimes, . . . yet the topic offers us something more: an interesting and fruitful window to language. "Race" can lead us to question our views of acceptable writing and appropriate style. It can change correct and safe writers into innovative risk takers—perhaps the defining essence of an advanced course.

The full text of this essay appears on the enclosed CD-ROM.

Course Description

In this advanced writing course, we will hone writing and editing skills in a workshop format. Students will write multiple drafts of four major and many shorter papers and review the work of their peers. The topics for writing will center on "race" and "ethnicity" and what these terms mean to American identity, in particular as expressed in language. We will examine how writers use colloquial and nonstandard language, or different varieties of language, in writing, and we will experiment with such practices in our own prose. Readings will be short essays, poems, and scholarly investigations of that topic. Students will select their best work to present in a portfolio at the end of the term.

Writing as a Means of Social Change

Patricia Bizzell

Teaching for contact zones rectifies the reasons for including multicultural material in the English class. No longer need one suggest that it is there simply to represent minority students or make them feel included. No longer need teacher and students be confused about how to handle the ethical and political issues that such material often raises. Now one can argue that such material must be there in order to accurately portray the richness of American rhetorical resources and to prepare students for what they will meet in public fora, within and beyond the academy. Everyone needs to know as much about all the diverse American cultures as possible. This means learning traditional cultural references, to be sure, but also mastering the registers and allusions of many other groups. Moreover, the focus in analyzing contact zone materials is rhetorical, not ethical. . . .

Teaching for contact zones enables the discussion of students' own writing to rise above such questions as whether their writing is logical or correct. Contact zone materials relativize such judgments, allowing us to talk about what different audiences are likely to accept as logical or what kinds of deviations from standard usage they are most likely to censure or welcome. Also, students can be encouraged to experiment with their own forms of hybrid discourse, that is, discourse that employs rhetorical strategies from mainstream, hegemonic discourses and from discourses that students bring from their home communities.

The full text of this essay appears on the enclosed CD-ROM.

Course Description

Expository Writing. Intensive reading and writing of expository essays to help students gain control over their own writing and to develop personal styles for use in a range of academic and nonacademic settings. Special attention is paid to issues in cross-cultural communication.

Writing for and About Business and Nonprofit Organizations

Kitty O. Locker

In this essay, I describe two related courses, one very old, one comparatively new. The first U.S. college course in business writing was offered in 1902; such courses . . . are now offered at most U.S. universities. Writing for and About Nonprofit Organizations is a course we have offered at Ohio State since 1997. . . .

I find these courses endlessly satisfying and endlessly new. As my interests evolve, as technology changes, as the world of work changes, I can incorporate what I'm learning into what I explore with my students. Interested in diversity? Well, everyone works. Interested in conflict resolution? Well, people have conflicts on the job as well as in personal relationships. Interested in justice? Well, the ways people treat one another within organizations and the ways that organizations treat their stakeholders have a real impact on our lives. . . . These courses can help students achieve their own aims as well as the goals of the organizations with which they work.

The full text of this essay appears on the enclosed CD-ROM.

Course Description

Solving problems in workplace settings through written, oral, graphic, and electronic discourse, and on understanding rhetorical situations, audiences, and purposes. Units include style, organization, document design, creating visuals and web pages, and strategies for composing, revising, and working on writing in groups.

Section 001: Writing for and About Nonprofit Organizations

Critical and rhetorical skills in the world of community action and service. Students volunteer at a local nonprofit community-service agency. Various sections focus on: literacy in the work of nonprofits; the rhetorical choices made by writers working for community change; the various stakeholders of nonprofits; the formats of standard genres; techniques needed to achieve organizational aims; methods for testing documents with intended audiences; and strategies for negotiating the claims of multiple audiences.

Constructive Communication

Community-Engagement Writing

H. Brooke Hessler

The advanced community-engagement writing course is essential to the civic dimension of the advanced writing curriculum because it exposes writing majors to professional applications of rhetoric and writing with considerable social impact. Furthermore, the course requires these students to demonstrate the real-world significance of their expertise—something that, over the years, English majors have felt increasingly challenged to do. They achieve this goal through a major writing project that contributes to the communication practices of a community, addressing such subjects as flaming on a community discussion board, the creation of a new forum for concerned citizens, or the use of reflective writing to train volunteers. As an experiential approach to many of the subjects explored in other advanced writing courses, such as Contrastive Rhetorics, Civic Literacy, and Genre Theory, the advanced community-engagement project is an appealing and appropriate capstone experience for the writing major.

The full text of this essay appears on the enclosed CD-ROM.

Course Description

A capstone course for Writing majors, open to upper-division students with the permission of the instructor.

An intensive examination of the use of writing for collaboration, negotiation, and community problem solving. Students will examine case studies of community-engagement writing in corporate, academic, and civic contexts, then draw upon a variety of tools and methods in the fields of rhetoric and composition to develop writing projects that contribute to the communication practices of a local community. Fieldwork and collaboration with people and organizations outside the classroom will be required for the successful completion of this capstone project.

Technical Communication

Mary M. Lay

To understand the place of the technical communication course in the advanced writing curriculum, one must understand its pedagogical history. The technical communication course has evolved from a course that taught students almost exclusively the forms and formats of the workplace to one that emphasizes critical thinking and the evolution of knowledge. As with other advanced writing courses, today the technical communication course teaches students how to make effective and ethical contributions to the modern world and how to assess the social construction of the knowledge that runs that world. Thus the technical communication course has an essential yet unique place in the advanced writing curriculum. It carries on the understanding that student writers gain in other courses within the curriculum that writing is a way of thinking or making decisions; that writing is a means of learning knowledge within the academy as well as preparing for a career; and that writing offers a way to enter into and affect different discourse communities. However, because of the content and nature of the assignments in the technical communication course, students may actually see the impact of their writing on other people's lives and welfare. Moreover, technical communication students can make a contribution to society's appreciation and application of scientific and technological information in maintaining those lives and that welfare. Finally, technical communication students not only develop the ability to convey that important scientific and technological information, but they also learn how to assess its value critically.

The full text of this essay appears on the enclosed CD-ROM.

Course Description

Technical and Professional Writing. Written and oral communication in professional settings. Gathering information; analyzing the audience; assessing conventional formats; drafting, testing, and revising documents; oral presentation of final reports.

Cultural Studies

The Rhetoric of Everyday Texts

Diana George

While the first-year course might draw on cultural practices in everyday life as the basis for analysis, research projects, and the like, the advanced course engages the questions and concerns of cultural studies on a more complex level. The language and theoretical underpinnings of cultural studies scholarship, for example, are not appropriate for a first-year course. In addition, though the advanced course is not a course in cultural studies per se, it does allow me to introduce students more fully than I could in the first-year course to the language, images, and cultural phenomena as signifying practices that make up what we call a culture.

An advanced writing course based in cultural studies is a course in communication practices of all sorts: how those communication practices function in the everyday world, how people use them and understand them, and how both the concerns of cultural studies and more traditional rhetorical training inform our understanding of them. More to the point for an advanced writing course, a cultural studies-based writing course moves students from writing as a school subject alone to communication practices of all sorts that occur both in and out of school and to the multidimensional texts that students will encounter and produce in their daily lives.

The full text of this essay appears on the enclosed CD-ROM.

Course Description

A third-year course in writing that examines the production of everyday texts such as image-texts, e-mail, web pages, signs, museum exhibits, architecture, and fashion in terms of their theoretical, historical, cultural, and technological contexts. Students are expected to produce "everyday texts" of their own as well as to write about texts examined in the course.

Taking the Rhetorical Turn
in Advanced Creative Writing

Mary Ann Cain and George Kalamaras

Traditionally, upper-division creative writing workshops focus primarily upon students' and instructors' critiques of student writing. Such courses tend to give little, if any, attention to problems surrounding the interpretation of student texts and their rhetorical contexts. In contrast, we argue that advanced courses in fiction and poetry writing should be reinvented with an eye toward their relationship to other forms and genres, other discourses and contexts for writing—particularly other courses in an advanced English curriculum. Such a reinvention, however, will depend upon not only an integration of rhetorical and literary contexts within creative writing's poetics but also a reciprocal integration of poetics into other writing, literature, and theory courses within an English studies curriculum, as we will discuss in our conclusion. Upper-division creative writing classes can be central to an undergraduate writing curriculum. Ideally, they are classes for all students of writing, not just those who want to focus primarily on literary genres. Like other courses described in this book, this course should be rhetorically situated, with argument embedded in the theory and practice of the creative writing workshop and enacted by the students and instructors in very immediate and consequential ways. Students will then learn the practice of argumentation as they exchange and develop their responses to written work.

The full text of this essay appears on the enclosed CD-ROM.

Course Description

This course begins with an invitation to write in a particular genre and extends into questions not only about that genre but also regarding interpretation, argumentation, and social contexts for writing. Students will respond to one another's work through oral and written comments. These responses will, in turn, become one of the texts in the course that will facilitate inquiry into the social dimensions of genre, discourse, and writing.

Writing About X

The Arts

Joseph Trimmer

Writing About X is a seminar for students who are comfortable with reflective learning, confident about their writing process, and curious about unfamiliar subjects. In other words, the course is designed for students who are *already* advanced writers—students who are eager to explore new resources and experiment with different rhetorical strategies. The seminar has focused on many subjects—Writing About Healing, Writing About the Family, Writing About the Environment, Writing About the Arts—but in each case, the scope of the curriculum and the sequence of the assignments have followed a similar pattern. I have elected to describe Writing About the Arts because students have been so enthusiastic about how this course enables them to make connections among the arts and, consequently, so adamant about the reasons writing teachers should integrate the visual and performing arts into courses in the language arts.

The full text of this essay appears on the enclosed CD-ROM.

Course Description

Instruction in the strategies and techniques of expository writing beyond that provided for the general student. Specific topics (X)—for example, arts, science, history—will vary by section, will be announced in advance, and will be open to students with upper-class standing, especially writing majors and those majoring in the discipline designated by the topic.

Teaching Writing Like a Lawyer

Richard Fulkerson

Day two of the semester: We're discussing a way to define *vehicle* in the context of a city ordinance that says "No vehicles allowed in the park." Tonya says her dictionary defines *vehicle* as "a device for carrying passengers, goods, or equipment." I ask her if that means a student knapsack full of books or a bag with groceries in it is illegal in the park. Other members chime in to help. "It has to have a motor," says one. "And wheels," says another. I ask if they think the city council members meant that it was all right to ride horses in the park. "And what about a motorized wheelchair, a riding lawnmower owned by the city, or an ambulance?" We conclude that simple words and simple laws can be treacherous when applied to concrete cases.

I am not a lawyer. I have never been to law school. Never taken the LSAT. But for the last twenty years, I have been teaching an upper-division course in pre-law composition. Teaching it, I believe, successfully. As a math major and college debater, turned compositionist, I have always been interested in logic, argument, and the public uses of rhetoric. When I noticed an ad for a new textbook, Norman Brand and John White's *Legal Writing,* in 1976, I thought it looked interesting and ordered an exam copy. As I read, I wrote most of the assignments, imaginary legal cases with simplified tort laws. Fortunately, the book came with a brief teacher's manual that included sample answers, so I could tell that my thinking wasn't too far off base. I told myself, "You could teach this."

The full text of this essay appears on the enclosed CD-ROM.

Course Description

This course is designed for any student planning to go on to law school or a paralegal career. It concentrates on clear, correct, and well-reasoned writing. The primary emphasis is on writing effective answers on hypothetical legal case problems. Analytic, logical, and problem-solving skills are stressed. Some attention is given to the nature of the law school and its admissions requirements.

Working in the Publishing Industries

Libby Miles

Perhaps the two most often-employed conversational gambits during interviews for jobs in the publishing industries are "I love reading," or language, or writing, or books, or words, and "I like to work with people." These are also probably the two most meaningless.

Students with writing, literature, and language majors are often attracted to jobs they believe they might find in publishing; conversely, such students carry credentials that potential employers will find highly desirable. Unfortunately, these expectations are built on employers' idealized notions of what English/language/writing majors bring with them to the job and on students' vague sense of what publishing jobs actually entail: time spent pondering great books or prospective manuscripts, lengthy conversations with like-minded peers debating the merits of a particular turn of phrase, days punctuated by flashes of brilliance that transcend the menial rituals of quotidian existence. But it just doesn't work that way—and it probably never did.

Nonetheless, many of our students do enjoy long careers in assorted avenues of the publishing industries, and no doubt they will continue to pursue options in publishing. Recognizing the gap . . . this course introduces writing students to the overall structure and function of publishing-related industries: their ideologies, their organizational hierarchies, their materials of existence, their many branches and incarnations, their purposes, their audiences, their daily work, and their potential for positive social change.

The full text of this essay appears on the enclosed CD-ROM.

Course Description

Senior Capstone Experience: Writing and Publishing
Examination of and practice in publishing. Focus is on editing and writing while studying the structure and function of publishing industries: daily practices, purposes, and audiences. Requires extended document and class publication.

Part Four

Designing and Protecting
the Advanced Writing Program

From Profession to Discipline

The Politics of Establishing a Writing Concentration

John Ramage

While establishing a writing certificate program within the Arizona State University English department over the past several years, my colleagues and I learned several useful political lessons. Somewhat surprisingly, the most useful of those lessons have less to do with garnering institutional support than with reconciling our newly emergent discipline with the English department's literature program and with achieving consensus among writing faculty about what it means to be a discipline. . . .

However singular our situation at ASU, anyone contemplating the development of an advanced undergraduate writing program should probably anticipate having to face one or more of the following issues touched on in this essay: resistance from your increasingly embattled literature colleagues worried that you are encroaching on their curricular turf or poaching their majors; the necessity of collectively defining and enacting a disciplinary identity that is necessarily "impure" from the perspective of any one of the major theoretical versions of that identity subscribed to by writing faculty; the likelihood of having to debate "secession" (from the English department) and "abolition" (of first-year composition) insofar as these moves have already been constructed by some theorists as logical extensions of the move to program status and necessary preconditions for full disciplinarity. . . .

Perhaps the most salient lesson to be learned from our experience is that finding support within a university for a writing concentration requires no special political acumen. . . . Our experience suggests that the larger community is eager for the program. . . . The major political issues are truly identity issues to be worked out within our departments and within our discipline. The emphasis here has been on forming those identities in ways that acknowledge local circumstances.

The full text of this essay appears on the enclosed CD-ROM.

Needs, Numbers, and the Creation
of a Writing Studies Major

Theresa Conefrey

In response to student requests for a writing studies major, together with a strong faculty desire to ensure that our English program remains relevant to the needs of our students, my colleagues and I in the English department at the University of Hawai'i at Hilo designed a writing studies major, which we are currently in the process of ratifying. To explain our decision to offer a writing major as an alternative to the more traditional literature major and to allow readers to evaluate whether our program would be replicable at their own institutions, I begin with brief details of our institution, our program, and our students, and then narrate the creation of our new program. . . .

Repeatedly soliciting input enabled me to increase understanding about the purpose of the new program and to address any objections as they arose. . . . Over time, I gained support by designing the program around practical rather than theoretical courses, with the aim of preparing students to be hired as technical writers, editors, reviewers, publishers, information designers, and so on. In addition, I structured the program to support and encourage our aspiring creative writers, together with students preparing for graduate work in primary and secondary education. . . . In keeping with current theory of composition and rhetoric, the professional writing courses were designed to stress the importance of defining the rhetorical setting: identifying readers, their needs, and the medium and document format that will best meet those needs. The professional writing courses were also designed to encourage students to learn how to work effectively in groups, how to coordinate and plan large-scale projects, how to use editorial critique, and how to negotiate with others in an organizational setting. . . . I built on relevant existing courses and the strengths of current faculty. . . . Rather than completely rewriting the requirements for the English major, I decided to model our writing major on existing requirements. . . . Basing the writing major on the existing program for English majors made it more comprehensible to faculty outside our department, which increased its chances of being accepted by the Curriculum Review Committee, the Academic Affairs Committee, and the Faculty Senate.

The full text of this essay appears on the enclosed CD-ROM.

Advancing Writing at GMU

Responding to Community Needs, Encouraging Faculty Interests

Ruth Overman Fischer and Christopher J. Thaiss

At George Mason University, while literary study is at the core of the English major, students have the option of concentrating in writing. In addition, George Mason has also recently implemented an undergraduate course in the teaching of writing, which supports its well-established writing-across-the-curriculum endeavors. The two writing concentrations in the English major, Creative Writing and Nonfiction Writing and Editing, plus the new course in pedagogy reflect a young university with a frankly entrepreneurial relationship with the Northern Virginia economy, based on a growing, diverse population, the nearby presence of the federal government, and burgeoning hi-tech industry. In this essay, we will describe and contextualize these programs within the history of the development of the university and the major. We will then offer implications of our experience for advanced writing options at other schools. . . .

The adage that says "Do what you can with what you have right where you are" seems appropriate in considering any new program. The undergraduate writing program at GMU grew out of a situation unique to this university. Still, our varied growth suggests these general principles:

- Consider the surrounding community.
- Start with faculty interests and strengths.
- Be willing to start small.
- Avoid, if possible, worshipping sacred cows.
- Continue to look for opportunities for program diversification.
- Look for outside funding, and cooperate with college development officers.

The full text of this essay appears on the enclosed CD-ROM.

Developing a Professional
and Technical Writing Major
That Integrates Composition Theory,
Literacy Theory, and Cultural Studies

Kathleen McCormick and Donald C. Jones

The [professional and technical writing] major [at the University of Hartford] is intellectually viable: it combines key work in technical writing theory and practice with work in composition, literacy theory, and cultural studies. This combination sometimes occurs through the juxtaposition of courses but more often within single courses so that students will learn critically literate approaches to professional and technical writing. Our major is also financially feasible: as we planned it, we drew on some existing courses and planned to develop collaborative relationships with colleagues in a variety of areas across the university in order to offer additional courses. Our major also reinforced and strengthened our relationships with other departments. Because our colleagues in other departments valued our first-year writing program, they were willing to support our new major. This had a further positive effect because as other departments came to understand our upper-level courses, they became more supportive of our first-year program.

In short, the establishment of our program became caught up in the typical 1990s institutional and disciplinary politics. This has, of course, long been the fate of writing and rhetoric programs as they have struggled within, against, or in harmony with departments of English. The establishment of the rhetoric and composition program at Carnegie Mellon in the 1970s and 1980s or the Syracuse writing program in the 1980s are classic instances. The annals of the Association of Departments of English (ADE) are full of visionary calls for action, accounts of successes, confessions of failure, compromise, and continued struggle.

The full text of this essay appears on the enclosed CD-ROM.

Getting Approval

David Schwalm

The process of developing a writing department, program, or concentration can generate imaginative thought, intellectual excitement, professional rejuvenation, and reawakened collegiality. Ultimately, however, a proposal must be written in the proper form and guided through complex institutional processes involving the department, college, and university committees, as well as boards of trustees or regents—units composed mostly of people who have not shared in the excitement of developing the program and who may have quite different agendas, not the least of which is thrift. As a faculty member and former writing program administrator (WPA), I have moved a number of program proposals through the approval process. As a central administrator, I have had the responsibility of viewing proposals from an institutional perspective. Based on this range of experience, I will offer some suggestions about discovering the best available means to get advanced undergraduate writing curricula through the approval process successfully, where success is possible. . . .

Most of the . . . suggestions are matters of common sense. In fact, it's mostly just good rhetorical practice. But like physicians who smoke and plumbers whose faucets leak, we often neglect to apply our professional knowledge to the conduct of our own affairs. Indeed, as a faculty proponent of new programs, I have failed to observe some of the strategies suggested above. As a member of reviewing committees and as a central administrator, I have almost ceased to be amazed at the strategic innocence of many of those proposing curricular or institutional change—even those proposing a program in rocket science. Perhaps what seems obvious might not be so obvious at all, and I hope that this brief reminder will contribute in some way to the success of proposals for advanced undergraduate writing courses and programs.

The full text of this essay appears on the enclosed CD-ROM.

Afterword

"Advanced Composition" and Advanced Writing
Robert J. Connors

Advanced Composition's History

The history of college rhetoric in the American nineteenth century is a curious movement that goes from professionalized discourse instruction—for bar and pulpit—in the classical curriculum, to nonprofessional general "composition" as the only requirement in an otherwise elective curriculum at the end of the nineteenth century. There had been, of course, sophomore-, junior-, and senior-level rhetoric courses in the classical curriculum, but with the elective system and the proliferation of the first-year composition requirement, all of the other rhetoric courses in the curriculum were forced to adjust themselves in relation to the potent newcomer that every student had to take. The result, as Kate Adams has discussed in her *History of Professional Writing Instruction in American Colleges,* was a move back toward innovation of new courses in advanced composition that would act as follow-ups or protests to the perceived "contentlessness" of the FY course. Creative writing, journalism, technical writing, and advanced composition courses were the result.

The relations of all these "advanced" courses with the first-year course have defined advanced composition for the last century, and it is difficult to consider them outside of the relationship. The FY requirement in American colleges was generally established between 1885 and 1900. It was established primarily in the new departments of English, departments populated by doctorally licensed philologists and literary critics rather than by rhetoricians. These literary and linguistic teachers, aware of both the power and the grinding work of the required FY course, were the key figures in the establishment of some new composition courses and the domestication of some older rhetoric courses. The choices they made would define the parameters of the writing curriculum. After the first-year course requirement had begun to bring thousands of new students each year before the English teaching staff, that staff—especially the powerful tenure-line professors—would naturally begin to create specialized subsets of the FY course as follow-ons, and thus the period from 1900 to 1920 was a heyday for the invention of various sorts of advanced composition in American colleges. The advanced composition curriculum that has come down to us was the result of those teachers' choices about interests, affiliations, and the institutional nature of English as a field.

There grew up three specific fields of advanced composition—journalism, creative writing, and technical/business writing—and one giant catchall generalist field, and they entered English through different doors. Journalism, though not "literary," was impossible to deny as a valid subfield of writing, even if it did not have a doctoral cachet, and teachers who had been working journalists were always available. Many flavors of creative writing came into existence after 1905 and found more hearty welcomes in literary departments whose citizens, devoted to the study and practice of literary appreciation, could hardly refuse a place to real authors and prospective producers of literature. Technical and business writing were probably the least native of these new advanced courses, based as they were on the alien needs of engineers and B-school students, but still a hardy cadre of subspecialists arose after 1910 to teach them, finding support from engineering colleges when denied it in the humanities (Connors 1982). Within the general field of "advanced composition" itself, the simplified taxonomic theories of modern composition-rhetoric, especially the modal classes, created conditions for post-FY comp writing courses based on narrative or descriptive or expository or argumentative writing (Harris 1916, 501). Teachers whose training was literary or philological gave free rein to their interests in literary-writing courses.

All of these courses sprang up in their earliest versions in the first two decades of this century as college English departments strove to capitalize on their problematical Brobdingnagian hostage, Freshman English. The institutional reasons for the rising of these courses are complex and must be seen in the larger historical context of changes in American higher education and culture: the establishment of the A&M colleges, the organization of engineering education and business schools, the rise of American business culture in general, changing perceptions of class and status, modernist conceptions of professional literary authorship, and media shifts such as magazine foundings and the rise of radio. But the changing socioculture of college English departments is central here, and it must be seen as the basis for the centrifugal forces that have traditionally kept advanced composition a congeries of unrelated courses taught by staffs with no essential mutual interests, courses related only in being composition beyond freshman English. We are all living in the backwash of the creation of an English curriculum that featured this unconnected and relatively primitive curricular lineup of writing courses, as juxtaposed to the God's Plenty of the literature curriculum, with its many proliferating mansions. We now have to try to understand where we are in today's rapidly changing English studies socioculture.

The general term *advanced composition,* as I have been using it here, came to be an impoverished term relatively quickly, and it is worth a closer look to understand why this is so. The three specific advanced course structures invented within English rather quickly established enough genre identity or vocational cachet to break away into status as special fields seen as preparations for careers in writing (Henry 1928, 138). As soon as any advanced composition genre had achieved a sufficiently developed formal character, it tended to split off into these separate formalized courses of instruction. In the case of journalism, this course of instruction sometimes defaulted into either a separate school or department or more often into a semiautonomous specialty within English studies, taught by a specialized caste of experienced journalists who passed along their knowledge of the story, the rewrite, the feature, and the editorial. Creative writing courses, often taught by another anomalous group of non-Ph.D. teachers within English, could promise no guaranteed deliverance into a world of vocational or monetary success. They thrived anyway, as a sort of side specialty of literary departments, fueled by a never-failing stream of romantic undergraduates set ablaze by Hemingway or Cather but more enamored of production than of consumption. They were taught to write the short story, the poem, the novel, sometimes the one-act play. Remaining usually within the general fold of English courses but separated from general "advanced composition" were courses featuring the formalized and vocational genres: technical writing, business writing, and professional writing. Taught by specialists and seldom taken by English majors, they offered the engineering and science and business students an entree into the world of professional advancement through communication skill. These courses featured the letter, the proposal, the survey, the research report, the memo, the progress report, the feasibility study, and so on.

We note here a curious trend. As soon as a genre was perceived as "useful" or preparatory or professionalized, it was plucked from "advanced composition" and apotheosized. A cache of specialized textbooks and a cadre of specialized teachers would grow up to take it over. The general advanced composition course was never able to escape a terrible unreal universality, a continuing curse of abstraction based upon the fact that it was defined as what was left over—a remnant culture. It was a course based on a dominant concept—"advancedness"—and a recessive concept—uselessness. General "advanced composition" is still inescapably defined by a relationship to first-year composition. What has such a course, after all, advanced away *from?* For many years the typical FY requirement consisted of two required courses, so, of course, the idea of advanced composition also became mixed with the idea of a second required course, usually in either literary writing or in argument (Smith 1921, 281). The standard advanced composition course, as a result, devoted itself to writing a higher level of what Robert Scholes calls "pseudo-non-literature"—nonprofessional expansions of the generalist impetus of the FY course: writing about literature, exposition, argument, narrative, description. They used the "types of exposition" if they did not use modal classes, and they were usually models-based courses that relied heavily on anthologies of "specimens of good writing" (Foerster 1950, 456). Thus "advanced composition" was what was left after all the actual kinds of advanced writing had evacuated the field.

As Adams has shown, English departments never evolved any more complex or complete advanced writing curricula than the disconnected worlds of general advancement, journalism, the creatives, and the vocationals. Throughout this century, these various advanced composition classes were offered in sprawling profusion throughout most American colleges; as Ralph Henry said in 1928, they "wax fat in the catalogue" (137). But the history of the advanced course in American composition has not been a happy one. Evolving through the last century as a remnant based on unusable genres, "advanced composition" has often seemed the least definable course in the entire composition curriculum. At its worst, the advanced composition course was programmatically indefinable, a complete hostage to the individual interests of each instructor, an uncontrollable hobbyhorse ridden to many different places for many different purposes. Teachers often loved the course; as Paul Wheeler said in 1930, "the compensations of thus leading a number of young writers are beyond all words" (566). But the arbitrary content of each individual version of the course was difficult to defend, and as a result the professional literature on advanced composition has been thin through most of this century. It has been the only course in the English catalog about the content of which teachers were often slightly reticent in public.

One result of this arbitrariness of content and resulting indefinableness has been that throughout most of the twentieth century, advanced composition courses have been small, widely cataloged but not widely offered, and relatively unpopular at most colleges (Hillway 1954, 177). "Advanced composition" was something we all knew about, occasionally got to teach, talked about vaguely in terms of our own imaginative inventions within its spacious field of play. But it was not something most composition teachers ever affiliated with in any powerful way. A few people got together in the late seventies to found ATAC, the Association of Teachers of Advanced Composition, but though ATAC's journal, the *JAC: Journal of Advanced Composition,* soldiers on today in its Ikeafied form as a "Journal of Composition Theory," the Association itself had miscarried by the early eighties. Advanced composition simply did not have enough gluten to sustain a group effort.

Throughout most of this century, then, the idea of an advanced composition *curriculum* beyond the individual courses was hardly conceived; there was no clear constituency for such an animal either on the tenured faculty or among students. A curious blindness has for many decades enveloped writing teachers—and then composition specialists—about this situation; we seem to have been so deeply interested in and defined by specialty upper-level courses or our first-year required course that larger curricular questions were elided. We assumed that either reality as we knew it was fixed—there was one FY requirement for all, followed by a ragbag of upper-level follow-up writing courses for a few—or that the literary nature of the English department made it as good as fixed on the level of realpolitik. Journalists, creatives, and vocationals cultivated their own gardens, and they were not—ahem!—our garden.

Advanced Writing: The Paradigm Shift of
Coming of Age: The Advanced Writing Curriculum

Things have now changed. We cannot think of the term "advanced" in quite the same way anymore. Though it may seem a relatively small semantic difference, the title wording of this book, *Coming of Age: The Advanced Writing Curriculum,* actually draws a powerful line between the concept of "advanced composition" as it has been practiced and the concept of advanced writing in a curricular context. This one changed word may be, as Mark Twain put it, the difference between the lightning bug and the lightning.

"Advanced writing," as opposed to "advanced composition," is not predicated on the idea of a fugitive two- or three-course selection that appears, sputters, and gives up the ghost to a literary undergraduate major. This idea is not, in other words, just another in a long line of reformist ideals that presuppose the first-year requirement as the basis and model of every other undergraduate writing idea. The advanced writing curriculum, for which this book is a prospectus and a menu, is a much more thoroughgoing and radical idea. It proposes and provides a program for an entirely new conception of undergraduate literacy education, one based on the centrality of writing rather than literature. This conception will be, in fact, the alternative English major for the twenty-first century.

The editors of this book have found that something larger than they originally expected has grown from the innocent seeds they planted. They thought they were putting together a book that might offer some useful possibilities for advanced composition or expository writing. This was a reasonable goal, although hardly a new one; good ideas for the advanced composition course have been a staple of staff room discourse for a long time. We have been so used to thinking of the undergraduate writing curriculum as a minimal and truncated phenomenon that a few new ideas about the advanced composition course have traditionally been all we could hope for if we were not working in a writing-across-the-curriculum (WAC) program. Thus do our terministic screens constrain us. It was only in the process of looking at the many varied course proposals that had begun to come in to them that the editors were suddenly struck by the fact that they had here aborning something completely different from their original intention. Like many of us, they were looking for a few good ideas for courses; unlike most of us, they were able to seek these ideas from the very best minds in the field. But somewhere within the process, the many good course ideas tumbling in over the transom and the historical point we have reached in conceiving of our discipline came together with a galvanic jolt. And the result, if I do not mistake myself, is the beginning of a whole new phase of composition studies.

Let me explain this sweeping statement a bit. As I have detailed elsewhere, dissatisfaction with the first-year requirement in composition has been obvious for over a century (1996). Almost since the day when freshman composition was invented, there have been forces critical of it and willing to do away with the institutional coercion that has long undergirded its primacy. Recently, however, abolition arguments have achieved a new cogency. Those who had traditionally argued against the first-year requirement often based their arguments in literary elitism and in a seeming carelessness about the nature and preparation of many college students, but the arguments for the abolition of the requirement that have been made since 1990 have come from respected scholars within our own field, people like Sharon Crowley and Lil Brannon. They have made telling political and economic arguments against the requirement, sparking a lively debate that has been going on now for more than eight years.

As one who has at times taken part in the debate, I have been aware both of the power of the abolitionist argument and of some of the lacunae within it. The abolition movement has been primarily a critical rather than an architectonic one. Very few abolitionists would wish to argue for no writing instruction at all in the college undergraduate curriculum, but abolitionism is essentially a negative ideal; it wishes to do away with one corrupt reality, but it has usually had only general ideas about what, if anything, should be put into its place. I mean this as an observation rather than as a criticism; we are reminded of the famous Nietzsche quote, "I love the great despisers, for they are the great adorers; they are the arrows of longing for the other shore."

We might think, then, while looking over the contents of this book, of the advanced writing curriculum as the counterpart or *antistrophe* of the abolition movement. The advanced writing curriculum is the fox to abolitionism's hedgehog; the abolition movement is about one great thing, but the advanced writing curriculum is about many small things—which, I would argue, cumulate into one great thing. The contents of this book take us on beyond abolitionism, into a landscape that is at once hauntingly familiar, exciting, and slightly scary. If the last forty years have been about composition studies reinventing itself as a respectable academic discipline, we may well be spending the next forty years defining exactly what that discipline looks like beyond the required first-year course.

This will not be a simple job. The conflicting goals and methods available within the advanced writing curriculum mirror those that Albert Kitzhaber found in first-year composition in the early 1960s, when he complained in *Themes, Theories, and Therapy* about the "bewildering diversity of freshman English courses" (1963, 4). Our task here is to evolve a coherent vision of a center. If we are to create a writing curriculum rather than just one requirement and a variegated herd of hobbyhorses, we will need to spend some hard time thinking about exactly what the undergraduate writing major that is currently falling into our laps should look like.

This book is your curriculum if you seek a way out. It offers, in addition to a huge menu of possible courses and approaches to teaching advanced writing, a remarkably developed professional discussion about what composition scholars and teachers will face in attempting to build an advanced writing undergraduate major. Relatively few of us have faced the political and cultural problem of attempting to construct our writing concentration within an established literature department; relatively few of us have argued a fully developed curriculum proposal up the line of administrative necessity. Most importantly, few of us have attempted to engage in the kinds of creative discussions with colleagues and the kind of intradepartmental bridge building that will be necessary for advanced writing curricula to work.

Coming of Age may initially be bought and used primarily as a collection of the best ideas for advanced composition courses. The book is that, of course, but it is much more than that. It will, I hope, be seen as a challenge to many of the ways English departments and specifically writing programs have been doing business as usual. The question this book asks is really nothing less than whether we can finally grow up as a discipline and take our natural place in the undergraduate curriculum. The task it assigns is to re-create and reorganize undergraduate writing offerings so that they are more than a fugitive scattering of separate enthusiasms. The challenge it makes is in asking us finally to force ourselves beyond the century-old model of composition as general, required, introductory, marginal, and service-based within literary English departments. We know this cave so well, we have been chained within it so long, that it has its own mythos, its own attractions and nostalgias. Moving out of its stuffy warmth is very difficult for many. As Erich Fromm noted many years ago, we are strangely attracted to institutional constraints that superimpose an identity on us. Though emerging from the cave of the first-year requirement will be liberating, we must also face the fear that comes with letting go of familiar chains. But *Coming of Age* shows us that we can move on. And it's time.

Works Cited

Abadi-Nagy, Z. 1998. "Beyond the Dictionary in Literary Translation." Paper presented at Texas Christian University, 2 November.

Adams, J. [pseud.]. 1999. Interview by L. K. Shamoon. 4 January.

Adams, K. H. 1993. *A History of Professional Writing Instruction in American Colleges.* Dallas: Southern Methodist Univ. Press.

Adams, K. H., & J. L. Adams, eds. 1991. *Teaching Advanced Composition: Why and How.* Portsmouth, NH: Heinemann–Boynton/Cook.

Adas, M. 1991. "Scientific Standards and Colonial Education in British India and French Senegal." In *Science, Medicine, and Cultural Imperialism,* ed. T. M. Meade & M. Walker. New York: St. Martin's.

Advances in the History of Rhetoric. Fort Worth: Texas Christian University.

Agee, J., & W. Evans. [1939] 1980. *Let Us Now Praise Famous Men.* Reprint, New York: Houghton and Mifflin.

———. 1989. "Introduction." In *A Way of Seeing,* by Helen Levitt, vii–xv. Durham, NC: Duke Univ. Press.

Alston, R. C. 1965–72. *A Bibliography of the English Language from the Invention of Printing to the Year 1800.* 20 vols. Menston: Scolar.

Alterman, E. 1992. *Sound & Fury: The Washington Punditocracy and the Collapse of American Politics.* New York: HarperCollins.

Anson, C. M. 1997. "On Reflection: The Role of Logs and Journals in Service-Learning Courses." In *Writing the Community: Concepts and Models for Service-Learning in Composition,* ed. L. Adler-Kassner, R. Crooks, & A. Watters, 167–80. Washington, D.C.: American Association for Higher Education.

Aristotle. *Poetics.*

Aristotle. *Rhetoric.*

Aristotle. 1991. *On Rhetoric: A Theory of Civic Discourse.* Trans. G. A. Kennedy. New York: Oxford Univ. Press.

Arnold, E. 1996. "History of Voice." In *The Arnold Anthology of Post-Colonial Literatures in English,* ed. J. Thieme. London: Arnold; NY: St. Martin's.

Aronoff, M., W. D. O'Grady, & M. Dobrovolsky. 1997. *Contemporary Linguistics: An Introduction,* 3d ed. New York: St. Martin's.

Aronowitz, S. 1977. "Mass Culture and the Eclipse of Reason: The Implications for Pedagogy." *College English* 38 (8): 768–74.

Ashcroft, B., G. Griffiths, & H. Tiffin. 1989. *The Empire Writes Back.* London: Routledge.

———. 1998. *Key Concepts in Post-Colonial Studies.* London: Routledge.

Atwan, R. 1986–93. *The Best American Essays, 1988–.* New York: Ticknor & Fields.

———. 1998. *Best American Essays.* College ed. 2d ed. Boston: Houghton Mifflin.

Augustine. 1997. *Confessions.* Trans. M. Boukling. Ed. J. E. Rotelle. London: Hodder and Stoughton.

Bâ, M. 1981. *So Long a Letter.* Trans. M. Bodé-Thomas. London: Heinemann.

Bacon, F. 1994. *Novum Organon.* Trans. P. Urbach & J. Gibson. Chicago: Open Court.

Bahri, D., & M. Vasudeva. 1996. *Between the Lines: South Asians and Postcoloniality.* Philadelphia: Temple Univ. Press.

Baker, S. 1998. *The Practical Stylist with Readings and Handbook.* New York: Longman.

Balester, V. M. 1993. *Cultural Divide: A Study of African-American College-Level Writers.* Portsmouth, NH: Boynton/Cook.

Ballif, M. 1997. "Seducing Composition: A Challenge to Identity-Disclosing Pedagogies." *Rhetoric Review* 16 (1): 76–91.

Baron, D. 1982. *Grammar and Good Taste: Reforming the American Language.* New Haven: Yale Univ. Press.

———. 1990. *The English-Only Question: An Official Language for Americans?* New Haven: Yale Univ. Press.

Barthes, R. 1997a. "Myth Today." In *Representation: Cultural Representations and Signifying Practices,* ed. S. Hall, 66–67. London: Sage.

———. 1997b. "Rhetoric of the Image." In *Representation: Cultural Representations and Signifying Practices,* ed. S. Hall, 68. London: Sage.

———. 1997c. "The World of Wrestling." In *Representation: Cultural Representations and Signifying Practices,* ed. S. Hall, 69. London: Sage.

Barton, B. F., & M. S. Barton. 1990. "Postmodernism and the Relation of Word and Image in Professional Discourse." *Technical Writing Teacher* 17 (3): 256–70.

Barton, D., & M. Hamilton. 1998. *Local Literacies: Reading and Writing in One Community.* New York: Routledge.

Bazerman, C. 1995. "Response: Curricular Responsibilities and Professional Definition." In *Reconceiving Writing, Rethinking Writing Instruction,* ed. J. Petraglia, 249–59. Mahwah, NJ: Erlbaum.

Beaud, M. 1984. *History of Capitalism 1500–1800.* Trans. by T. Dickman & A. Lefebvre. London: MacMillan.

Bedford, S. 1992. *Yoruba Girl Dancing.* New York: Viking.

Belenky, M. F., B. McVicker Clinchy, N. R. Goldberger, & J. M. Tarule. [1986] 1997. *Women's Ways of Knowing: The Development of Self, Voice, and Mind.* Reprint, Basic Books.

Berger, J. 1972. *Ways of Seeing.* London: Penguin.

Berlin, J. A. 1982. "Contemporary Composition: The Major Pedagogical Theories." *College English* 44: 765–77.

———. 1984. *Writing Instruction in Nineteenth-Century American Colleges.* Carbondale, IL: Southern Illinois Univ. Press.

———. 1988. *Rhetoric and Reality.* Carbondale, IL: Southern Illinois Univ. Press.

———. 1996. *Rhetorics, Poetics, and Cultures.* Urbana, IL: NCTE.

Bhabha, H. 1994a. *The Location of Culture.* NY: Routledge.

———. 1994b. "Of Mimicry and Man." In *The Location of Culture.* New York: Routledge.

Bhatt, S. 1996. "Different History." In *The Arnold Anthology of Post-Colonial Literatures in English,* ed. J. Thieme. London: Arnold; New York: St. Martin's.

Bierut, M., W. Drenttel, S. Heller, & D. K. Holland, eds. 1994. *Looking Closer: Critical Writings on Graphic Design.* New York: Allworth.

Bishop, W. 1990. "Learning Our Own Ways to Situate Composition and Feminist Studies in the English Department." *JAC: A Journal of Composition Theory* 10 (2): 339–58.

Bizzell, P. 1994. " 'Contact Zones' and English Studies." *College English* 56: 163–69.

Bizzell, P., & B. Herzberg, eds. 1990. *The Rhetorical Tradition: Readings from Classical Times to the Present.* Boston: Bedford.

———. 1996. *Negotiating Difference: Cultural Case Studies for Composition.* Boston: Bedford.

Black, L. J. 1998. *Between Talk and Teaching: Reconsidering the Writing Conference.* Logan, UT: Utah State Univ. Press.

Block, G. 1992. *Effective Legal Writing.* 4th ed. Mineola, NY: Foundation.

Bloom, L. Z. 1990. "Why Don't We Write What We Teach? And Publish It?" *JAC: A Journal of Composition Theory* 10 (1): 87–100.

———. 1994. *Fact and Artifact: Writing Nonfiction.* 2d ed. Englewood Cliffs, NJ: Prentice-Hall.

———. 1996. "Freshman Composition as a Middle-Class Enterprise." *College English* 58 (6): 654–75.

Blumler, J. G., J. M. McLeod, & K. E. Rosengren, eds. 1992. *Comparatively Speaking: Communication and Culture Across Space and Time.* Newbury Park, England: Sage.

Booth, W., G. Colomb, & J. Williams. 1995. *The Craft of Research.* Chicago: Univ. of Chicago Press.

Bourdieu, P. 1986. "The Forms of Capital." In *Soziale Ungleichheiten,* ed. R. Kreckel, 183–98. Goettingen, Germany: Otto Schartz, 1983. Reprinted in *Handbook of Theory and Research for the Sociology of Education,* ed. J. G. Richardson, trans. R. Nice, 241–60. New York: Greenwood.

Bourke-White, M., & E. Caldwell. 1937. *You Have Seen Their Faces.* New York: Macmillan.

Braddock, R. 1971. *A Little Casebook in the Rhetoric of Writing.* Englewood Cliffs, NJ: Prentice-Hall.

Bradford, R. 1997. *Stylistics.* New York: Routledge.

Brady, L. 1998. "The Reproduction of Othering." In *Feminism and Composition Studies: In Other Words,* ed. S. C. Jarratt & L. Worsham, 21–44. New York: MLA.

Brand, N., & J. O. White. 1976. *Legal Writing: The Strategy of Persuasion.* New York: St. Martin's.

———. 1994. *Legal Writing: The Strategy of Persuasion.* 3d. ed. New York: St. Martin's.

Brantlinger, P. 1976. "Mass Communication and Teachers of English." *College English* 37 (5): 490–509.

Brathwaite, K. 1996. "Selection from *History of the Voice.*" In *The Arnold Anthology of Post-Colonial Literatures in English,* ed. J. Thieme, 550–53. London: Arnold; New York: St. Martin's.

Braverman, H. 1998. *Labor and Monopoly Capital: The Degradation of Work in the Twentieth Century.* New York: Monthly Review.

Brereton, J. C. 1988. *The Origins of Composition Studies in the American College, 1875–1925, A Documentary History.* Pittsburgh: Univ. of Pittsburgh Press.

Broeder, P. 1999. *Language, Ethnicity, and Education: Case Studies on Immigrant Minority Groups and Immigrant Minority Languages.* Philadelphia: Multilingual Matters.

Bruffee, K. 1980. *A Short Course in Writing.* Winthrop.

———. 1998. "Closing Remarks." Presented at the Conference of the Council of Writing Program Administrators, 19 July, at Tucson, AZ.

———. 1999. "Thoughts of a Fly on the Wall." *WPA* 23:55–64.

Bryson, B. 1991. *The Mother Tongue: English and How It Got That Way.* New York: Avon.

Bullock, R. 1998. "First-Year Composition: What to Expect, How to Prepare." Paper presented at the National Council of Teachers of English National Convention, 22 November, at Nashville, TN.

Burke, K. [1950] 1969. *A Rhetoric of Motives.* Reprint, Berkeley, CA: Univ. of California Press.

———. 1957. "The Rhetoric of Hitler's 'Battle.'" In *The Philosophy of Literary Form.* New York: Vintage.

———. 1966. "Terministic Screens." In *Language as Symbolic Action: Essays on Life, Literature, and Method,* 44–62. Berkeley, CA: Univ. of California Press.

———. 1984. *Permanence and Change: An Anatomy of Purpose.* 3d. ed. New York: New Republic.

Burke, R. K., ed. 1992. *American Public Discourse: A Multicultural Perspective.* Lanham, MD: Univ. Press of America.

Butler, J. 1990. *Gender Trouble: Feminism and the Subversion of Identity.* New York: Routlege.

———. 1993. *Bodies That Matter: On the Discursive Limits of "Sex."* New York: Routledge.

Butler-Bowdon, W., ed. 1944. *The Book of Margery Kempe.* New York: Devin-Adair.

C-SPAN. Available at *http://www.c-span.org*

Cameron, D. 1995. *Feminism and Linguistic Theory.* New York: St. Martin's.

Cameron, D., ed. 1990. *The Feminist Critique of Language: A Reader.* New York: Routledge.

Campbell, G. 1988. *The Philosophy of Rhetoric,* ed. L. F. Bitzer. Carbondale, IL: Southern Illinois Univ. Press.

Carter, L. 1998. *Reason in Law.* 5th ed. New York: Longman.

Caywood, C. L., & G. R. Overing, eds. 1987. *Teaching Writing: Pedagogy, Gender, and Equity.* New York: State Univ. of New York Press.

Cicero. 1967. *De Oratore.* Trans. E. W. Sutton & H. Rackham. Loeb Classical Library.

———. 1986. *On Oratory and Orators.* Trans. J. S. Watson. Carbondale, IL: Southern Illinois Univ. Press.

Cixous, H. [1976] 1990. "The Laugh of the Medusa." Trans. and revised by K. Cohen and P. Cohen in *The Rhetorical Tradition: Readings from Classical Times to the Present,* ed. P. Bizzell & B. Herzberg, 1232–44. Reprint, Boston: Bedford.

Cleveland, J. H., 3d. 1996. "On Writing English." Letter. *New York Times* 21 March, late ed., A24.

Cliff, M. 1988. "If I Could Write This in Fire, I Would Write This in Fire." In *The Graywolf Annual Five: Multicultural Literacy,* ed. R. Simonson & S. Walker, 63–81. St. Paul: Graywolf.

Clifford, J. 1986. "Introduction: Partial Truths." In *Writing Culture: The Poetics and Politics of Ethnography,* ed. J. Clifford & G. E. Marcus, 1–26. Berkeley, CA: Univ. of California Press.

Clyne, M. 1994. *Intercultural Communication at Work: Cultural Values in Discourse.* Cambridge: Cambridge Univ. Press.

Coe, R. 1980. *Form and Substance.* New York: Wiley.

———. 1990. *Process, Form and Substance: A Rhetoric for Advanced Writers.* Englewood Cliffs, NJ: Prentice-Hall.

Colley, L. 1986. "Whose Nation? Class and National Consciousness in Britain 1750–1830." *Past and Present* 113: 97–117.

Committee Reports on Advanced Composition. 1954–1976. *College Composition and Communication* vols. 5–27.

Conference on College Composition and Communication. 1974. "Students' Right to Their Own Language." Special Issue. *College Composition and Communication* 25.

Connor, U. 1996. *Contrastive Rhetoric: Cross-Cultural Aspects of Second-Language Writing.* Cambridge: Cambridge Univ. Press.

Connors, R. J. 1982. "The Rise of Technical Writing Instruction in America." *Journal of Technical Writing and Communication* 12: 329–52.

———. 1996. "The Abolition Debate in Composition: A Short History." In *Composition in the Twenty-First Century: Crisis and Change,* ed. L. Z. Bloom, D. Daiker, & E. White, 47–63. Carbondale, IL: Southern Illinois Univ. Press.

———. 1997. *Composition-Rhetoric: Backgrounds, Theory, and Pedagogy.* Pittsburgh: Univ. of Pittsburgh Press.

Contemporary Postcolonial & Postimperial Literature in English at Brown University. *http://landow.stg.brown.edu/post/misc/postov.html.*

Conway, J. K. 1989. *The Road from Coorain.* New York: Knopf.

Copy Editor: Language News for the Publishing Profession. December 1997–December 1998.

Corbett, E. P. J. 1965. *Classical Rhetoric for the Modern Student.* New York: Oxford Univ. Press.

Corbett, E. P. J., & R. J. Connors. 1999. *Classical Rhetoric for the Modern Student.* 4th ed. New York: Oxford Univ. Press.

Council of Writing Program Administrators. 1998. "Evaluating the Intellectual Work of Writing Administration." *WPA: Writing Program Administration* 22 (1–2): 85–104.

Court, F. E. 1992. *Institutionalizing English Literature: The Culture and Politics of Literary Study.* Stanford: Stanford Univ. Press.

Creative Nonfiction. 1993–.

Crowley, S. 1989. "Linguistics and Composition Instruction, 1950–1980." *Written Communication* 6 (4): 480–505.

———. 1990. *The Methodical Memory: Invention in Current-Traditional Rhetoric.* Carbondale, IL: Southern Illinois Univ. Press.

———. 1991. "A Personal Essay on Freshman English." *Pre/Text* 12: 156–76.

———. 1995. "Composition's Ethic of Service, the Universal Requirement and the Discourse of Need." *JAC: A Journal of Composition Theory* 15: 227–39.

———. 1998. *Composition in the University: Historical and Polemical Essays.* Pittsburgh: Univ. of Pittsburgh Press.

Crowley, S., & D. Hawhee. 1999. *Ancient Rhetorics for Contemporary Students,* 2d. ed. Boston: Allyn & Bacon.

Curtis, J. 1989. *Mind's Eye, Mind's Truth: FSA Photography Reconsidered.* Philadelphia: Temple Univ. Press.

Daley, K. [pseud.]. 1999. Interview by L. K. Shamoon. 12 January.

Dangarembga, T. 1996. *Nervous Conditions.* London: Women's, 1988. Reprint, Seattle: Seal Press Feminist.

Daniels, H. A. 1983. *Famous Last Words: The American Language Crisis Reconsidered.* Carbondale, IL: Southern Illinois Univ. Press.

Dawkins, J. 1995. "Teaching Punctuation as a Rhetorical Tool." *College Composition and Communication* 46 (4): 533–46.

deFrancis, J. 1989. *Visible Speech: The Diverse Oneness of Writing Systems.* Honolulu: Univ. of Hawaii Press.

de Pisan, C. 1990. "From the Treasure of the City of Ladies." In *The Rhetorical Tradition: Readings from Classical Times to the Present,* ed. P. Bizzell & B. Herzberg, 488–93. Boston: Bedford.

Derrida, J. 1974. *Of Grammatology.* Trans. G. Chakravorty Spivak. Baltimore: Johns Hopkins Univ. Press.

Dewey, J. [1923] 1954. *The Public and Its Problems.* Athens, OH: Ohio Univ. Press.

Diamond, E., & R. A. Silverman. 1995. *White House to Your House: Media and Politics in Virtual America.* Cambridge: MIT Press.

Dicks, B. W. 1982. "State of the Art in Advanced Expository Writing: One Genus, Many Species." *Journal of Advanced Composition* 3 (1–2): 172–91.

Dittmar, N. 1976. *A Critical Survey of Sociolinguistics: Theory and Application.* Trans. P. Sand, P. A. M. Seuren, & K. Whiteley. New York: St. Martin's.

Douglass, F. [1846] 1993. *Narrative of the Life of Frederick Douglass, an American Slave: Written by Himself.* Reprint, Boston: Bedford.

Dreifus, C. 1999. "Going Ape." *Ms.* August/September: 48–54.

Eagleton, T. 1983. "The Rise of English." In *Literary Theory: An Introduction,* 17–53. Minneapolis: Univ. of Minnesota Press.

————. 1990. *The Ideology of the Aesthetic.* Oxford: Blackwell.

————. 1991. *Ideology: An Introduction.* London: Verso.

Ede, L. 1996. "Writing Centers and the Politics of Location." *Writing Center Journal* 16 (Spring): 111–30.

Ede, L., C. Glenn, & A. Lunsford. 1995. "Border Crossings: Intersections of Rhetoric and Feminism." *Rhetorica: A Journal of the History of Rhetoric* 13: 401–41.

Edwards, P., ed. 1967. *The Encyclopedia of Philosophy.* 8 vols. New York: Macmillan.

Ehrenreich, B. 1999. "She Got Game." *Ms.* June/July: 64–71.

Eisenstein, E. 1979. *The Printing Press as an Agent of Change.* Cambridge: Cambridge Univ. Press.

Elbow, P. 1991. "Some Thoughts on Expressive Discourse: A Review-Essay." *Journal of Advanced Composition* 11 (1): 83–94.

Emerson, R. M., R. I. Fretz, & L. L. Shaw. 1995. *Writing Ethnographic Fieldnotes.* Chicago: Univ. of Chicago Press.

Epstein, J., ed. 1997. *The Norton Book of Personal Essays.* New York: Norton.

Evans, W. 1973. *Photographs for the Farm Security Administration, 1935–1938.* New York: Da Cappo.

Farrell, T. B. 1993. *Norms of Rhetorical Culture.* New Haven: Yale Univ. Press.

Fell, M. 1990. "Women's Speaking Justified, Proved, and Allowed by the Scriptures." In *The Rhetorical Tradition: Readings from Classical Times to the Present,* ed. P. Bizzell & B. Herzberg, 677–85. Boston: Bedford.

Fields, W. 1996. *Union of Words: A History of Presidential Eloquence.* New York: Free.

Finegan, E. 1980. *Attitudes Toward English Usage: The History of a War of Words.* New York: Teachers College Press.

Fish, S. E. 1996. "What Is Stylistics and Why Are They Saying Such Terrible Things About It?" In *Approaches to Poetics,* ed. Seymour Chatman. New York: Columbia Univ. Press, 1973. Reprinted in *The Stylistics Reader: From Roman Jakobson to the Present,* ed. J. J. Weber, 94–116. New York: St. Martin's.

Fishkin, J. S. 1995. *The Voice of the People: Public Opinion and Democracy.* New Haven: Yale Univ. Press.

Fishman, J. 1999. *Handbook of Language and Ethnic Identity.* New York: Oxford Univ. Press.

Fishman, S. M., & L. McCarthy. 1998. *John Dewey and the Challenge of Classroom Practice.* New York: Teachers College Columbia Univ. Press.

Fliegelman, J. 1993. *Declaring Independence: Jefferson, Natural Language, and the Culture of Performance.* Stanford: Stanford Univ. Press.

Fleischer, C., & D. Schaafsma, eds. 1998. *Literacy and Democracy: Teacher Research and Composition Studies in Pursuit of Habitable Spaces.* Urbana, IL: NCTE.

Fleming, D. 1998. "Rhetoric as a Course of Study." *College English* 61 (2): 169–91.

Flower, L. 1997. "Partners in Inquiry: A Logic for Community Outreach." In *Writing the Community: Concepts and Models for Service-Learning in Composition,* ed. L. Adler-Kassner, R. Crooks, & A. Watters, 95–117. Washington, D.C.: American Association for Higher Education.

———. 1998. *Problem-Solving Strategies for Writing in College and Community.* Fort Worth, TX: Harcourt.

Flower, L., & E. Long, eds. Forthcoming. *The Community Literacy Primer.*

Foerster, D. M. 1950. "Expository Writing for Advanced Students." *College English* 12: 456.

Foerster, N., & J. M. Steadman. 1931. *Writing and Thinking: A Handbook of Composition and Revision.* Boston: Houghton Mifflin.

Foucault, M. [1980] 1998. "What Is an Author?" In *Language, Countermemory, Practice.* Ithaca, NY: Cornell Univ. Press. Reprinted in *Contemporary Literary Criticism: Literary and Cultural Studies,* ed. R. C. Davis & R. Schliefer. New York: Longman.

Frank, R. [1959] 1998. *The Americans.* Zurich, Switzerland: Scalo Verlag AG.

Freire, P. 1970. *Pedagogy of the Oppressed.* New York: Continuum.

Friedman, D. 1973. "Introductory Education in Typography." *Visible Language* 7 (2): 129–44.

Friedson, E. 1994. *Professionalism Reborn: Theory, Prophecy, and Policy.* Chicago: Univ. of Chicago Press.

Fulkerson, R. 1979. "Four Philosophies of Composition." *College Composition and Communication* 30: 343–48.

Fulwiler, T. 1986. "Freshman English: It's the Best Course in the University to Teach." *Chronicle of Higher Education* 31 (5 February).

Gale, F. G. 1994. *Political Literacy: Rhetoric, Ideology, and the Possibility of Justice.* Albany: SUNY Press.

Gamson, W. A. 1992. *Talking Politics.* New York: Cambridge Univ. Press.

Gandhi, L. 1998. *Postcolonial Theory.* New York: Columbia Univ. Press.

Gauer, A. 1984. *A History of Writing.* London: British Library.

Gelb, I. J. 1963. *A Study of Writing.* Chicago: Univ. of Chicago Press.

Genung, J. F. 1886. *The Practical Elements of Rhetoric with Illustrative Examples.* Boston: Ginn.

George, D. 1999. "The 'Communication Battle,' or Whatever Happened to the 4th C?" *College Composition and Communication* 50: 125–41.

George, D., & J. Trimbur. 1999. *Reading Culture: Contexts for Critical Reading and Writing.* 3d ed. New York: Longman.

Ghosh, A. 1990. *The Shadow Lines.* New York: Penguin.

Gibson, W. 1966. *Tough, Sweet, and Stuffy: An Essay on Modern American Prose Styles.* Bloomington, IN: Indiana Univ. Press.

———. 1969. *Persona: A Style Study for Readers and Writers.* New York: Random House.

Gilyard, K. 1991. *Voices of the Self: A Study of Language Competence.* Detroit: Wayne State Univ. Press.

Glenn, C. 1997. *Rhetoric Retold: Regendering the Tradition from Antiquity Through the Renaissance.* Carbondale, IL: Southern Illinois Univ. Press.

Goggin, M. 1995. "The Disciplinary Instability of Composition." In *The Politics of Writing Instruction: Postsecondary,* ed. R. Bullock & J. Trimbur, 27–48. Portsmouth, NH: Boynton/Cook. Reprinted in *Reconceiving Writing, Rethinking Writing Instruction.* ed. J. Petraglia. Mahwah, NJ: Lawrence Erlbaum, xi–xvii.

Goodman, Y. 1988. "The Development of Initial Literacy." In *Awakening to Literacy,* ed. H. Goelman, A. Oberg, & F. Smith, Portsmouth, NH: Heinemann Educational, 1984. Reprinted in *Perspectives on Literacy,* ed. E. Kintgen, B. Kroll, & M. Rose. Carbondale, IL: Southern Illinois Univ. Press.

Gordimer, N. 1994. *The Lying Days.* New York: Penguin.

Gorgias. 1990. "Encomium of Helen." In *The Rhetorical Tradition: Readings from Classical Times to the Present,* ed. P. Bizzell & B. Herzberg, 40–42. Boston: Bedford.

Gould, S. J. 1993. "American Polygeny and Craniometry Before Darwin: Blacks and Indians as Separate, Inferior Species." In *The "Racial" Economy of Science: Toward a Democratic Future: Race, Gender, and Science,* ed. S. Harding, 84–115. Bloomington, IN: Indiana Univ. Press.

Graddol, D., & J. Swann. 1989. *Gender Voices.* Oxford, UK: Blackwell's.

Graff, G. 1987. *Professing English Literature: An Institutional History.* Chicago: Univ. of Chicago Press.

Grimke, S. 1990. "Letters on the Equality of the Sexes and the Condition of Woman, Letters III, IV, and XIV." In *The Rhetorical Tradition: Readings from Classical Times to the Present,* ed. P. Bizzell & B. Herzberg. 685–96. Boston: Bedford.

Gross, J. 1991. *The Oxford Book of Essays.* New York: Oxford Univ. Press.

Guerrilla Girls. 1998. *The Guerrilla Girls' Companion to the History of Western Art.* New York: Penguin.

Haas, C. 1996. *Writing Technology: Studies on the Materiality of Literacy.* Mahwah, NJ: Lawrence Erlbaum.

Habermas, J. 1989. *The Structural Transformation of the Public Sphere: An Inquiry into a Category of Bourgeois Society.* Trans. T. Burger. Cambridge: MIT Press.

Hacker, D. 1997. *The Bedford Handbook for Writers.* 5th ed. Boston: Bedford.

Hahn, D. F. 1998. *Political Communication: Rhetoric, Government, and Citizens.* State College, PA: Strata.

Hairston, M. 1981. *Successful Writing.* New York: Norton.

———. 1986. *Successful Writing.* 2d ed. New York: Norton.

———. 1992. *Successful Writing.* 3d ed. New York: Norton.

Hall, K., & M. Bucholtz, eds. 1995. *Gender Articulated: Language and the Socially Constructed Self.* New York: Routledge.

Hall, S. 1989. "Ideology and Communication Theory." In *Rethinking Communication,* ed. B. Dervin, 41–52. Newbury Park: Sage.

———. 1991. "The Local and the Global: Globalization and Ethnicity." In *Culture, Globalization and the World-System,* ed. A. D. King, 19–39. London: MacMillan.

———. 1996. *Representation and the Media.* Boston: The Media Education Foundation.

———. 1997a. "The Spectacle of the 'Other.' " In *Representation: Cultural Representations and Signifying Practices,* 223–79. London: Sage.

Hall, S., eds. 1997b. *Representation: Cultural Representations and Signifying Practices.* London: Sage.

Hall, S., & P. Whannel. 1964. *The Popular Arts.* Boston: Beacon.

Halliday, M. A. K. 1978. *Language as Social Semiotic: The Social Interpretation of Language and Meaning.* Baltimore: University Park.

Halloran, S. M. 1993. "Rhetoric in the American College Curriculum: The Decline of Public Discourse." *PRE/TEXT* 3: 245–69, 1983. Reprinted in *PRE/TEXT: The First Decade,* ed. V. Vitanza, Pittsburgh: Univ. of Pittsburgh Press.

Hamilton, P. 1997. "Representing the Social: France and Frenchness in Post-War Humanist Photography." In *Representation: Cultural Representations and Signifying Practices,* ed. S. Hall, 75–150. London: Sage.

Harris, J., & J. Rosen. 1995. *Media Journal: Reading and Writing About Popular Culture.* Boston: Allyn and Bacon.

Harris, L. H. 1916. "A Proposed Course in Advanced Exposition for College Students." *English Journal* 5: 501–3.

Harris, R. 1980. *The Language Makers.* Ithaca, NY: Cornell Univ. Press.

Haswell, R. H. 1991. *Gaining Ground in College Writing: Tales of Development and Interpretation.* Dallas: Southern Methodist Univ. Press.

Hatch, E. 1992. *Discourse and Language Education.* Cambridge: Cambridge Univ. Press.

Havelock, E. 1986. *The Muse Learns to Write: Reflections of Orality and Literacy from Antiquity to the Present.* New Haven: Yale Univ. Press.

Heller, S. 1999. "The Shrinking Scholarly Book." *The Chronicle of Higher Education* 26 (February): A15–A17.

Henry, R. L. 1928. "A College Course in Advanced Composition." *English Journal* 17: 137–46.

Herring, S. C., ed. 1996. *Computer-Mediated Communication: Linguistic, Social and Cross-Cultural Perspectives.* Amsterdam: Benjamins.

Herzberg, B. 1994. "Community Service and Critical Teaching." *College Composition and Communication* 45 (3): 307–19.

Hillway, T. 1954. "Present Status of Advanced Composition and Rhetoric." *College English* 16: 177–80.

Hine, L. N. Library of Congress Collection of Photographs. *http://lcweb.loc.gov/spcoll/169.html.*

Hine, L. N., & R. Freedman. 1998. *Kids at Work: Lewis Hine and the Crusade Against Child Labor.* Boston: Houghton Mifflin.

Hirschberg, S., & T. Hirschberg, eds. 1992. *One World, Many Cultures,* 3d ed. Boston: Allyn & Bacon.

Hodge, M. 1981. *Crick, Crack, Monkey.* London: Heinemann.

Hogan, M. P. 1980. "Advanced Composition: A Survey." *Journal of Advanced Composition* 1 (1): 21–29.

Hollis, R. 1994. *Graphic Design: A Concise History.* London: Thames and Hudson.

Homer. *Iliad.*

———. *Odyssey.*

hooks, b. 1991. "Narratives of Struggle." In *Critical Fictions: The Politics of Imaginative Writing,* ed. P. Mariani, 53–61. Seattle: Bay.

Horace. *Roman Odes.*

"How Not to Write English." 1996. Editorial. *New York Times* 14 March, late ed., A22.

Howell, W. S. 1971. *Eighteenth-Century British Logic and Rhetoric.* Princeton: Princeton Univ. Press.

Hull, G. T., P. B. Scott, & B. Smith, eds. 1982. *All the Women Are White, All the Blacks Are Men, But Some of Us Are Brave.* New York: Feminist.

Illich, I., & B. Sanders. 1988. *ABC: The Alphabetization of the Human Mind.* San Francisco: North Point.

Intercollegiate Electronic Democracy Project (IEDP). 1999. Available at: *http://www.trincoll.edu/depts/writcent/edproject.html.*

Irons, P., & S. Guitton, eds. 1993. *May It Please the Court: The Most Significant Oral Arguments Made Before the Supreme Court Since 1955.* New York: New.

Jackall, R., ed. 1998. *Propaganda.* New York: New York Univ. Press.

Jacobs, S. 1997. "Reflections on Pedagogical Study." *College English* 59 (4): 461–69.

Jacobus, L. A. 1998. *Substance, Style, and Strategy.* New York: Oxford Univ. Press.

Jamieson, K. H. 1988. *Eloquence in an Electronic Age: The Transformation of Political Speechmaking*. New York: Oxford Univ. Press.

Jarratt, S. C. 1991. "Feminism and Composition: The Case for Conflict." In *Contending with Words: Composition and Rhetoric in a Postmodern Age*, ed. P. Harkin & J. Schilb, 105–23. New York: MLA.

Jarratt, S. J. 1995. "In Excess: Radical Extensions of Neopragmatism." In *Rhetoric, Sophistry, Pragmatism*, ed. S. Mailloux, 206–27. Cambridge: Cambridge Univ. Press.

Jolliffe, D. 1996. "Twelve Readers Reading: Exemplary Responses, Thorny Problems." *Assessing Writing* 3 (2): 221–33.

Joyce, M. 1995. *Of Two Minds: Hypertext, Pedagogy and Poetics*. Ann Arbor: Univ. of Michigan Press.

Kane, H. 1972. *Ambiguous Adventure*. Trans. K. Woods. London: Heinemann.

Kells, M. H., & V. Balester, eds. 1999. *Attending to the Margins: Writing, Researching, and Teaching on the Front Lines*. Portsmouth, NH: Boynton/Cook.

Kennedy, G. A. 1999. *Comparative Rhetoric: An Historical and Cross-Cultural Introduction*. New York: Oxford Univ. Press.

Kinneavy, J. 1971. *A Theory of Discourse*. New York: W.W. Norton.

Kinneavy, J., W. McCleary, & N. Nakadate. 1985. *Writing in the Liberal Arts Tradition*. New York: Harper.

Kipling, R. 1899. "The White Man's Burden," *McClure's Magazine* 12 (February).

Kirszner, L. G., & S. R. Mandell. 1994. *Common Ground: Reading and Writing About American's Cultures*. New York: St. Martin's.

Kitzhaber, A. R. 1963. *Themes, Theories, and Therapy: The Teaching of Writing in College: The Report of the Dartmouth Study of Student Writing*. New York: McGraw-Hill.

———. 1990. *Rhetoric in American Colleges, 1850–1900*. Dallas: Southern Methodist Univ. Press.

Klein, R. 1996. "Text and Subtext." *New York Times* 18 March, late ed., A15.

Kolln, M. 1999. *Rhetorical Grammar: Grammatical Choices, Rhetorical Effect*. 3d. ed. Boston: Allyn & Bacon.

Kozol, J. 1991. *Savage Inequalities*. New York: Crown.

Kress, G., & T. van Leeuwen. 1997. *Reading Images: The Grammar of Visual Design*. New York: Routledge.

Kristeva, J. 1990. "Women's Time." In *The Rhetorical Tradition: Readings from Classical Times to the Present*, ed. P. Bizzell & B. Herzberg, 1251–66. Boston: Bedford.

Labov, W. 1966. *The Social Stratification of English in New York City*. Washington, D.C.: Center for Applied Linguistics.

———. 1972. *Language in the Inner City: Studies in the Black English Vernacular*. Philadelphia: Univ. of Pennsylvania Press.

———. 1973. *Sociolinguistic Patterns*. Philadelphia: Univ. of Pennsylvania Press.

laGuardia, D., & H. P. Guth, eds. 2000. *American Voices: Culture and Community.* 4th ed. Mountain View, CA: Mayfield.

Lamb, C. 1996. "Other Voices, Different Parties: Feminist Responses to Argument." In *Perspectives on Written Argument,* ed. D. P. Berrill, 257–69. Cresskill, NJ: Hampton.

Lamming, G. 1991. *In the Castle of My Skin.* Univ. of Michigan Press.

Lange, D., & P. S. Taylor. 1939. *American Exodus: A Record of Human Erosion in the Thirties.* New York: Reynal and Hitchcock.

Lanham, R. 1979. *Revising Prose.* Englewood Cliffs, NJ: Prentice-Hall.

———. 1983. *Analyzing Prose.* New York: Scribner's.

———. 1999. *Revising Prose.* 4th ed. Boston: Allyn and Bacon.

Larson, G. J., & E. Deutsch, eds. 1988. *Interpreting Across Boundaries: New Essays in Comparative Philosophy.* Princeton: Princeton Univ. Press.

Laurence, P. 1975. "Error's Endless Train: Why Students Don't Perceive Errors." *Journal of Basic Writing* 1 (1): 23–42.

Leavis, F. R., & D. Thompson. 1933. *Culture and Environment.* London: Chattus and Windus.

LeClercq, T. 1995. *Guide to Legal Writing Style.* Boston: Little, Brown.

Leppert, R. 1996. *Art and the Committed Eye: The Cultural Function of Imagery.* Boulder: Westview.

Levi, E. 1949. *An Introduction to Legal Reasoning.* Chicago: Univ. of Chicago Press.

Levitt, H. 1989. *A Way of Seeing.* Durham, NC: Duke Univ. Press.

Lewis, A. 1966. *Gideon's Trumpet.* New York: Vintage.

Lidchi, H. 1997. "The Poetics and Politics of Exhibiting Other Cultures." In *Representation: Cultural Representations and Signifying Practices,* ed. S. Hall, 151–208. London: Sage.

Little, S. B., & S. K. Rose. 1994. "A Home of Our Own: Establishing a Department of Rhetoric and Writing Studies at San Diego State University." *WPA: Writing Program Administration* 18 (1–2): 16–28.

Livia, A., & K. Hall, eds. 1997. *Queerly Phrased: Language, Gender, and Sexuality.* New York: Oxford Univ. Press.

Livy. *Ab Urbe Condita.*

Locke, J. 1959. *Essay Concerning Human Understanding,* ed. A. C. Fraser. New York: Dover.

Locker, K. O. 2000. *Business and Administrative Communications,* 5th ed. Boston: Irwin/McGraw-Hill.

Lofty, J. S. 1992a. *Time to Write: The Influence of Time and Culture on Learning to Write.* Albany: SUNY Press.

———. 1992b. "Time to Write: Resistance to Literacy in a Maine Fishing Village." *Time to Write: The Influence of Time and Culture on Learning to Write,* Albany: SUNY Press.

Logan, S. W. 1995. *With Pen and Voice: A Critical Anthology of Nineteenth-Century African-American Women.* Carbondale, IL: Southern Illinois Univ. Press.

———. 1999. "We Are Coming." In *The Persuasive Discourse of Nineteenth-Century Black Women.* Carbondale, IL: Southern Illinois Univ. Press.

Loomba, A. 1998. *Colonialism/Postcolonialism.* London: Routledge.

Lopate, P., ed. 1994. *The Art of the Personal Essay.* New York: Anchor/Doubleday.

———. 1997. *The Anchor Essay Annual.* New York: Anchor.

Lu, M-Z. 1999. "The Vitality of the Ungrateful Receiver: Making Giving Mutual Between Composition and Postcolonial Studies." *JAC: A Journal of Composition Theory* 19 (3): 335–58.

Lunsford, A. A. 1990. "Composing Ourselves: Politics, Commitment, and the Teaching of Writing." *College Composition and Communication* 41: 71–82.

Lunsford, A. A., ed. 1995. *Reclaiming Rhetorica: Women in the Rhetorical Tradition.* Pittsburgh: Univ. of Pittsburgh Press.

Lunsford, A. A., & R. Connors, eds. 1999. *The New St. Martin's Handbook,* 4th ed. New York: Bedford/St. Martin's.

Maasik, S., & J. Solomon. 1994. *Signs of Life in the USA: Readings on Popular Culture for Writers.* Boston: St. Martin's.

Macaulay, T. B. 1835. "Minute on Indian Education." *Thomas Babington Macaulay: Selected Writings,* ed. J. Clive & T. Pinney, 237–51. Chicago: Univ. of Chicago Press.

MacIntyre, A. 1984. *After Virtue: A Study in Moral Theory.* 2d ed. Notre Dame: Univ. of Notre Dame Press.

MacLeod, M. 1937. "The 'Thinking' Examination for Advanced Compositions." *English Journal* 26: 215–18.

Mani, L. 1990. "Multiple Mediations." *Feminist Review* 35: 24–41.

———. 1998. *Contentious Traditions: The Debate on Sati in Colonial India.* Berkeley, CA: Univ. of California Press.

Maraire, J. N. 1996. *Zenzele: A Letter to My Daughter.* New York: Crown.

McCrum, R., W. Cran, & R. MacNeil. 1986. *The Story of English.* New York: Viking.

McGann, J. 1998. "The Dawn of the Dead: Dante Gabriel Rossetti at the End of the Twentieth Century." Paper presented at the conference "The Sociomaterial Turn: Excavating Modernism," 6 March, at the University of Tulsa, Tulsa, OK.

Millar, J. 1773. *Observations Concerning the Distinctions of Ranks in Society.* 2d ed. London: NP.

Miller, C. R. 1984. "Genre as Social Action." *Quarterly Journal of Speech* 70: 151–67.

———. 1993. "Rhetoric and Community: The Problem of the One and the Many." In *Defining the New Rhetorics,* ed. T. Enos & S. C. Brown, 79–94. Newbury Park, CA: Sage.

Miller, T. P. 1993. "Teaching the Histories of Rhetoric as a Social Praxis." *Rhetoric Review* 12: 70–82.

———. 1997. *The Formation of College English: Rhetoric and Belles Lettres in the British Cultural Provinces.* Pittsburgh: Univ. of Pittsburgh Press.

Mills, J. [pseud.]. 1999. Interview by L. K. Shamoon. 20 January.

Mnthali, F. "The Stranglehold of English Lit." Unpublished manuscript available from the author.

Moore-Gilbert, B. J. 1997. *Postcolonial Theory: Contexts, Practices, Politics.* London: Verso.

Morgan, G. 1997. *Images of Organization.* 2d ed. Thousand Oaks, CA: Sage.

Mulvey, L. 1989. *Visual and Other Pleasures.* London: Macmillan.

Mutnick, D. 1998. "Rethinking the Personal Narrative: Life-Writing and Composition Pedagogy." In *Under Construction: Working at the Intersections of Composition Theory, Research, and Practice,* ed. C. Farris & C. M. Anson. Logan, UT: Utah State Univ. Press.

National Education Association. 1958. *Education Policies Commission. Mass Communication and Education.* Washington, D.C.: National Education Association.

New London Group. 1996. "A Pedagogy of Multiliteracies: Designing Social Futures." *Harvard Educational Review* 66 (1): 60–92.

Ngugi wa Thiong'o. 1986a. *Decolonising the Mind: The Politics of Language in African Literature.* London: J. Currey; Portsmouth, NH: Heinemann.

———. 1986b. "Literature and Society." In *Decolonising the Mind: The Politics of Language in African Literature,* London: J. Currey; Portsmouth, NH: Heinemann.

North, S. 1987. *The Making of Meaning in Composition: Portrait of an Emerging Field.* Upper Montclair, NJ: Boynton.

Nystrand, M., with A. Gamoran, R. Kachur, & C. Predergast. 1997. *Opening Dialogue: Understanding the Dynamics of Language and Learning in the English Classroom.* New York: Teachers College Press.

Ogbu, J. 1988. "Literacy and Schooling in Subordinate Cultures: The Case of Black Americans." In *Literacy in Historical Perspective,* ed. D. Resnick, Washington, D.C.: Library of Congress, 1983. Reprinted in *Perspectives on Literacy,* ed. E. Kintgen, B. Kroll, & M. Rose. Carbondale, IL: Southern Illinois Univ. Press.

Ogundipe-Leslie, M. 1996. "To a Jane Austen Class at Ibadan University." In *The Arnold Anthology of Post-Colonial Literatures in English,* ed. J. Thieme, London: Arnold; New York: St. Martin's.

Ohmann, R. 1979. "Use Definite, Specific, Concrete Language." *College English* 41: 390–97.

Ong, W. 1971. *Rhetoric, Romance, and Technology.* Ithaca, NY: Cornell Univ. Press.

———. 1982. *Orality and Literacy: The Technologizing of the Word.* New York: Methuen.

Orwell, G. [1977] 1984. *1984.* Reprint, San Diego: Harcourt Brace Jovanovich.

Ouchi, W. G. 1981. *Theory Z: How American Business Can Meet the Japanese Challenge.* Reading, MA: Addison Wesley.

Oxford English Dictionary. 1971. 2 vols. Oxford: Oxford Univ. Press.

Paine, C. 1997. "The Composition Course and Public Discourse." *Rhetoric Review* 15: 282–98.

Patterson, T. E. 1993. *Out of Order.* New York: Knopf.

Pavalko, R. M. 1985. *Sociology of Occupations and Professions.* 2d ed. Itasca, IL: F. E. Peacock.

Pemberton, G. 1992. "Antidisestablishmentarianism." In *One World, Many Cultures,* 3d. ed., ed. S. Hirschberg & T. Hirschberg, 18–25. Boston: Allyn & Bacon.

Penfield, E. 1991. "Freshman English/Advanced Writing: How Do We Distinguish the Two?" In *Teaching Advanced Composition,* ed. K. H. Adams & J. L. Adams, 17–30. Portsmouth, NH: Heinemann–Boynton/Cook.

Peterson's Guide to Four Year Colleges 1998. 1997. 28th ed. Princeton, NJ: Peterson's.

Petraglia, J. 1995. "Introduction." In *Reconceiving Writing, Rethinking Writing Instruction,* ed. J. Petraglia, xi–xvii. Mahwah, NJ: Erlbaum.

Plato. 1971. *Gorgias.* Trans. W. Hamiliton. London: Penguin.

———. *Ion.*

———. 1995. *Phaedrus.* Trans. A. Nehamas & P. Woodruff. Indianapolis: Hackett.

Ponsot, M., & R. Deen. 1982. *Beat Not the Poor Desk.* Upper Monclair, NJ: Boynton/Cook.

Pooley, R. C. 1974. *The Teaching of English Usage.* Urbana, IL: NCTE.

Postcolonial and Colonial Studies at the University of California, Santa Barbara. *http://humanitas.ucsb.edu/shuttle/cultural.html#postcolonial.*

Postcolonial Studies at Emory. http://www.emory.edu/ENGLISH/Bahri/Contents.html.

Postman, N. 1985. *Amusing Ourselves to Death: Public Discourse in the Age of Show Business.* New York: Penguin.

Postman, N., & the Committee on the Study of Television of the National Council of Teachers of English. 1961. *Television and the Teaching of English.* New York: Appleton-Century-Crofts.

Pratt, M. L. 1992. *Imperial Eyes: Travel Writing and Transculturation.* London: Routledge.

Procopiow, N., & W. Covino. 1999. *The Elements of Legal Prose.* Boston: Allyn and Bacon.

Qualley, D. J. 1994. "Being Two Places at Once: Feminism and the Development of 'Both/And' Perspectives." In *Pedagogy in the Age of Politics: Writing and Reading (in) the Academy,* ed. P. A. Sullivan & D. J. Qualley, 25–42. Urbana, IL: NCTE.

Quinn, J. 1980. *American Tongue and Cheek: A Populist Guide to Our Language.* New York: Pantheon.

Quintilian. *Institutio Oratoria.*

Ramage, J. D., & J. C. Bean. 1998. *Writing Arguments: A Rhetoric with Readings.* 4th ed. Boston: Allyn and Bacon.

Rampton, M. B. H. 1992. "Scope for Empowerment in Sociolinguistics." In *Researching Language: Issues of Power and Method,* ed. D. Cameron, E. Frazer, P. Harvey, M. B. H. Rampton, & K. Richardson. London: Routledge.

Rheingold, H. 1994. *The Virtual Community: Homesteading on the Electronic Frontier.* New York: Harper Perennial.

Rhetorica: A Journal of the History of Rhetoric. Berkeley, CA: Univ. of California Press.

Rich, A. 1978a. *On Lies, Secrets, and Silence: Selected Prose, 1966–1978.* New York: Norton.

———. 1978b. "Toward a Woman-Centered University." In *On Lies, Secrets, and Silence,* A. Rich, 125–55. New York: Norton.

———. 1978c. "When We Dead Awaken: Writing as Re-Vision." In *On Lies, Secrets, and Silence: Selected Prose, 1966–1978,* A. Rich, 33–49. New York: Norton.

———. 1993. "As If Your Life Depended on It." In *What Is Found There: Notebooks on Poetry and Politics.* New York: W.W. Norton.

Riis, J. [1890] 1996. *How the Other Half Lives.* Reprint, Boston: Bedford.

Robertson, L. R., S. Crowley, & F. Lentricchia. 1987. "The Wyoming Conference Resolution Opposing Unfair Salaries and Working Conditions for Post-Secondary Teachers of Writing." *College English* 49: 274–80.

Robinson, A., & R. Tallia. 1998. *The Princeton Review: Cracking the LSAT.* New York: Random House.

Rose, M. 1989. *Lives on the Boundary: The Struggles and Achievements of America's Underprepared.* New York: Free.

———. 1995. *Possible Lives: The Promise of Public Education in America.* Boston: Houghton Mifflin.

Roskelly, H., & K. Ronald. 1998. *Reason to Believe: Romanticism, Pragmatism, and the Possibility of Teaching.* New York: SUNY Press.

Rubin, G. S. [1984] 1993. "Thinking Sex: Notes for a Radical Theory of the Politics of Sexuality." In *Pleasure and Danger: Exploring Female Sexuality,* ed. C. S. Vance. New York: Routledge. Reprint in *The Lesbian and Gay Studies Reader,* ed. H. Abelove, M. A. Barale, & D. M. Halperin, 3–44. New York: Routledge.

Rushdie, S. 1991a. "Commonwealth Literature Does Not Exist." In *Imaginary Homelands: Essays and Criticism 1981–1991,* 61–70. London: Granta; New York: Penguin.

———. 1991b. *Imaginary Homelands: Essays and Criticism 1981–1991.* London: Granta; New York: Penguin.

Russell, D. R. 1991. *Writing in the Academic Disciplines, 1970–1990: A Curricular History.* Carbondale, IL: Southern Illinois Univ. Press.

———. 1995. "Activity Theory and Its Implications for Writing Instruction." In *Reconceiving Writing, Rethinking Writing Instruction,* ed. J. Petraglia, 51–77. Mahwah, NJ: Lawrence Erlbaum.

———. 1997. "Rethinking Genre in School and Society: An Activity Theory Analysis." *Written Communication* 14: 504–54.

———. 1999. "Activity Theory and Process Approaches: Writing (Power) in School and Society." In *Post-Process Theory: Beyond the Writing-Process Paradigm,* ed. T. Kent, 80–95. Carbondale, IL: Southern Illinois Univ. Press.

Sadker, M., & D. Sadker. 1994. *Failing at Fairness: How America's Schools Cheat Girls*. New York: Scribner's.

Samovar, L. A., & R. E. Porter, eds. 1997. *Intercultural Communication: A Reader*. 8th ed. Belmont, CA: Wadsworth.

Schiffman, S. 1994. *25 Sales Habits of Highly Successful Salespeople*. Holbrook, MA: B. Adams.

Schiffrin, D. 1994. *Approaches to Discourse*. Cambridge: Basil Blackwell.

Schilb, J. 1990. "The Role of Ethos: Ethics, Rhetoric, and Politics in Contemporary Feminist Theory." *Pre/Text* 11: 212–34.

Schon, D. 1987. *Educating the Reflective Practitioner*. San Franciso: Jossey-Bass.

Schuster, C. I. 1991. "The Politics of Promotion." In *The Politics of Writing Instruction: Postsecondary*, ed. R. Bullock & J. Trimbur, 85–95. Portsmouth, NH: Boynton/Cook.

Schwegler, R. A. "150 Years of English Curriculum Development: Eight Colleges and Universities." Unpublished manuscript.

Scott, J. 1991. "The Evidence of Experience." *Critical Inquiry* 17: 773–97.

Scribner, S., & M. Cole. 1973. "The Cognitive Consequences of Formal and Informal Education." *Science* 182: 553–59.

Search for Common Ground. 1999. Available at *http://www.sfcg.org/toolbox.htm*.

Seligman, J. 1978. *The High Citadel: The Influence of Harvard Law*. Boston: Houghton Mifflin.

Selvadurai, S. 1997. *Funny Boy*. San Diego: Harcourt Brace.

Seth, V. 1982a. "Diwali." In *Mappings*. Calcutta: Writer's Workshop.

———. 1982b. *Mappings*. Calcutta: Writer's Workshop.

Showalter, E. 1999. "Regeneration." *PMLA* 114: 318–28.

Shumaker, R. C., L. Dennis, & L. Green. 1990. "Advanced Exposition: A Survey of Patterns and Problems." *Journal of Advanced Composition* 10 (1): 136–44.

Sledd, J. 1991. "Why the Wyoming Resolution had to be Emasculated: A History and a Quixotism." *JAC: Journal of Advanced Composition* 11.2: hypertext. 2 June 1999 *http://nosferatu.cas.usf.edu/JAC/112/sledd.html*.

Slevin, J. F. 1991. "Depoliticizing and Politicizing Composition Studies." In *The Politics of Writing Instruction: Postsecondary*, ed. R. Bullock & J. Trimbur, 1–22. Portsmouth, NH: Boynton/Cook.

Smart, W. 1965. *Eight Modern Essayists*. New York: St. Martin's.

———. 1995. *Eight Modern Essayists*. 6th ed. New York: St. Martin's.

Smith, A. 1978. *Lectures on Jurisprudence*. Oxford: Clarendon.

———. 1987a. *An Inquiry into the Nature and Causes of the Wealth of Nations*. Oxford: Clarendon.

———. 1987b. *The Theory of Moral Sentiments*. Oxford: Clarendon.

Smith, M. E. 1921. "A Basis for Advanced Freshman Composition." *English Journal* 10: 281–283.

Steinem, G. 1999. "Supremacy Crimes." *Ms.* August/September: 44–47.

Stevenson, H. A. 1951. "Facing the Problem in Upperclass English." *College English* 13: 32–37.

Strunk, W., & E. B. White, Jr. 1979. *The Elements of Style.* 3d ed. New York: Macmillan.

———. 1999. *The Elements of Style.* 4th ed. Boston: Allyn & Bacon.

Summerfield, J., & G. Summerfield. 1986. *Texts and Contexts: A Contribution to the Theory and Practice of Teaching Composition.* New York: Random House.

Sunder Rajan, R. 1992. "Fixing English: Nation, Language, Subject." In *The Lie of the Land: English Literary Studies in India,* 7–28. New York: Oxford Univ. Press.

Tannen, D. 1984. *Conversational Style: Analyzing Talk Among Friends.* Norwood, NJ: Ablex.

———. 1990. *You Just Don't Understand: Women and Men in Conversation.* New York: William Morrow.

———. 1998. *The Argument Culture: Moving from Debate to Dialogue.* New York: Random House.

Thieme, J. ed. 1996. *The Arnold Anthology of Post-Colonial Literatures in English.* London: Arnold; New York: St. Martin's.

Thompson, D., ed. 1964. *Discrimination and Popular Culture.* Hammondsworth, NY: Penguin.

Thompson, H. S. 1995. *Better Than Sex: Confessions of a Political Junkie.* New York: Ballantine.

Trask, R. L. 1999. *Key Concepts in Language and Linguistics.* London: Routledge.

Trimbur, J. 1994. "Review: Taking the Social Turn: Teaching Writing Post-Process." *College Composition and Communication* 45 (1):108–18.

———. 1999. *The Call to Write.* New York: Longman.

Trudgill, P. 1983. *Sociolinguistics: An Introduction to Language and Society.* Rev. ed. Penguin.

Tufte, E. 1983. *The Visual Display of Quantitative Information.* Chesire, CT: Graphics.

———. 1990. *Envisioning Information.* Chesire, CT: Graphics.

———. 1997. *Visual Explanations.* Chesire, CT: Graphics.

Turkle, S. 1995. *Life on the Screen: Identity in the Age of the Internet.* New York: Simon and Schuster.

———. 1996. "Who Am We?" *Wired* 4 (1): Also available at: *http://www.wired.com/wired/archive/4.01/turkle.html.*

Turow, S. 1977. *One L.* New York: Warner.

Uchmanowicz, P. 1997. "Lessons from the Margins of the Academic Grove, or 'Hoop Dreams.'" *WPA: Writing Program Administration* 20: 31–43.

Ullman, E. 1997. *Close to the Machine: Technophilia and Its Discontents.* San Francisco: City Lights.

van Dijk, T. A., ed. 1985. *Handbook of Discourse Analysis.* 4 vols. London: Academic.

———. 1998a. *Discourse as Structure and Process.* Vol. 1, *Discourse Studies: A Multi-disciplinary Introduction.* London: Sage.

———. 1998b. *Discourse as Social Interaction.* Vol. 2, *Discourse Studies: A Multi-disciplinary Introduction.* London: Sage.

Vaughn, T. [pseud.]. 1998. Interview by L. K. Shamoon. 15 December.

Vergil. *Aeneid.*

Villanueva, V., Jr. 1993. *Bootstraps: From an American Academic of Color.* Urbana, IL: NCTE.

Villanueva, V., Jr., ed. 1997. *Cross-Talk in Comp Theory: A Reader.* Urbana, IL: NCTE.

Viswanathan, G. 1988. "Currying Favor: The Politics of British Educational and Cultural Policy in India, 1813–1854." *Social Text* 7 (1–2) (Fall): 85–104.

———. 1989. *Masks of Conquest.* New York: Columbia Univ. Press.

Walker, A. 1983. "In Search of Our Mother's Gardens." In *In Search of Our Mothers' Gardens,* 231–243. New York: Harcourt Brace Jovanovich.

Web White & Blue, a site sponsored by the Markle Foundation and Harvard's Shorenstein Center on Press, Politics, and Public Policy. Available at *http://webwhiteblue.org.*

Weber, J. J., ed. 1996. *The Stylistics Reader: From Roman Jakobson to the Present.* New York: St. Martin's.

Welch, N. 1997. *Getting Restless: Rethinking Revision in Writing Instruction.* Portsmouth, NH: Boynton/Cook.

Wells, S. 1996. "Rogue Cops and Health Care: What Do We Want from Public Writing?" *College Composition and Communication* 47 (3): 325–41.

Wendt, A. 1996. "Colonialism: The Wounds." In *The Arnold Anthology of Post-Colonial Literatures in English,* ed. J. Thieme, 646–49. London: Arnold; New York: St. Martin's.

Wheeler, P. M. 1930. "Advanced English Composition." *English Journal* 19: 557–66.

Wiley, M., B. Gleason, & L. W. Phelps, eds. 1996. *Composition in Four Keys: Inquiring into the Field.* Moutain View, CA: Mayfield.

Williams, G. 1992. *Sociolinguistics: A Sociological Critique.* London: Routledge.

Williams, J. M. 1981a. "The Phenomenology of Error." *College Composition and Communication* 32: 152–68.

———. 1981b. *Style: Ten Lessons in Clarity and Grace.* New York: Longman.

———. 1997. *Style: Ten Lessons in Clarity and Grace.* 5th ed. New York: Longman.

———. 1999. *Style: Ten Lessons in Clarity and Grace.* 6th ed. New York: Addison Wesley Longman.

Williams, R. 1961. *The Long Revolution.* London: Chatto and Windus.

Witte, S. P., & L. Faigley. 1983. *Evaluating College Writing Programs.* Carbondale, IL: Southern Illinois Univ. Press.

Wittig, M. [1981] 1993. "One Is Not Born a Woman." In *The Straight Mind.* Beacon. Reprinted in *The Lesbian and Gay Studies Reader,* ed. H. Abelove, M. A. Barale, & D. M. Halperin, 103–9. Reprint, New York: Routledge.

Wolfe, T. 1973. *The New Journalism,* Anthology ed. T. Wolfe & E. W. Johnson. New York: Harper.

Woolf, V. [1929] 1977. *A Room of One's Own.* Reprint, London: Granada.

"The WPA Annual Bibliography of Writing Textbooks." Spring 1981–. WPA: Writing Program Administration.

Wright, A. 1998. "Sentence Fragments: Elements of Style, Postcolonial Edition." *JAC: A Journal of Composition Theory* 18 (1): 91–104.

Wydick, R. 1998. *Plain English for Lawyers.* 4th ed. Durham, NC: Carolina Academic.

"Wyoming Resolution." 1987. *College English* 49: 274–80.

X, Malcolm. 1965. *The Autobiography of Malcolm X.* New York: Grove.

Yancey, K. B. 1997. "Teacher Portfolios: Lessons in Resistance, Readiness, and Reflection." In *Situating Portfolios: Four Perspectives,* eds. K. B. Yancey & I. Weiner, 244–62. Logan, UT: Utah State Univ. Press.

Young, R., A. Becker, & K. Pike. 1970. *Rhetoric: Discovery and Change.* New York: Harcourt.

Zinsser, W. 1995. *On Writing Well.* 5th ed. New York: HarperCollins.

Contributors

Chris M. Anson (*chris_anson@ncsu.edu*) is professor of English and director of the campuswide Writing and Speaking Program at North Carolina State University, Raleigh, North Carolina. His research interests, on which he has published widely, include writing to learn, response to writing, the social construction of error, and the nature of literacy in and out of schools.

Deepika Bahri (*dpetrag@emory.edu*) teaches postcolonial literature and theory at Emory University, Atlanta, Georiga. She has co-edited *Between the Lines: South Asians and Postcoloniality* (Bahri and Vasudeva) and has published articles in edited collections as well as in various journals, including *Ariel: A Review of International English Literature, Postmodern Culture,* and *College English.* She is on the editorial board of *Jouvert: A Journal of Postcolonial Studies* and *The Journal of Commowealth and Postcolonial Literature* and has developed an extensive postcolonial studies website available at: *http://www.emory.edu/ENGLISH/Bahri.*

Valerie Balester (*v-balester@tamu.edu*) is associate professor of English at Texas A&M University, College Station, Texas and co-editor, with Michelle Hall Kells, of *Attending to the Margins: Writing, Researching, and Teaching on the Front Lines* (1999). She is also author of *Cultural Divide: A Study of African-America College-Level Writers* (1993) and *The Holt Guide to Using Daedalus.* She has had articles published in *The Writing Lab Newsletter, Language and Education,* and *Computers and Composition.* Her professional credits include administering a writing center and a writing program at Texas A&M University, and her research interests center on literacy and culture, technology, and writing. Most recently, her research concerns the history of how we teach grammar, mechanics, and usage.

Dennis Baron (*debaron@uiuc.edu*) is professor of English and linguistics and head of the Department of English at the University of Illinois at Urbana-Champaign. His books included *Grammar and Good Taste: Reforming the American Language* (Yale Univ. Press, 1982), *Grammar and Gender* (Yale, 1986), *The English-Only Question: An Official Language for Americans?* (Yale, 1990), *Declining Grammar* (NCTE, 1989), and *Guide to Home Language Repair* (NCTE, 1994). His current book project is *The New Technologies of Literacy.*

John C. Bean (*jbean@seattleu.edu*) is a professor of English at Washington's Seattle University, where he holds the title of consulting professor of academic and professional writing. He has a B.A. degree from Stanford and a Ph.D. from the University of Washington. He is the author of *Engaging Ideas: The Professor's Guide to Integrating Writing, Critical Thinking, and Active Learning in the Classroom* (Jossey-Bass, 1996) and coauthor of *Writing Arguments,* 5th ed. (Allyn & Bacon, forthcoming) and *The Allyn &*

Bacon Guide to Writing, 2d ed. (Allyn & Bacon, 2000). In addition to articles on writing across the curriculum and composition pedagogy, he has published articles on Renaissance literature, including Shakespeare and Spenser.

David Beard (*bear0043@tc.umn.edu*), a Ph.D. student in rhetoric, scientific, and technical communication, is the advisee of Dr. Arthur Walzer. He is primarily interested in modernism in rhetoric, aesthetics, and the human sciences; his interests of late have circled around ethical and rhetorical components of scholarly discussion of the Holocaust and fascism.

Patricia Bizzell (*pbizzell@holycross.edu*) is professor of English at the College of the Holy Cross, Worcester, Massachusetts, where she teaches courses in expository writing, composition theory, and American literature. She has directed the college's Writing-Across-the-Curriculum Program, Writers Workshop (a peer tutoring facility), and Honors Program, and next year she will teach in the First Year Program. Among her publications are, with Bruce Herzberg, *The Bedford Bibliography for Teachers of Writing* (5th ed. in press) and *The Rhetorical Tradition: Readings from Classical Times to the Present* (2d ed. in press).

Lynn Z. Bloom (*lbloom@uconnvm.uconn.edu*), University of Connecticut (Storrs) Board of Trustees Distinguished Professor of English and Aetna Chair of Writing since 1988, explains in a recent essay on "Writing and Cooking" (under editorial review), "Writing and cooking are two of the things I like to do best. Indeed, they're a lot alike— a messy mix of knowledge and improvisation, experience and innovation, and continual revision with a lot going on in between the lines." "For years I've toyed with writing a cookbook," she continues, but she is unwilling to revise her cooking indefinitely until she gets it right, so she sticks to writing books (*Composition Studies as a Creative Art* 1998), articles ("The Essay Canon," 1999—41 drafts, no kidding), and essays ("Writing *Blue Berries:* Once More to My Summer Vacation" 1998).

Richard Bullock (*richard.bullock@wright.edu*) is a professor of English at Wright State University, Dayton, Ohio, where he directs the writing programs and the Institute on Writing and Teaching. He has edited or co-edited three books: *Why Workshop? Changing Course in 7–12 English* (Stenhouse, 1998); *Seeing for Ourselves: Classroom Research by Teachers of English* (with Glenda Bissex, Heinemann, 1987); and *The Politics of Writing Instruction: Postsecondary* (with John Trimbur and Charles Schuster, Heinemann, 1991).

Mary Ann Cain (*cain@ipfw.edu*) is associate professor of English at Indiana University–Purdue University Fort Wayne, where she teaches courses in creative writing, rhetoric and composition, and women's studies. Her book *Revisioning Writers' Talk: Gender and Culture in Acts of Composing* was published by SUNY Press in 1995. Her articles have appeared in journals such as *College Composition and Communication, Dialogue,* and *Composition Studies.* Her creative writing has appeared in numerous literary journals, including *First Intensity, Nebraska Review,* and *13th Moon.*

Theresa Conefrey (*conefrey@hawaii.edu*) is assistant professor of English at the University of Hawai'i at Hilo. As a writing specialist, she teaches courses in professional and technical writing, language and gender, and beginning, intermediate, and advanced composition. Her research focuses on how gender, discourse, and power interact with academic access and career choice. She has published articles on women in science and is currently researching the impact of tertiary education on Micronesian women's changing societal roles.

Robert J. Connors was professor of English and director of the Writing Center at the University of New Hampshire, Durham. A recipient of the Richard Braddock Award (CCCC) and the Mina P. Shaughnessy Award (MLA), he authored *Composition-Rhetoric: Backgrounds, Theory, and Pedagogy* (Univ. of Pittsburg Press, 1997) and *Selected Essays of Edward P. J. Corbett*. His other publications include *Essays on Classical Rhetoric and Modern Discourse* (co-edited with Lisa Ede and Andrea Lunsford, Southern Illinois Univ. Press, 1984); *The New St. Martin's Handbook* (1999), *The Everyday Writer* (Bedford, 1988), and *Easywriter* (St. Martins, 1997) (both coauthored with Andrea Lunsford); *The New St. Martin's Guide to Teaching Writing* (coauthored with Cheryl Glenn, Bedford, 1999); *Classical Rhetoric for the Modern Student* (Oxford Univ. Press, 1998) and *Style and Statement* (Oxford Univ. Press, 1998) (both coauthored with Edward P. J. Corbett). His interests included the relation of pedagogical and cultural movements to theoretical movements in academic culture, and the question of the rhetorical decline of the sentence and of style. Bob Connors died on June 22, 2000, long before we were ready to let him go.

Richard Leo Enos (*r.enos@tcu.edu*), who received his Ph.D. from Indiana University in 1973, is professor and holder of the Lillian B. Radford Chair of Rhetoric and Composition at Texas Christian University, Fort Worth. His research emphasis is in the history of rhetoric with a specialization in classical rhetoric. Much of his work deals with understanding the relationship between thought and expression in antiquity.

Ruth Overman Fischer (*rfischer@gmu.edu*) is director of composition and visiting assistant professor in English at George Mason University, Fairfax, Virginia. She earned her Ph.D. in English with an emphasis in rhetoric and linguistics from Indiana University of Pennsylvania. Her dissertation investigated the long-term effects on teachers of their participation in a summer institute of a National Writing Project site. She has presented at the conventions of the Conference on College Composition and Communication, the National Council of Teachers of English, and the Modern Language Association, and at Writing Across the Curriculum conferences. She is a faculty member in the Women's Studies Program, a teacher/consultant with the Northern Virginia Writing Project, and a member of the GMU chapter of the National Coalition Building Institute.

Richard Fulkerson (*dick_fulkerson@tamu-commerce.edu*) received a Ph.D. in Victorian literature from the Ohio State University in 1970. He joined the faculty of East Texas State University, now Texas A&M–Commerce, where he migrated into composition. He is director of English graduate studies and coordinator of composition and specializes in argumentative writing.

Diana George (*dgeorge@mtu.edu*) is professor of humanities at Michigan Technological University, Houghton. She is coauthor with John Trimbur of *Reading Culture: Contexts for Critical Reading and Writing* (1999) and editor of *Kitchen Cooks, Plate Twirlers, and Troubadours: Writing Program Administrators Tell Their Stories* (Heinemann, 1999). With Dennis Lynch and Marilyn Cooper, she was awarded the 1998

CCCC Richard Braddock Award for her essay "Moments of Argument: Agonistic Inquiry and Confrontational Cooperation" (*College Composition and Communication* vol. 48.1, Feb. 1997).

Bruce Herzberg (*bherzberg@bentley.edu*) is chair of the English department at Bentley College, Waltham, Massachusetts, where for many years he served as director of the writing program. He is the author of a number of articles on composition and rhetoric and, with Patricia Bizzell, co-editor of *The Rhetorical Tradition: Readings from Classical Times to the Present* (1990) and *Negotiating Difference: Cultural Case Studies for Composition* (1996).

H. Brooke Hessler (*hessler@writetosucceed.org*) teaches community-engagement writing at Texas Christian University, Fort Worth. She is cofounder and president of Write to Succeed, a nonprofit corporation that supports and develops collaborative communication programs in local and virtual communities.

Rebecca Moore Howard (*rehoward@syr.edu*) is associate professor of writing and rhetoric at Syracuse University, New York. Her scholarly work explores the role of composition in the university insofar as it negotiates the tension between gatekeeping and student empowerment. *Standing in the Shadow of Giants* (Ablex, 1999) explicates how that tension informs pedagogical approaches to plagiarism.

Sandra Jamieson (*sjamieso@drew.edu*) is associate professor of English and director of composition at Drew University, Madison, New Jersey, where she teaches graduate and undergraduate courses in composition theory, upper-level writing courses, first-year composition, and writing classes in the doctor of letters program. She also supervises the academic component of internship projects conducted as part of Drew's writing minor. Her publications include *The Bedford Guide to Teaching Writing in the Disciplines: An Instructor's Desk Reference,* with Rebecca Moore Howard (Bedford, 1995). Her research explores the relationship between theory and pedagogy within the field of writing.

Johndan Johnson-Eilola (*johndan@purdue.edu*) works as the director of professional writing and teaches in the graduate rhet/comp and undergraduate professional writing programs at Purdue University, West Lafayette, Indiana. He has published extensively on computers and communication, including pieces in numerous books and journals, such as *Computers and Composition, Technical Communication Quarterly,* and *Journal of Advanced Composition.* He is the author of *Nostalgic Angels: Rearticulating Hypertext Writing* (Ablex, 1997).

Donald C. Jones (*djones@mail.hartford.edu*) is an Assistant Professor of rhetoric, language, and Culture at Connecticut's University of Hartford. He has published on John Dewey's pragmatic philosophy, postmodern questions of agency, writing process theories, and the teaching of academic discourse. He also is the coauthor of two chapters of *Reading Our Histories, Understanding Our Cultures* (K. McCormick, C. Lipke, eds. Allyn and Bacon, 1998).

George Kalamaras (*kalamaraci@ipfw.edu*) is associate professor of English at Indiana University–Purdue University Fort Wayne, where he teaches courses in creative writing and rhetoric and composition. He is the author of *Reclaiming the Tacit Dimension: Sym-*

bolic Form in the Rhetoric of Silence (SUNY Press, 1994), and his articles have appeared in *College Composition and Communication, Composition Studies,* and *International Journal of Hindu Studies,* among others. He has also published his poetry widely, including a book, *The Theory and Function of Mangoes,* winner of the 1999 Four Way Books Intro Series in Poetry Award.

Mary R. Lamb (*mlamb@mindspring.com*) is a Ph.D. candidate at Texas Christian University, Fort Worth, specializing in rhetoric and composition. Her research and teaching interests include feminist rhetoric and composition, twentieth-century American women's fiction, and African American women's fiction. She is completing a dissertation on the rhetoric of reading communities, specifically Oprah's Book Club and academic classrooms. Locating her work in the recent reexamination of reading as collective and collaborative practice, she examines the cultural work accomplished in reading groups by tracing the circulation of feminist ideas in the discussion of literature.

Mary M. Lay (*mmlay@tc.umn.edu*) is Professor of Rhetoric and Director of Graduate Studies at the University of Minnesota, Minneapolis, in the Scientific and Technical Communication Program. She is coauthor of the textbook *Technical Communication* (McGraw-Hill, 2d ed., 2000), author of *The Rhetoric of Midwifery: Power, Knowledge, and Gender* (Rutgers Univ. Press, 2000), and co-editor of *Body Talk: Rhetoric, Technology, and Reproduction* (Wisconsin Univ. Press, 2000). She is co-editor of *Technical Communication Quarterly,* the official journal of the Association of Teachers of Technical Writing and past president of the association.

Kitty O. Locker (*locker.1@osu.edu*) is an associate professor of English at The Ohio State University, Columbus. She is a former President of the Association for Business Communication (ABC) and is the current editor of *The Journal of Business Communication.* Two of her articles have received ABC's award for Distinguished Publications; she received the Outstanding Researcher Award from ABC in 1992 and ABC's Meada Gibbs Outstanding Teacher Award in 1998.

Andrea Abernethy Lunsford (*lunsford@stanford.edu*) is Distinguished Professor of English and acting director of the Center for the Study and Teaching of Writing at The Ohio State University, Columbus. Her recent publications include *Reclaiming Rhetorica: Women in the Rhetorical Tradition* (1995), *The New St. Martin's Handbook* (1999), and *Everything Is an Argument* (with J. Rusakiewicz, Bedford, 1998).

Kathleen McCormick (*kmpurchase@aol.com*) is professor of rhetoric, language, and culture and director of freshman reading and writing at Connecticut's University of Hartford. She is the winner of the Mina Shaughnessy Award (1995) for *The Culture of Reading and the Teaching of English* (Manchester Univ. Press, 1994) and the University of Hartford's Bent Award for Creativity (1998). She is also the editor of *Reading Our Histories, Understanding Our Cultures* (Allyn and Bacon, 1998), *Reading Text* (Heath, 1987), and other books on rhetoric, theory, and modern literature.

Libby Miles (*lmiles@uri.edu*) is an assistant professor at the University of Rhode Island, Kingston, where she also directs the Writing Center. There she teaches all levels of undergraduate writing courses, emphasizing public consumption, as well as graduate rhetoric seminars. Prior to her doctoral work at Purdue University, she worked in the textbook publishing industry, which continues to be the focus of her research. She is the cochair of the CCCC Caucus for Intellectual Property, and she has published articles in *College Composition and Communication, College English, Works & Days, Composition Chronicle,* and *Technical Communication Quarterly.*

Thomas P. Miller (*tpm@u.arizona.edu*) teaches at the University of Arizona, Tucson. His most recent book, *The Formation of College English: Rhetoric and Belles Lettres in the Eighteenth-Century Provinces* (Univ. of Pittsburg Press, 1997), won the Mina Shaughnessey Award from the Modern Language Association.

John Ramage (*ramage@asu.edu*) is associate professor of English at Arizona State University, Tempe, where he has taught and served in a variety of administrative positions since 1990. He is coauthor with John Bean of several writing textbooks, most recently the *Allyn & Bacon Guide to Writing* (Allyn and Bacon, 1999).

David E. Schwalm (*david.schwalm@asu.edu*) is currently vice provost for academic affairs and dean of East College at Arizona State University East, a new campus of ASU in Mesa. Previously, he held faculty positions at UC Berkeley, the Ohio State University, the University of Texas at El Paso, and Arizona State University Main. He was a WPA at both UTEP and ASU Main and vice provost for academic affairs at ASU West.

Robert A. Schwegler (*rschweg@uri.edu*) is professor of English at the University of Rhode Island, Kingston. He teaches first-year composition, scientific and technical communication, writing about culture, and a number of other advanced courses. His research currently focuses on concepts of error and correctness and their social consequences.

Linda K. Shamoon (*shamoon@uri.edu*) is professor of English, director of the College Writing Program, and director of the Faculty Institute on Writing at the University of Rhode Island, Kingston. She has published articles on the research paper, on writing across the curriculum, on the place of rhetoric in composition programs, and on writing center practices. She has received numerous major grants to develop and support writing with electronic technology at the University of Rhode Island, and she is a founding member of the Intercollegiate Electronic Democracy Project. In addition to directing the writing program, she serves as a regional consultant for writing across the curriculum.

Gail Stygall (*stygall@u.washington.edu*) is director of expository writing at the University of Washington, Seattle, where she teaches courses on writing, rhetoric, English language, and discourse analysis. She continues working in legal discourse, basic writing, and discourse analysis. Recently, she and Ellen Barton have edited a collection of essays, *Discourse Studies and Composition,* forthcoming from Hampton Press.

Christopher J. Thaiss (*cthaiss@gmu.edu*) chairs the English department at George Mason University, Fairfax, Virginia, where he has taught since 1975 and where for many years he directed the English composition and writing-across-the-curriculum programs. Active as a consultant to college and university writing programs, he also works with K–12 teachers through the Northern Virginia Writing Project. He has written, coauthored, or edited nine books, most recently a series of writing texts for students in theatre, psychology, and law enforcement. He is also at work on a book on youth baseball, which he coaches.

John Trimbur (*jtrimbur@wbi.edu*) is Paris Fletcher Distinguished Professor of humanities and director of technical, scientific, and professional communication at Worcester Polytechnic Institute, Massachusetts. He has published extensively in writing theory and cultural studies of literacy, including the CCCC Outstanding Book Award collection *The Politics of Writing Instruction* (with R. Bullock and R. Ohmann, Heinemann, 1991).

Joseph Trimmer (*jtrimmer@bsu.edu*) is professor of English and director of the Writing Program at Ball State University, Muncie, Indiana. His books include *Narration as Knowledge: Tales of the Teaching Life* (Greenwood-Heinemann, 1997), *FICTIONS* (Harcourt, 1997), and *Writing with a Purpose* (Houghton Miflin, 1997). In the summers, he teaches at the Martha's Vineyard Institute on Teaching and Writing.

Beverly Wall (*beverly.wall@trincoll.edu*) is associate professor and director of the Allan K. Smith Center for Writing and Rhetoric at Trinity College in Hartford, Connecticut. She does commentary on American political rhetoric for BBC Radio London and has appeared on C-SPAN's *Washington Journal.* Her scholarship and teaching interests include writing with multimedia technologies, the art of argument, and the rhetoric of Supreme Court opinions. The Intercollegiate Electronic Democracy Project can be found at this web address: *http://www.trincoll.edu/depts/writcent/edproject. html.*

Arthur E. Walzer (*awalzer@tc.umn.edu*) is an associate professor in the rhetoric department at the University of Minnesota, Minneapolis, where he teaches courses in eighteenth-century rhetorical theory, technical communication, and humanities. With Edward A. Schiappa, he is serving as editor for the series "Rhetoric in the Modern Era," sponsored by SUNY Press. His articles have appeared in the *Quarterly Journal of Speech, College English, Rhetoric Review, College Composition and Communication,* and *Argumentation,* among others. He is currently writing a book on George Campbell.

Yameng Liu (*yameng@andrew.cmu.edu*) is associate professor of rhetoric and English at Carnegie-Mellon University, Pittsburg, Pennsylvania. His articles addressing issues in rhetorical theory and cross-cultural studies of rhetoric have been published in journals such as *College English, Philosophy and Rhetoric, Philosophy East and West, Rhetoric Review,* and *Argumentation.* Among the courses he teaches regularly at CMU is Comparative Rhetoric, which was first offered in 1994.

Kathleen Blake Yancey (*kyancey@clemson.edu*) is Pearce Professor of professional communication at Clemson University, in Clemson, South Carolina, where she teaches an undergraduate course in composition and literature and graduate courses in rhetoric and professional communication. Prior to joining the faculty at Clemson, she taught at UNC Charlotte, where she developed the course portrayed and described here. Yancey has edited or co-edited five collections of essays, most recently *Self Assessment and the Development of Writing* (Hampton Press, 2000); she co-edits the journal *Assessing Writing;* and she has authored *Reflection in the Writing Classroom* (Utah State Univ. Press, 1998), a study theorizing uses of reflection in the teaching of writing. Her current projects include work in the assessment of electronic texts such as e-mails and websites, and continuing (often collaborative) practice and theory of alternative texts similar to the one apprearing here.